IMAGES
of America

Stephenville Yellow Jacket Football

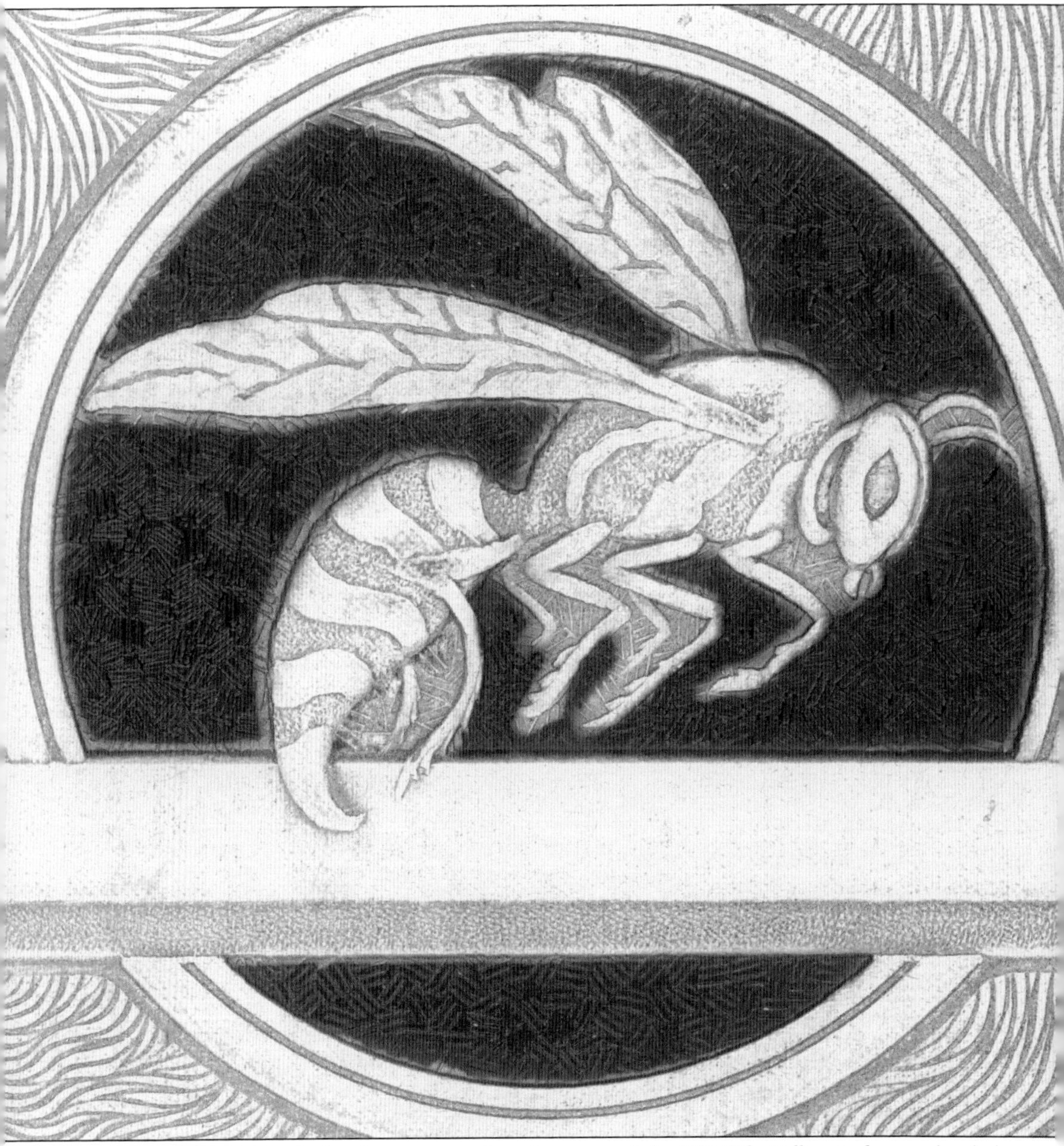

The familiar Yellow Jacket logo, pictured on the cover of the 1938 *The Yellow Jacket* yearbook, has evolved over time. The 1999 logo (page 77) is a more modern version that noticeably features four stars representing 1990s state football titles. Over nine decades, the logo has become recognized across the Lone Star State as emblematic of one of the finest football programs in Texas.

On the Cover: The 1940 Yellow Jacket offensive huddle is pictured from the ground looking up. Clockwise from the lower left-hand corner are Barney Welch (no. 61 and future Aggie great), C.B. Rushing, John "Whit" Whitacre, Verne Scott Jr., Charles Williams, Donald "Smitty" Smith, Oliver Griffin (three-year letterman, *Star-Telegram* All-State Team, and District 9-2A coaches' selection as Outstanding Lineman), C.V. Tate, Connie Jones, Jackson "Cracky" Allen, and Aaron Autry. These Jackets went undefeated and tied Temple High School in the bi-district playoff round.

IMAGES
of America

STEPHENVILLE YELLOW JACKET FOOTBALL

Ricky L. Sherrod
Foreword by Art Briles

ARCADIA
PUBLISHING

ISBN 978-0-7385-8493-5

Published by Arcadia Publishing
Charleston, South Carolina

Printed in the United States of America

Library of Congress Control Number: 2011923573

For all general information, please contact Arcadia Publishing:
Telephone 843-853-2070
Fax 843-853-0044
E-mail sales@arcadiapublishing.com
For customer service and orders:
Toll-Free 1-888-313-2665

Visit us on the Internet at www.arcadiapublishing.com

To Annette—my wife, my muse, and the inspiration of all that flows from my computer keyboard

CONTENTS

FOREWORD

Dear Yellow Jacket Fans,

I hope that you will enjoy reading this book, as I believe it will give new perspective and insight into the rich history and tradition that is Yellow Jacket football. The years that I spent as athletic director and head football coach were filled with outstanding moments on and off the field, not only for our teams, but for the community, too.

There is no doubt that the community support we enjoyed played a vital role in the Yellow Jackets' rise to prominence, and that outpouring continues to this day. All you "can fans" should be proud of the inspiration you provided to our players on the field and those fans cheering in the stands. It impacted our program's success and has been well documented throughout the state.

The Stephenville football program has been a tremendous source of community pride for many years. Quite honestly, the support all Stephenville teams receive is remarkable, especially when taking into account the community's size. I experienced firsthand the right way for a community and school district to work together in support of its youth, which in turn allows young people the opportunity to achieve academic and athletic success.

In my opinion, the program's turning point was the Yellow Jackets' 1990 win over Brownwood; this was when the skies turned blue for our football program. This signature win propelled the Yellow Jackets to four state championships in the 1990s and signaled the dawn of a new era, not only for our community, but for our opponents, too. Other memorable moments include the 1993 state semifinal win over Waxahachie at Baylor's Floyd Casey Stadium and the playoff victories at Pennington Field in the Dallas–Fort Worth Metroplex.

Thank you for helping establish Stephenville's City of Champions tradition. Everyone in the community—players, parents, coaches, the administration, and the many loyal fans—should take great pride in the Yellow Jackets' past gridiron accomplishments and their role in helping turn those dreams into reality!

—Art Briles
Head Football Coach
Baylor University

ACKNOWLEDGMENTS

During the summer of 2010, I battled to meet a deadline for *Stephenville*, the Arcadia publication preceding this present work. My beautiful, wonderful wife gazed compassionately at me and lovingly observed, "You know, what you *really* need to do is write an Arcadia history about the Yellow Jacket football program!" That lightbulb moment marks the conception of the volume in your hands. Historians should write about their passions, and Yellow Jacket football is one of my most cherished, treasured indulgences.

My love for the program dates from wide-eyed childhood, when I examined my father's 1937 football letter jacket and listened to his tales about the 9-1 Jacket team that barely missed the playoffs. Members of that team achieved great athletic feats in their schoolboy days. Some shortly thereafter had storied intercollegiate careers. Second only to my wife, Annette, my dad, Marshall Sherrod, provided the inspiration for this book.

Next in importance is my acquisitions editor, Winnie Rodgers. She deftly guided me to complete my first Arcadia publication. Her tireless, unstinting advocacy of a Yellow Jacket history transformed the project from the thinking stage into a wonderful finished product. It was delightful to work with her, and I will miss our regular cyberspace correspondence.

Four of my colleagues—Tammy Jones, Nancy McIntyre, Debbie Cashell, and Kathy Slemmons—rendered invaluable service in locating representative images. Stephenville High School (SHS) principal Travis Stilwell supported the idea of the book from the thinking stage to the finish line and so has Stephenville Independent School District (SISD) superintendent Dr. Darrell Floyd, who graciously contributed "About the Organization" (page 127) and granted permission to use school-district images. I am especially grateful to coaches Joseph Gillespie and Michael Copeland, my colleagues and friends. Their historical memory helped me distinguish the significant from the trivial.

Others who contributed significantly include the founder of the Yellow Jacket and Honey Bee webpage, Cody Derrick; businessman Brad Thompson; retired Tarleton State University professor Stuart Chilton; Glenda Stone of Tarleton State University's Dick Smith Library; local photographers Bud Jones, Ellen Skipper, and her mother, Louise Jarratt Skipper; and the sports editor of the *Stephenville Empire-Tribune*, Brad Keith. Managing editor Sara Vanden Berge also enthusiastically supported the project, granting access to *Empire-Tribune* photograph files and permission to publish special and unique images. Boots Elliott, the radio voice of the Stephenville Yellow Jackets, provided encouragement and help, as did his mother and my colleague, Stephany Elliott. Finally, thanks to the Stephenville Historical Museum in general for making available several rare, significant photographs of early Yellow Jacket football.

Unless otherwise noted, images are provided courtesy of SISD.

From the Sidelines

"The Stephenville High School (SHS) football program sets a high standard of excellence throughout the state of Texas, and it also provides positive role models for the youth of our community. They see what it takes to achieve excellence. They see the tremendous work ethic and drive that our high school athletes have, and they, in turn, want to do their part to uphold SHS's tradition of excellence and do their part to maintain Stephenville's motto of continuing to be the City of Champions."

—Dr. Darrell Floyd

"I feel sure that the SHS football program has had an impact on the young men's lives who have participated in the program. It has allowed them to see the importance of setting goals, working to achieve those goals, and then seeing those goals come to be reality. It is something they will carry with them the rest of their adult lives. The football program has given this community a sense of pride and identity that we are all part of the Yellow Jacket program, a sense that it takes all of us to become a City of Champions."

—Michael Copeland

"The program instills a sense of pride, accomplishment, and a tradition of excellence."

—Dr. Cheryl Floyd

"The work ethic we had been trying to instill in our children was reinforced and encouraged by the coaches that they encountered in their high school football experiences. This serves them well as adults who are now parents themselves and contributing members of their respective communities."

—Michael Odell

"The only thing I heard when I arrived at Stephenville was, 'Do you think we could beat Brownwood?' There was never any talk about playoff—just, 'Could we beat Brownwood?' [page 26]. After 1988, beating Brownwood would be important, but the mindset changed to making the playoffs. It's amazing when you have vision and high expectations. What a turnaround! We finally did beat Brownwood in 1990, but making the playoffs . . . we had already done that the year before. Looking back, wow, what a ride. Players weighing 140 pounds, playing defensive end in a state championship game, thought that they were studs. That's what it's all about. Players playing above their ability, giving all they had, developing a work ethic, and having a positive attitude. Stephenville has had its share of studs, but we have also had 7th and 8th C and D teamers grow into all-district varsity players their senior year. What can I say about a program that gives every kid a chance to find success?"

—Bob Cervetto

"The SHS football program has had a profound effect on my family personally. As our son has progressed through the program, it has instilled in him a sense of accomplishment, pride, determination, teamwork, and a work ethic that is unparalleled in most high schools. Separate and apart from the family pride issue, the success of the SHS football program has (among other successful programs) helped put Stephenville on the map. Serving as superintendent of schools in Stephenville ISD for the past 11 years and attending various state and national meetings, inevitably someone always wants to talk about Stephenville Yellow Jacket football and the success the program has enjoyed over the years. I always take pride in that."

—Dr. Darrell Floyd

"The success of the football program sets great examples for the youth of our community. The high school players serve as role models for the youth."

—Dr. Cheryl Floyd

"When I came to Stephenville in the fall of 1981, I was just hoping to learn a little football and then move on. I felt my stay would be no longer than five years. This is my 30th year, and I feel fortunate to have been a part of a program that was definitely a rags-to-riches story. You see, for the first seven years, all everyone would say is that we were not able to compete because we were one of the smallest 4A schools and did not have enough kids to compete. All that changed when Coach Briles came to town. In the spring of 1988, an attitude shift came to Stephenville. Coaching positive and upbeat gave every kid a chance to do something special. From the smallest to the tallest, the mindset was 'I could do anything if I work hard enough.' "

—Bob Cervetto

"When we moved to Erath County in the summer of 1991, Glenn was an incoming freshman who had never played organized football because the small town in Arizona where he had lived his whole life did not offer football until high school. Nonetheless, he was welcomed to the premier football program in the state of Texas as though he was an all-state prospect [page 46]."

—Michael Odell

"My most memorable moment occurred during the 2009 season. First—Tyler's interception for a touchdown during the Granbury game [page 116]. Second—the playoff game against Aledo at Cowboys Stadium."

—Dr. Cheryl Floyd

"There are many great memories over the last 30 years, but the one that stands out the most, regarding the program, is beating no. 6 state-ranked Belton [pages 31 and 80] in the first round of the playoffs in 1989. That, to me, was the game that elevated the program to a new level, and we have never looked back!"

—Bob Cervetto

"My most memorable moment came in December 1993 at our first state championship game. Standing in the middle of Memorial Stadium as state champions after 25 years of coaching, my mind wandered back to the hundreds of young men over those 25 years who had fought so hard to achieve this goal. My heart and eyes filled with tears. This one was for every young man who had worn the blue and gold, all who had laid the groundwork, all who strived so hard. This one was for them [page 78]."

—Michael Copeland

"From the time my son Connor was old enough to walk, he has been on the sidelines at the Yellow Jacket football games. Watching him realize his childhood dream [page 52], being the quarterback of the Jackets, is something I will always hold dear to my heart."

—Kristi Washington

"As a football mom, I am proud to be a part of a program that provides my son with a strong work ethic, character, determination, and pride. The program has taught him more than how to be a good player. It has also taught him how to succeed in life by being a leader, overcoming adverse situations, by working hard, and by being a team player."

—Dr. Cheryl Floyd

INTRODUCTION

At its best, high school football is a crucible in which character can be positively shaped and formed. It can set an auspicious tone for impressionable young men. A good athletic program can even have a beneficent, transforming impact on an entire community. So it has been in Stephenville, where Yellow Jacket football is the passion of young and old alike.

In Texas, Stephenville's love affair with high school football is not unique. Since 1960, Dave Campbell's *Texas Football* has satisfied legions of Texans eager for the latest predictions about the local schoolboy team. What is unique about Stephenville football is its remarkable success and near universal popularity dating from its early-20th-century introduction as an extracurricular student activity.

From the town's mid-19th-century founding on the raw Cross Timbers frontier, Stephenville has had strong interest in recreational diversions. Earliest residents satisfied their cravings with local horse races or cockfights. As the 20th century advanced, the new option of high school athletics became available. Reporting on the first SHS football game under University Interscholastic League (UIL) sponsorship, the local newspaper reported Stephenville's 57-0 victory over neighboring Dublin. The October 8, 1920, *Tribune* reports that the October 1 contest "was the first football the local high school has engaged in for three years and the interest by students seems much aroused. Mobley, Kay, Belcher, and Poteet played consistently for Stephenville."

By the 1930s, Stephenville's high school football teams generated great excitement. There were old-timers, of course, who longed for bygone pastimes. In a January 1936, 66th Anniversary Edition *Stephenville Empire-Tribune* article, "Football Games Are Play Compared to Rooster Fight," Ben Compton muses, "You can talk about your exciting football games if you want to, but for real excitement, you should see a chicken fight like we used to stage around here." Nostalgia notwithstanding, Compton's reminiscence reflects the birth of a new era in local entertainment, one gaining powerful momentum even as he spoke. Even before those Great Depression years, Stephenville teams were competitive against some of the best football programs in Texas.

No one today in Stephenville would be surprised to read the declaration "Stephenville is football crazy." No one would dispute the claim "Stephenville High School continues as one of the outstanding teams in Texas" or the "Yellow Jackets look good to go into the final for the state championship." What might surprise many is that these assertions appeared in the *Stephenville Empire* on September 26 and November 21, 1924 and on November 20, 1925.

At 2:30 p.m. on November 23, 1923, the Yellow Jackets played against Pete Shotwell's Abilene High School team for the District No. 3 title and a playoff berth. The Eagles averaged 162 pounds per player, outweighing the Jackets by a dozen pounds a man. That day's *Stephenville Tribune* notes, "Stephenville Hi's big brother—Tarleton College—graciously volunteered their playing field, the forty-piece band, and dressing rooms for the game." One *Tribune* headline declaimed, "Local Business Men Will Close for the Game." The price of admission was 25¢ to 35¢. In a pattern heralding the fan support that exploded after Art Briles's 1988 arrival in Stephenville, this 1923 contest drew what the November 30 *Tribune* called a "record crowd" estimated at "more than 2000 rip-snorting adherents of the Stephenville team," including "many visitors from surrounding towns." The crowd "overflowed the field as the play began."

From the beginning, townspeople jumped on the football bandwagon. By the 1930s, eager Jacket fans devoured regular, multicolumn front-page newspaper coverage of high school games. Coach Joe Brown (1926–1933) earned three district championships, including a 1933 title. Eleven lettermen graduated after that season, leaving Brown's successor, Pleas Stanley, the formidable task of turning a small, light, disorganized, and inexperienced squad into a contender. The Jackets won their first game over heavily favored Eastland. The October 5, 1934, *Empire-Tribune* reports that the victory roused initially pessimistic fans "to new heights of frenzy. . . . The whole town is talking about the high school: they are singing the praises of Pleas Stanley." The coach's peculiarly deceptive "spin formation" anticipated trickery like Art Briles's 1990s starburst kickoff return or quarterbacks Branndon Stewart (1992–1994) and Kevin Kolb (2000–2002) taking snaps while in motion. The Jacket 1934 win over Eastland converted "halfhearted fans." Overflow crowds followed the team the rest of the season.

A 1934 boldfaced, four-columns-wide headline in the *Empire-Tribune* proclaims, "Stephenville Defeats Dublin, 7-6." This season-ending victory, on the day before Thanksgiving, over their Irish adversaries, guaranteed the Jackets a share of the district title. "The game ended and pandemonium broke loose on the side of the field occupied by Stephenville," according to the November 30 article. When the district committee voted 4-1 for Dublin, not Stephenville, to advance to the playoffs, the same *Empire-Tribune* issue cynically opines, "From an unofficial source, it was learned that the committee favored Dublin because . . . Stephenville had won [district] for a period of years. This is the first district championship for Dublin." When SHS played for the 1936 Class B Regional title, public schoolchildren received a half holiday. The *Empire-Tribune* predicted on December 4, 1936, that most of SISD's 1,200 students would attend the game. This policy of early dismissal on game day foreshadowed what became standard during the 1990s playoffs.

Traditional rivalry matches attracted the greatest attention. In early years, SHS and the Dublin Lions were, according to *Empire-Tribune* articles on November 9 and 28, 1930, the bitterest "rivals—ancient rivals" who frequently scheduled contests on Thanksgiving Day. In due course, a different kind of Lion—one from Brownwood—displaced Dublin as "our most hated" opponent. Before that transition during the 1940s and 1950s, Breckenridge became the most formidable Jacket foe. By the late 1980s, the focus shifted 60 miles south down Highway 377 to Brownwood. In more recent times, Aledo, one hour away down Interstate 20, has become the new Brownwood. The Yellow Jacket 31-28 victory in 2007 is the only loss sustained by Aledo at home since the Bearcat Stadium opened that year. Whoever Stephenville's main rival has been over time, a state championship was always the ultimate prize.

Class B schools in the 1920s and 1930s could not advance beyond a regional title. In 1936, the Class B Jackets won the regional crown. The December 18, 1936, *Empire-Tribune* enthusiastically reported, "The town has become extremely football-minded and a number are advocating a some-kind-of-bowl game here in January. . . . It will take a long time for fans of this area to forget the achievement of the high school team of 1936 and, along with it, the good work done by Coach Jim Mobley in his first season as head coach." A groundswell of local expectation anticipated SHS's 1937 elevation to Class A, where the Jackets could contend for a state title. Local newspaper coverage about the coming change bears striking similarity to 2009 articles expressing a similar expectation. Many townsfolk hoped that the 2009 biannual realignment would move SHS from Conference 4A into the presumably less-difficult 3A classification. Similarly, 1937 fans resembled their modern-day spiritual descendants hoping for the best possible chance to bring a state championship trophy back home.

Regarding fan support, twice during the 1937 season, special trains were chartered to transport spectators to games in Duncanville and San Angelo. For those unable to make the latter trip, a loudspeaker was set up on the town square outside Rexall Drugstore where Belknap and Washington Streets intersected. Clinton Cox received phone updates from San Angelo and reported the game's progress over the sound system to a crowd of some 150 eager fans.

Yellow Jacket gridiron success has not, of course, been uniform across nine decades. Mike Copeland, whose SHS coaching tenure dates from 1969, once reflected, "I've seen the good, the bad, and the ugly. The good is better." Good times came not long after the football program began in 1920. Both then and now, when the Jackets have been competitive, huge crowds follow the team to games at home and away. This Stephenville football obsession was part of the inspiration for one-time Stephenville recording artist Mike Graham's "Sacking a Small Town" (2001), the lyrics of which colorfully describe a mass exodus of game-bound city residents leaving a town of vacated houses. In the most dramatic illustration of this phenomenon to date, a full 39,102 spectators—at the time, the sixth largest crowd in Texas schoolboy football history—gathered at Houston's Astrodome to watch the 1999 4A Division 2 (D-2) state title game between Stephenville and Port Neches-Groves.

Not everyone would agree that the Texas fixation on football is favorable. Without doubt, high school football placed under the microscope is not perfect. But neither is any human pursuit or person. H.G. Bissinger's 1990 book *Friday Night Lights* (and the subsequent 2004 movie and 2006–2011 television series) shines light on the darker side of high school sports. Controversy has always existed. For instance, an excellent 1925 Class B Yellow Jacket team, one that shutout recent state champion Abilene 13-0, was denied the opportunity to advance. The Texas Interscholastic League, over a matter of player eligibility, disqualified SHS from participation "in the championship game in district." The November 13, 1925, edition of the local *Tribune* challenged the ruling, writing that football games "are supposed to be played and won on the field of honor rather than behind closed doors." The editor puzzled over why the larger Class A schools Electra, Wichita Falls, and Vernon were reinstated after alleged rule violations, yet SHS was denied "for a smaller offense." He concluded, "probably what the Yellow Jackets need is a 'lobbyist' in Austin. Surely they don't need a football team—they have that and a team that is willing to meet anybody."

Whatever its flaws, a persuasive, valid body of evidence suggests high school football, imperfections and all, creates great good under the direction of an administration and coaching staff right in motive and noble in intent. Ty Cashion, author of *Pigskin Pulpit* (1998), eloquently describes a "commonly held belief among coaches that football still teaches the timeless lessons of character." Good coaches exploit their occupation as a bully pulpit. They become "protectors of traditional values," thereby sowing seeds that yield bountiful societal benefits as the younger generation comes of age.

Today at SHS, many Gillespie era T-shirts worn by Jacket athletes bear the slogan "Old School." Present head coach Joseph Gillespie explains Old School as a philosophy pointing back in time to an outlook on life—a work ethic—lying at the heart of success, not only for high school football programs but in every life endeavor. From ancient Rome to modern America, the formula for a winning society has always been the same. In the rural Stephenville setting, Old School is shorthand for a familiar country belief in rolling up the sleeves of one's flannel shirt and getting down to business. Stephenville's triumphant football tradition has roots in this simple approach to life in general and to ball games in particular.

In the little Cross Timbers, Texas, town of Stephenville, Yellow Jacket football has been a powerful force shaping the community self-image. It brings young and old together in a common cause and interest. High school football has taken Stephenville and its residents to Friday night heights, to places they would otherwise never have gone. As Texas UIL schoolboy football moves toward its centennial anniversary, the Yellow Jacket program remains alive and well, promising to make the next decade of Stephenville football history just as exciting as the nine decades that came before it.

One

In the Beginning

The origins of SHS football are not entirely certain. As early as 1902, photographic evidence exists that at least a few SHS students played on some kind of city team, although the squad was perhaps no more than a collection of uniformed rogue athletes. The program widely known today got its start in 1920 and won its first five games. That year, UIL, formed in 1909 to "provide educational extracurricular academic, athletic, and music contests," initiated a sustained, organized supervision of high school football that led ultimately to the grand prize of crowning a single Texas state champion football team.

In that inaugural year, Stephenville's Johnson County neighbor, Cleburne, battled Houston Heights to a scoreless tie in the championship game. It would be some time before SHS would ascend to ultimate playoff glory. Nevertheless, the high school fielded a 1920 team of 16 players drawn from a student body of 133. By the 1990s, more than 200 SHS students reported in late August every year to compete for spots on the varsity, junior varsity, sophomore, and freshman teams.

Other differences abound. In the beginning, there was no double-digit coaching staff with specialized division of labor. Rather, every single aspect of the game came under the supervision of a single head coach. As late as the 1930s, team members numbered fewer than the modern-day coaching staff. At SHS, during six of the first seven seasons, coaching duties fell to the high school principal. He perceived his role as an extension of other administrative duties and, perhaps more importantly, an opportunity to educate his charges in principles of duty, honor, sportsmanship, and fair play.

However, some things remain the same. For instance, SHS awarded "the letter" for membership and participation on the team. In Stephenville, conferring letter sweaters was a recognizable tradition no later than 1922. Football lettermen proudly sported this acknowledgement of athletic prowess. By 1941, they were commonly known by fellow students as "sweater boys." On the foundation of these small beginnings, the SHS administration and coaching staff built a mighty program.

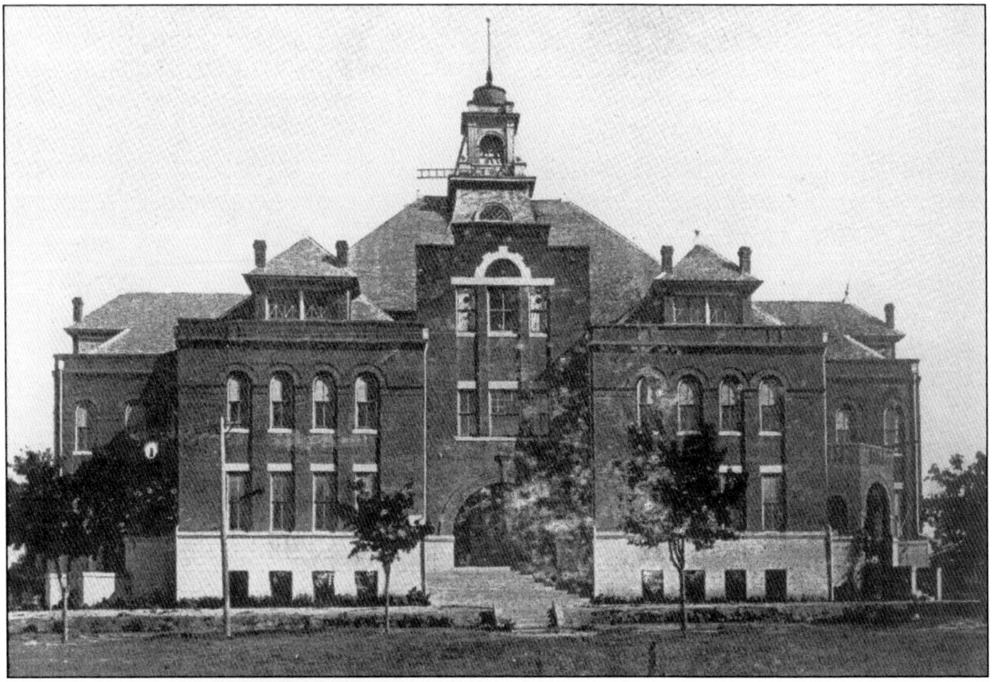

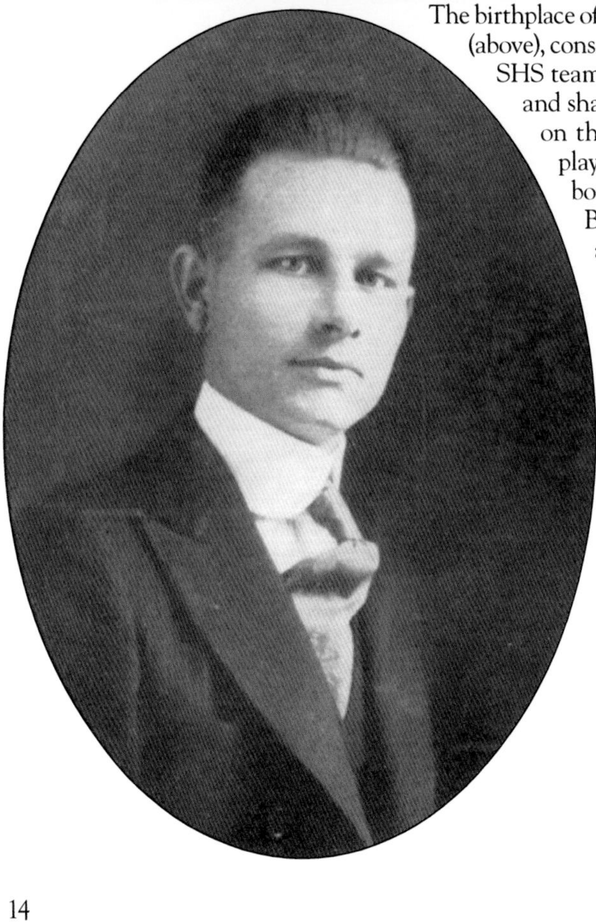

The birthplace of SHS football was Central Ward School (above), constructed in 1908. There, in 1920, the first SHS team under the auspices of UIL took form and shape. Obviously, with a mere 16 players on the squad, most team members had to play both offense and defense, and playing both became a pattern persisting until Art Briles came to Stephenville in 1988. In a school where females outnumbered males four to one, almost half the boys enrolled were part of the football program. Principal Joe B. Preston (left) assumed coaching responsibilities.

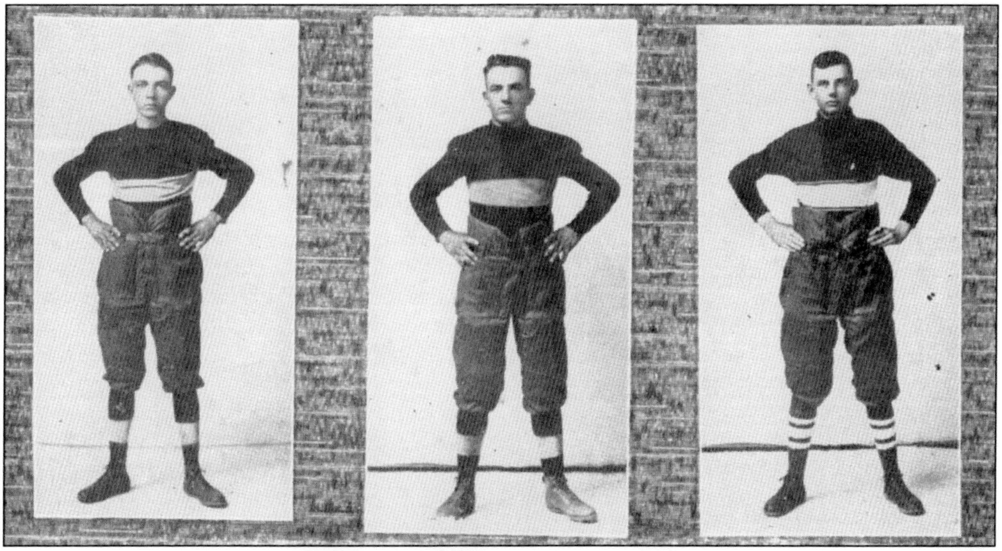

Preston guided his players to a 5-2-0 season. The three team members pictured (above) are, from left to right, senior Jim Mobley (end), Clarence Kay (fullback), and Charlie Ward (guard). They model the original SHS uniform typical of the high school football program at this early stage. When team members reconvened for practices in the fall of 1921, not only did they enter a brand new season, they also entered a brand new building. A new Stephenville High School (right) replaced Central Ward School that year.

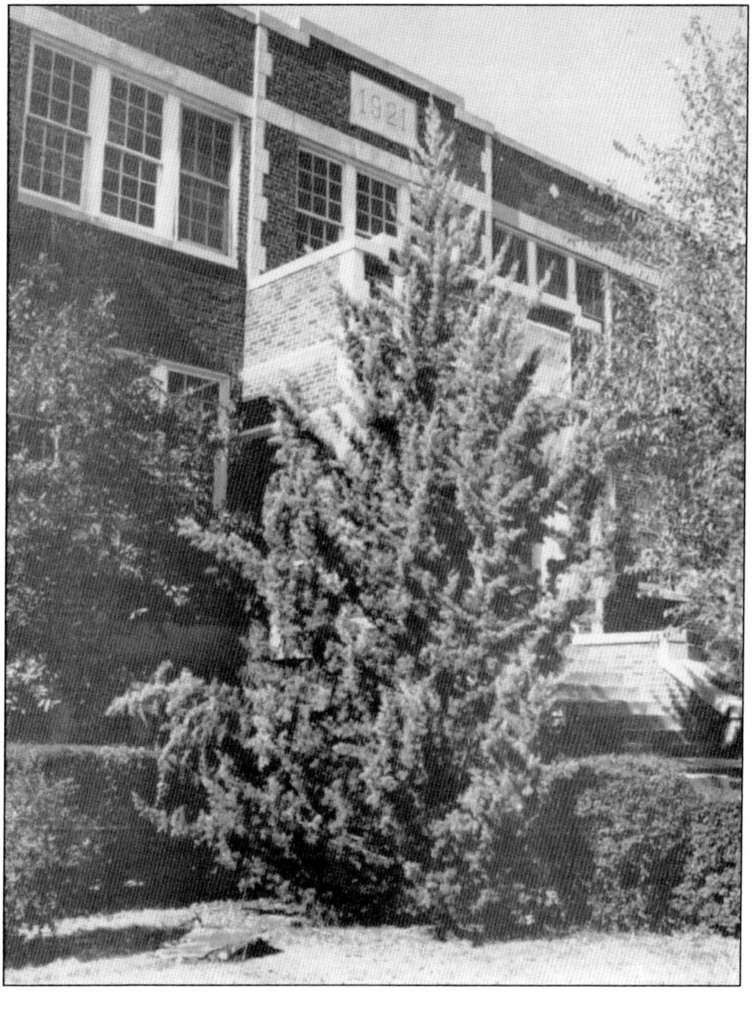

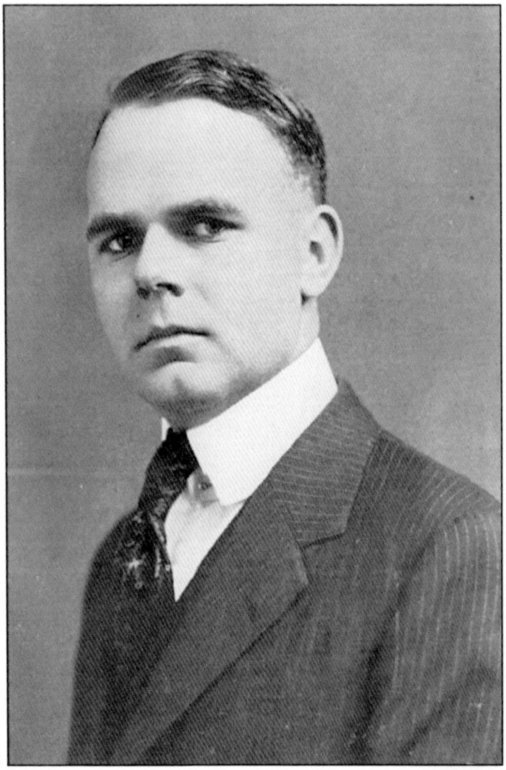

In 1921, Stephenville students also had a new principal, J.C. Dykes (left). He coached the team for four years (1921–1923, 1925), compiling a 23-13-1 cumulative record. Below are eight players from the 17-member 1921 team. Those pictured are, clockwise from the top, Littleton Presslar, Neil Arendell, Lambuth Sellers, John Culpepper, George Carlton, Clifford Fulkerson, Tullis Hall, and Charlie Ward. Coach Dykes and Mascot Wayne "Chicken" McCluskey are at the center. The 1921 squad was 3-7-0. In the school's most ignominious defeat, SHS lost to the DeLeon Fightin' Bearcats. Explaining the contest in perhaps the greatest understatement ever gracing a high school yearbook, the 1922 *Aviator* observes, "De Leon's splendid team carried us away to the tune of 122-0." In contrast, the 1951 SHS team had the lowest scoring, narrowest win in the program's history, defeating a forfeiting Graham 1-0.

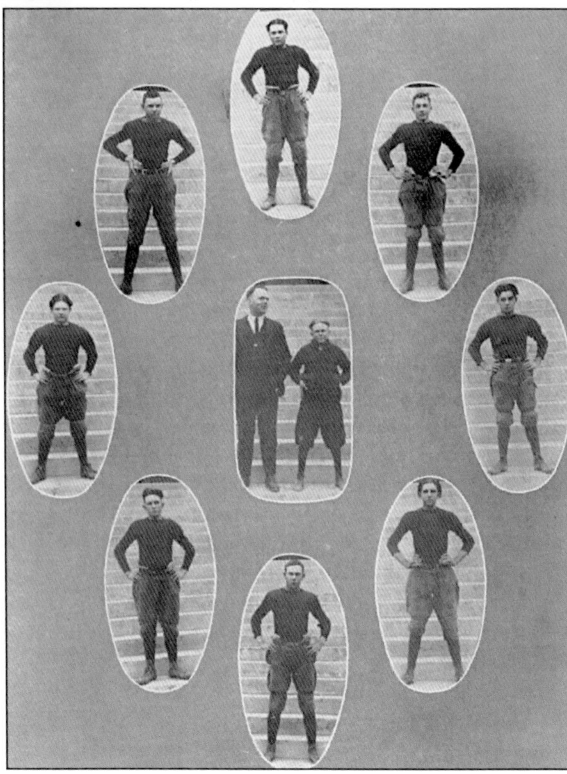

If the 1922 season of 5-6 proved disappointing, the local *Empire* on November 2, 1923, declared, "It's a far different tale as Stephenville has one of the best teams in the country." By 1922, team members received the coveted athletic letter. The 1923 yearbook identified recipients as "members of the 'S' club." Letter sweaters were awarded about a month after the season. Of the 21 lettermen in 1921–1922, 16 were football players, including Alton McMillan (top center), Jasper Webb (middle right), Olen Fenner (lower right), and team captain Albert Whitacre (bottom middle). Arnold Johnson's 1936 SHS letter sweater survives (below) and is held by, from left to right, Mitch, Mike, and Matt Copeland, the first Jacket quarterback to experiment with the wishbone formation. The Copeland family owns and operates Stephenville's Barefoot Athletics. (Below, author.)

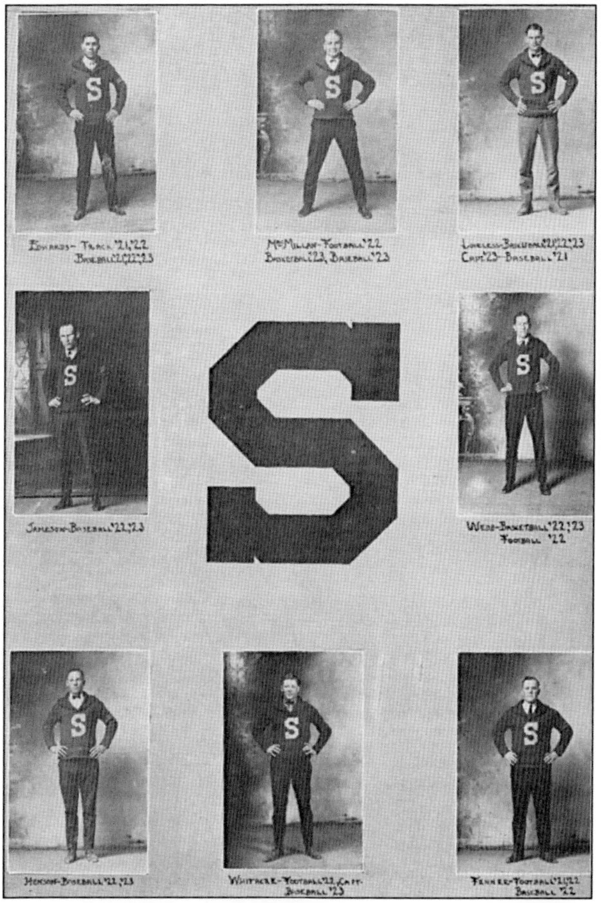

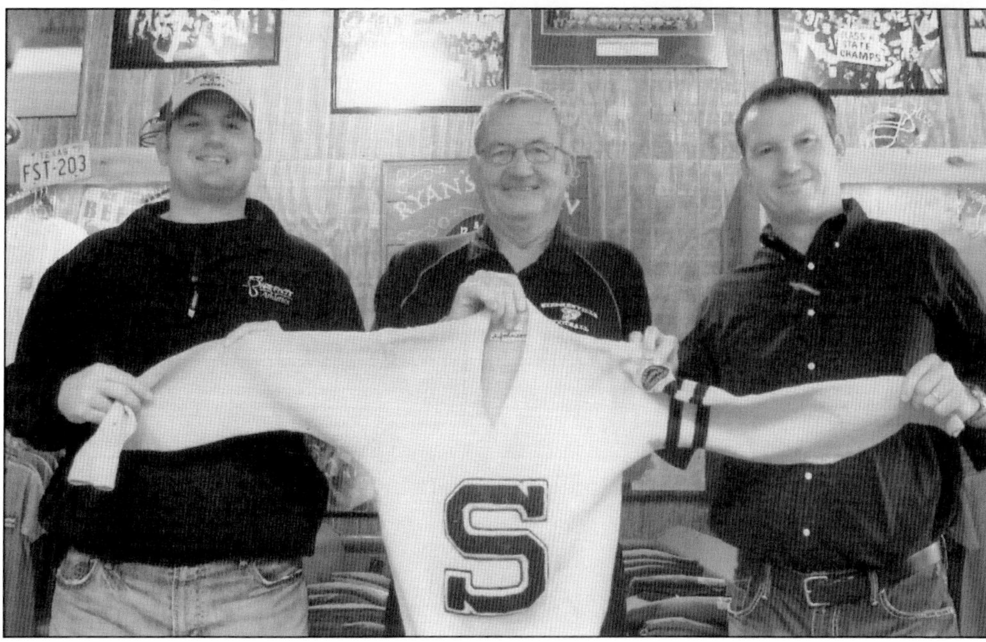

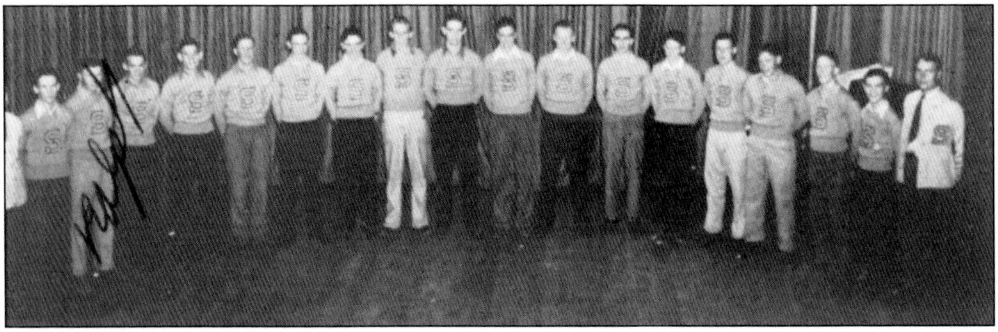

For the 1922–1923 school year, there were 40 total letters awarded for all high school sports. Football accounted for 40 percent of the total. In 1941, football lettermen were referred to simply as sweater boys (above). More recently, the players receive letter jackets like the one worn below by Brad Mills. During his four-year career (2005–2008), Mills helped his team win 2005 and 2006 district titles and is the Jacket all-time leader in career touchdowns (49), career rushing touchdowns (40), career points scored (327), and single-season rushing attempts (293). (Below, author.)

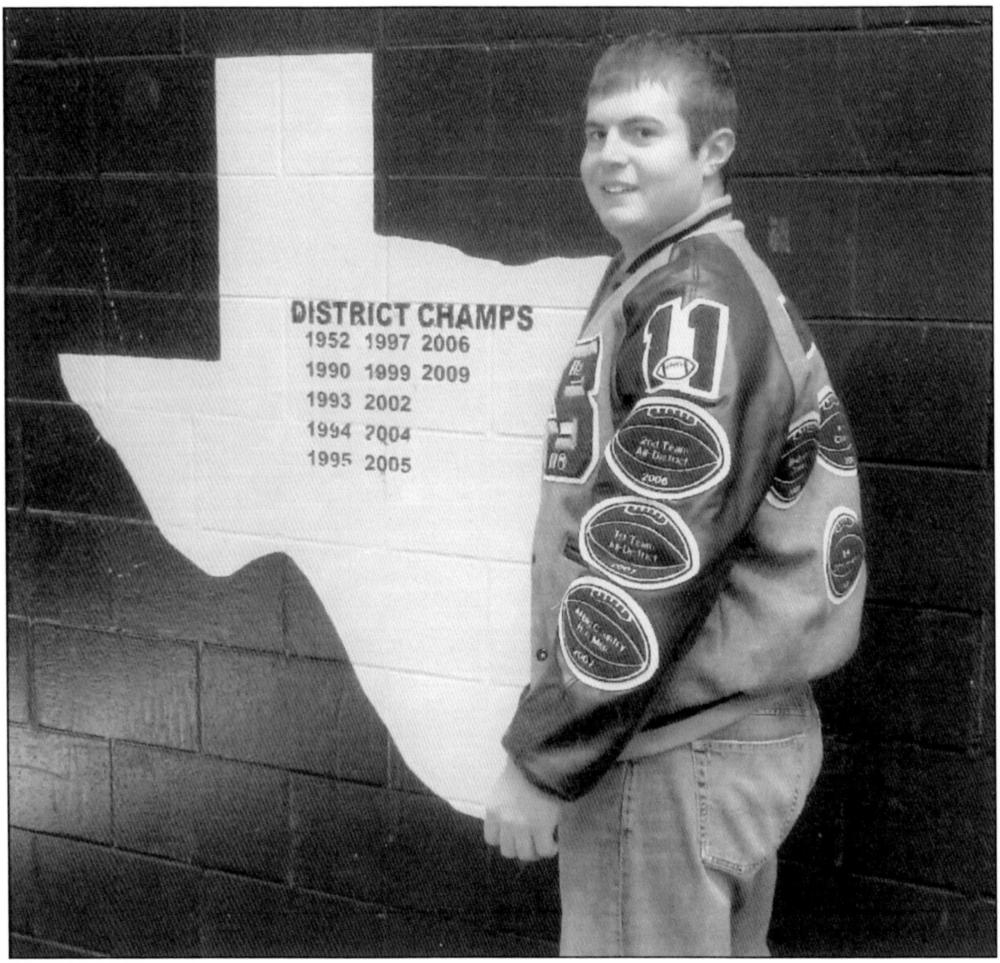

Two

No "I" in Team

Since 1920, 21 different men have coached the Yellow Jackets to a 59.8 win percentage (567-352-28). It took more than seven decades to get to the top, but head coach Art Briles (1988–1999) and his defensive coordinator Mike Copeland (1969–2002, 2008–present), turned the 1990s into a Stephenville "decade of dominance." Twice, the Jackets won back-to-back state titles (1993–1994, 1998–1999). Briles took his teams to the playoffs 11 seasons (1989–1999). His successors nurtured the playoff-making machine, adding another 10.

If the state championships of the 1990s are the pinnacle of Yellow Jacket achievement thus far, they rest on accomplishments of many worthy predecessors. Assuredly, the modern program is the house that Briles built. But other quality teams appeared before, bringing the total number of Yellow Jacket postseason playoff runs to 28. On average, over 90 years, an SHS team has been playoff-bound almost every third season. During the mid-1920s through the late 1930s, coaches Joe Brown (1926–1932) and Jim Mobley (1936–1937) put the Yellow Jackets on the Texas football map.

Playoff qualifiers are not, however, the only teams deserving inclusion in the SHS football pantheon. Jimmy Marshall's 1938–1942 teams were among the best in Texas but won district only once, falling victim to powerhouse district opponent Breckenridge, which eventually gathered four state crowns. Before UIL's present qualifying system allowing more than one team to advance from each district, only district champions made the postseason. The introduction of multiple playoff-district berths made a monumental difference. Indeed, Stephenville's 1998 team that set a national record for single-season total offense would never even have advanced in an era when only district champion teams entered postseason play.

This chapter features a smorgasbord of high-performance Yellow Jacket teams. Their accomplishments are all the more impressive because historically, SHS players have been drawn from a population base smaller than Stephenville's Dallas–Fort Worth Metroplex neighbors 75 miles east-northeast. If the state's city slickers sometimes relished contests with their smaller country cousins, they frequently found that country boys could survive and play with a vengeance, coming out winners more times than not.

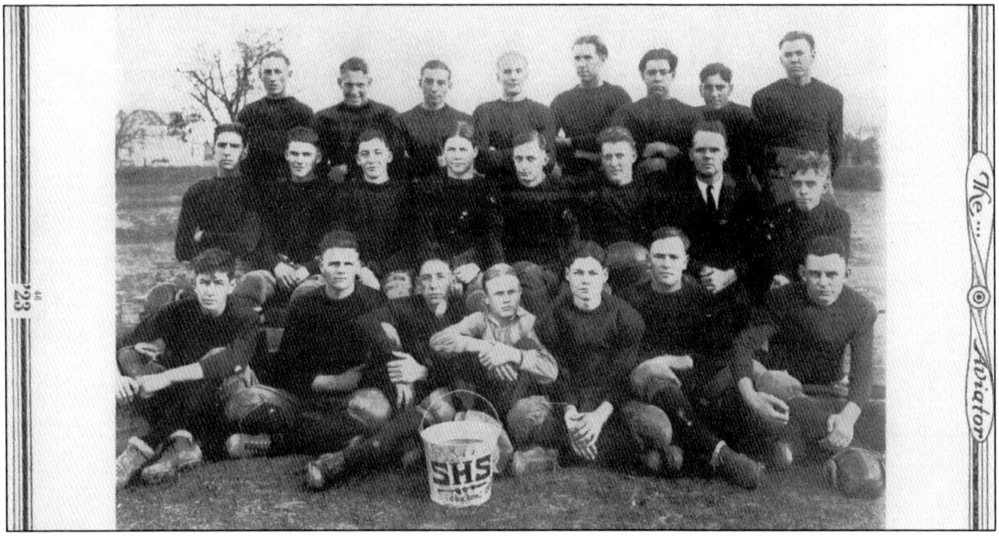

In spite of a team that looked like a "crutch brigade" (1923 yearbook), coach J.C. Dykes improved his 1921 record, ending the 1922 season at 5-6-0 (and happily, holding all of Stephenville's opponents below triple digits). The image above is of a 21-member squad drawn from a student body of 211 (54 were male). In this photograph, Dykes is in the second row, second from the right, and team mascot Wayne McCluskey is in the first row, in the middle. McCluskey's water bucket bears his distinctive nickname, Chicken. Senior team captain Albert Whitacre is to the left of Coach Dykes. Below, the 1924 team is pictured. Its claim to fame is bringing the first district title and playoff run to Stephenville. (Below, Brad Thompson.)

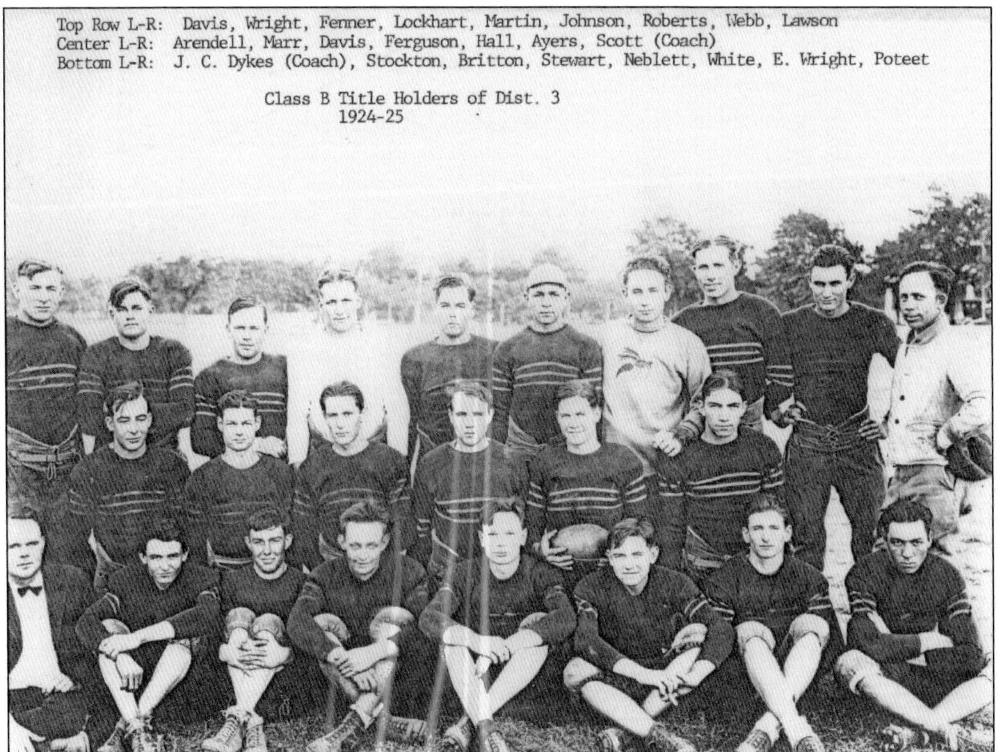

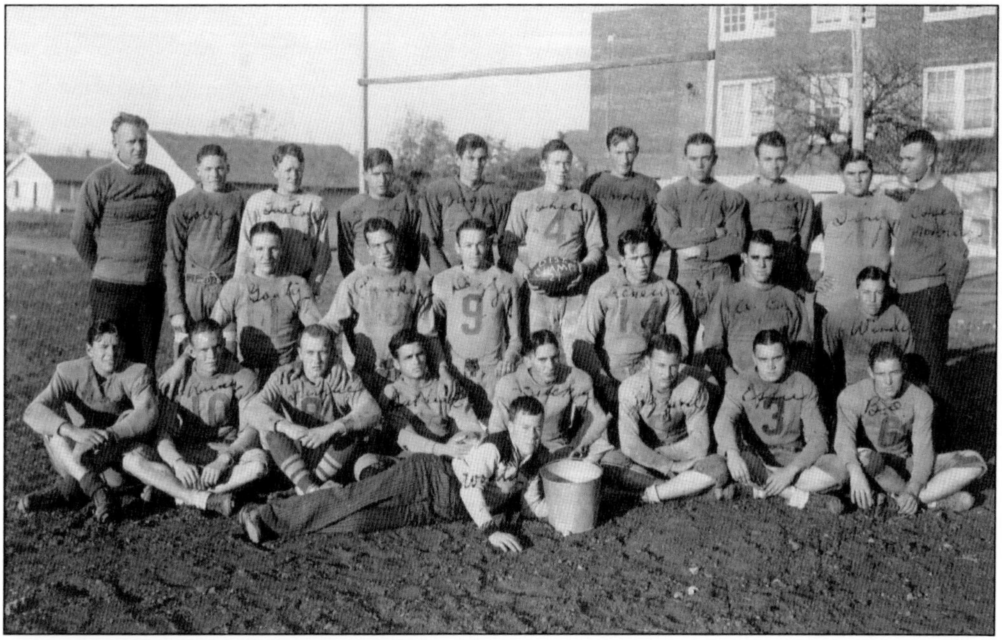

The 1929 district champions coached by Joe Brown are pictured above. During the 1929 and 1930 seasons, his Jackets only lost one regular-season contest and put together back-to-back district championships. Below is the 1930 team, a squad that included 11 returning lettermen from the previous season's district champions. Brown (right) and his assistant coach, Jim Mobley, recline in the first row. The team's most notable member was Hugh "Here" Wolfe (second row, fourth from left) who played both college and professional football. Disappointingly, the Jackets fell to Albany in the 1930 Bi-District contest, in spite of the fact that SHS gained 32 first downs to Albany's 11. (Both, Stephenville Historical Museum.)

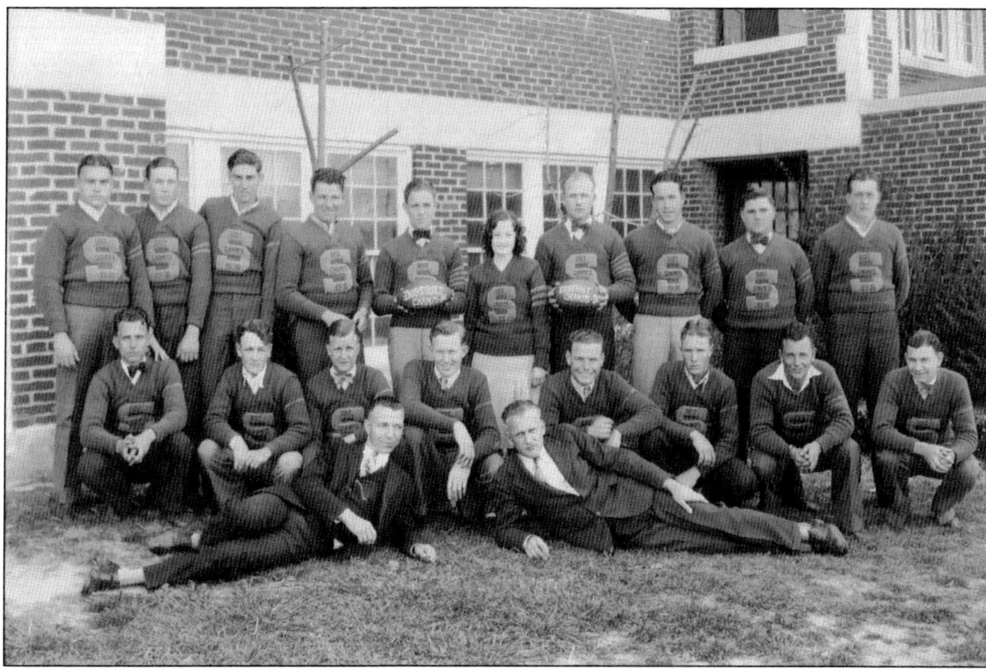

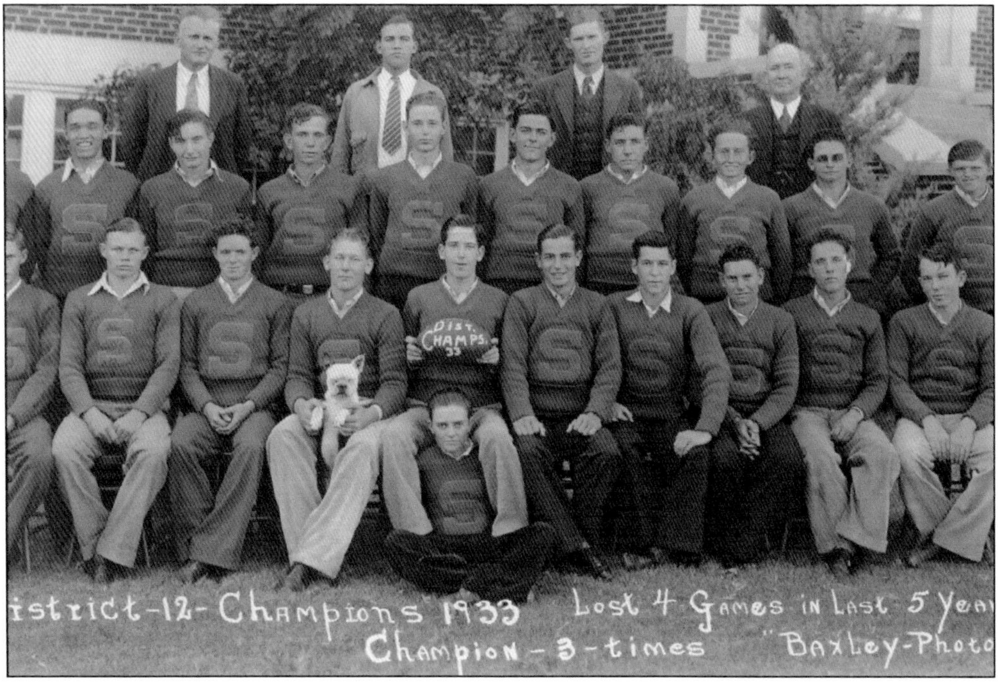

Posing in front of the high school, Brown's sweater boys (above) performed well again in 1933, bringing Stephenville its third District 12 title in five years. In 1936, the tight-lipped, soft-spoken, sportsmanship-minded Jim Mobley coached the Jackets to an undefeated 9-0-0 season. His team (below) outscored opponents 283 to 12, posting seven shutouts, including a 45-0 bi-district win over the Winter Blizzards and an 18-0 win over Rock Springs for Stephenville's first ever Class B Regional title. Admission to the title game was 75¢. (Above, Stephenville Historical Museum.)

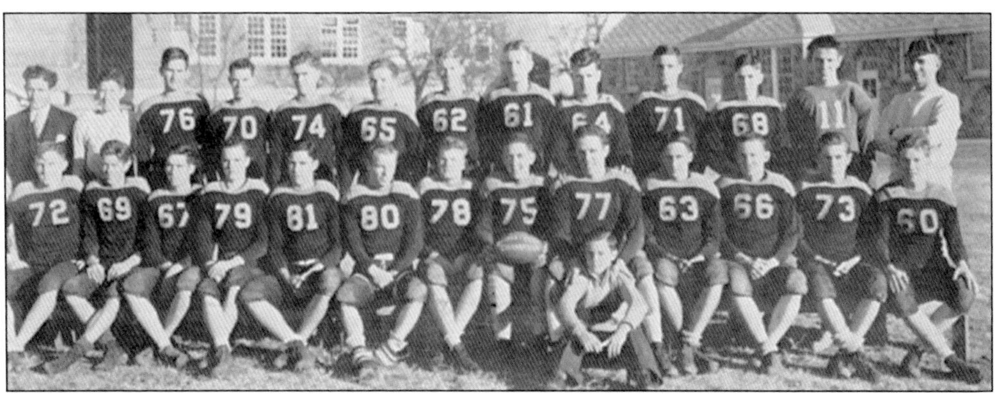

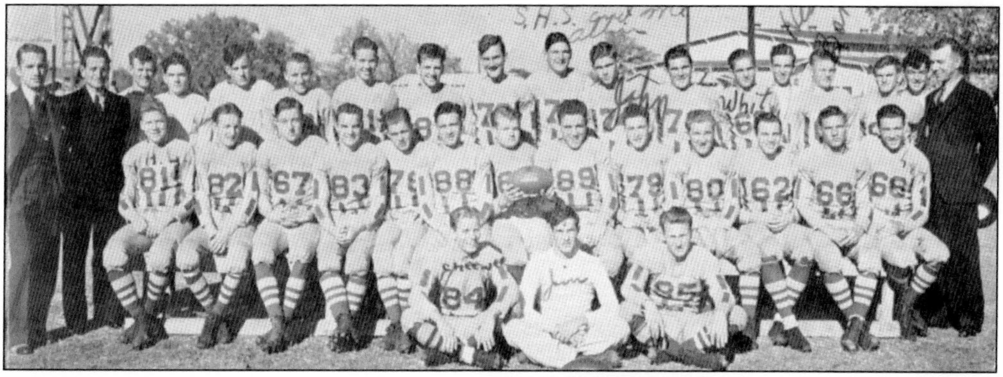

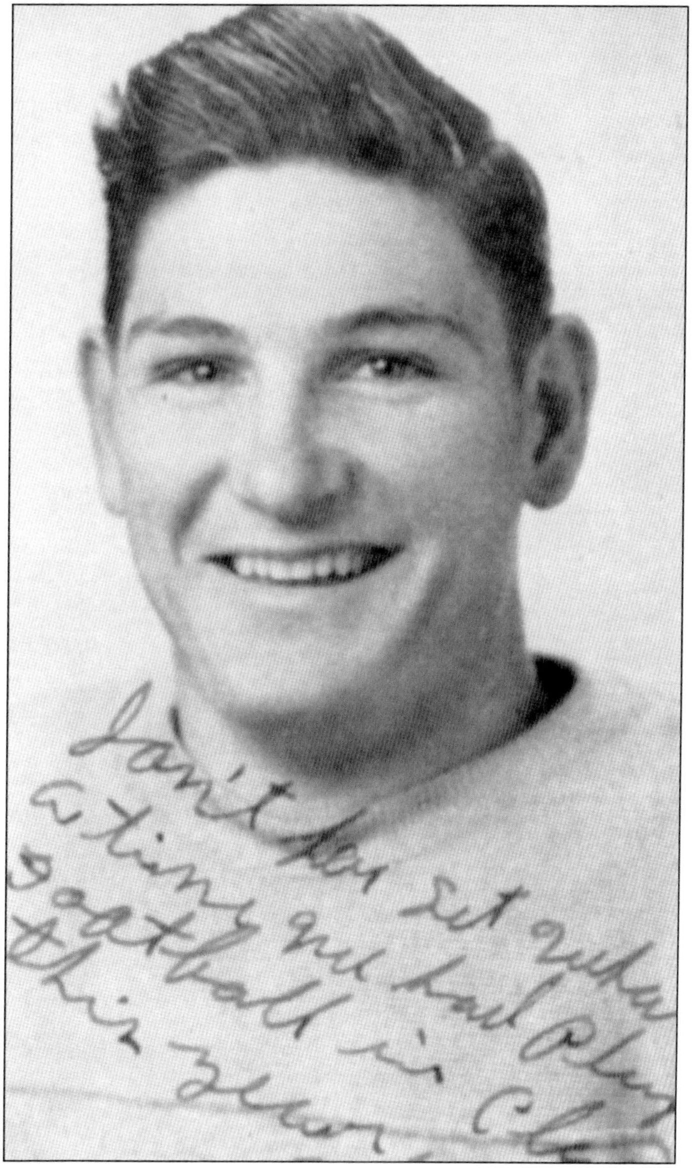

In 1937, Mobley's Jackets moved to the Class A Oil Belt District. At season's midpoint at their Hays Field home venue, SHS upset Sweetwater before 5,000 fans, the largest crowd ever gathered there. Noted for speed and power, SHS outscored its 1937 opponents 237-51. The team (above) went 9-1-0, their only defeat being a 7-6 loss to Abilene. While the Jackets and Eagles finished the regular seasons with identical records, the district committee granted Abilene, not Stephenville, the sole district playoff berth. In the 1930s, Texas coaches everywhere often encouraged strong, athletic farm boys from the hinterland to move to town to play football. Albin Ramsey (right) and Marshall Sherrod were two such 1937 recruits. In 1940, Bill Hicks came from nearby Bluff Dale to Stephenville for precisely the same reason. These out-of-town additions often enhanced Yellow Jacket play.

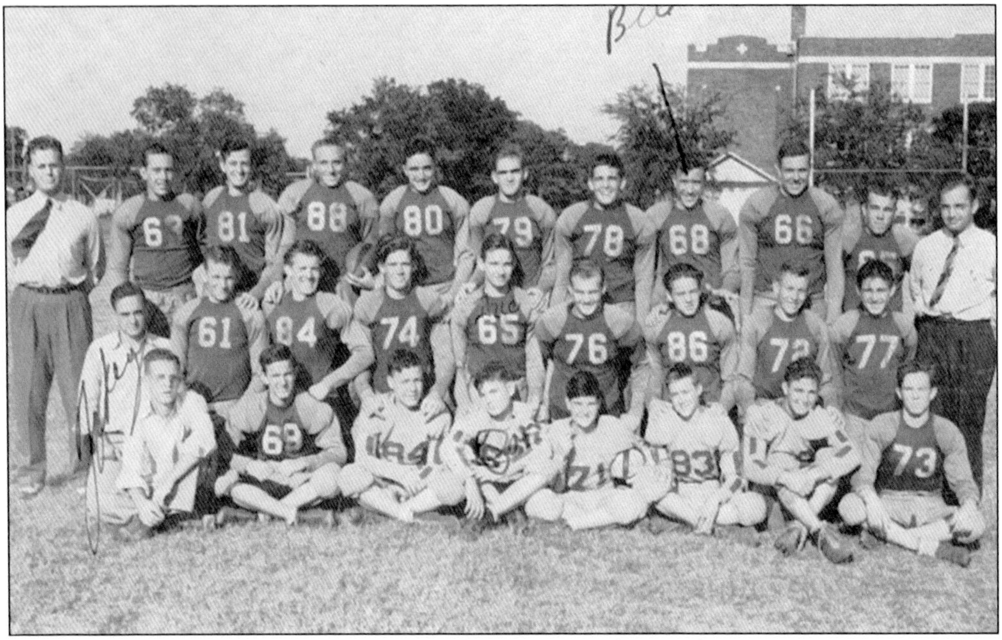

By the late 1930s, team sizes were twice as large as were their early-1920s counterparts. Jimmy Marshall took over the Jackets in 1938. The 1940 preseason poll ranked Marshall's team at no. 9. Beating District 9-2A nemesis Breckenridge 26-6 during the regular season, the team (above) went 8-0-1 and advanced to bi-district. There, SHS tied Temple 7-7, but in the days prior to overtime play, they lost by three to two on penetrations (the tie-breaking system of the time). Below are Jacket 1940 All-District selections. They are, from left to right, (first row) second teamers C.B. Rushing, Donald "Smitty" Smith, and John "Whit" Whitacre; (second row) first teamers Barney Welch (back), Connie Jones (guard), Oliver Griffin (guard), and Aaron Autry (end).

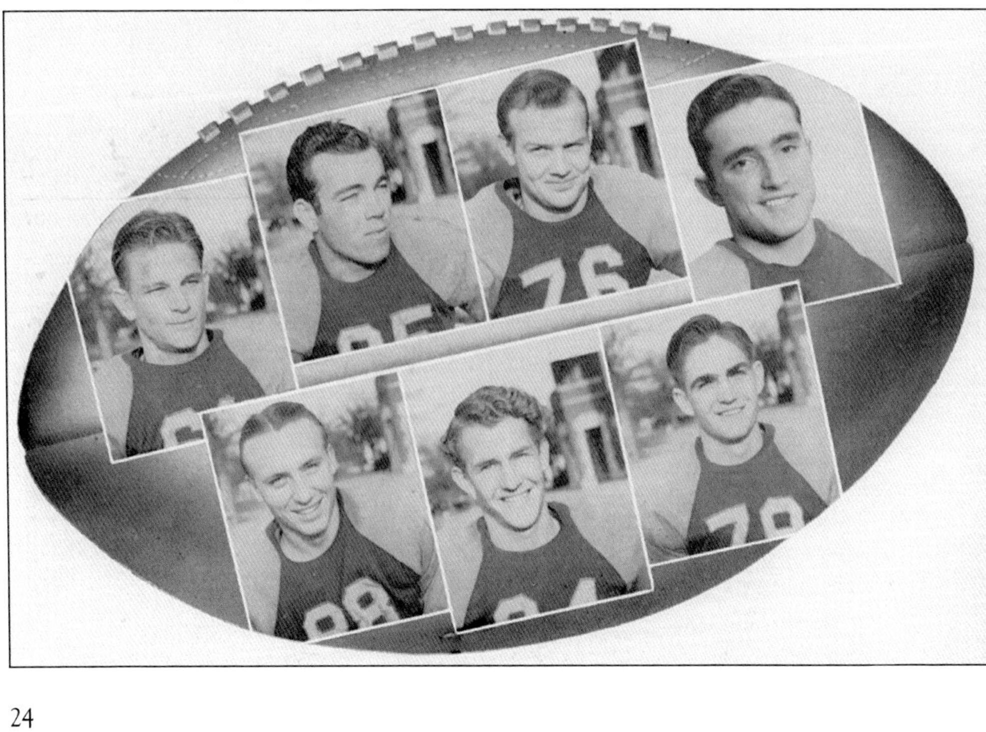

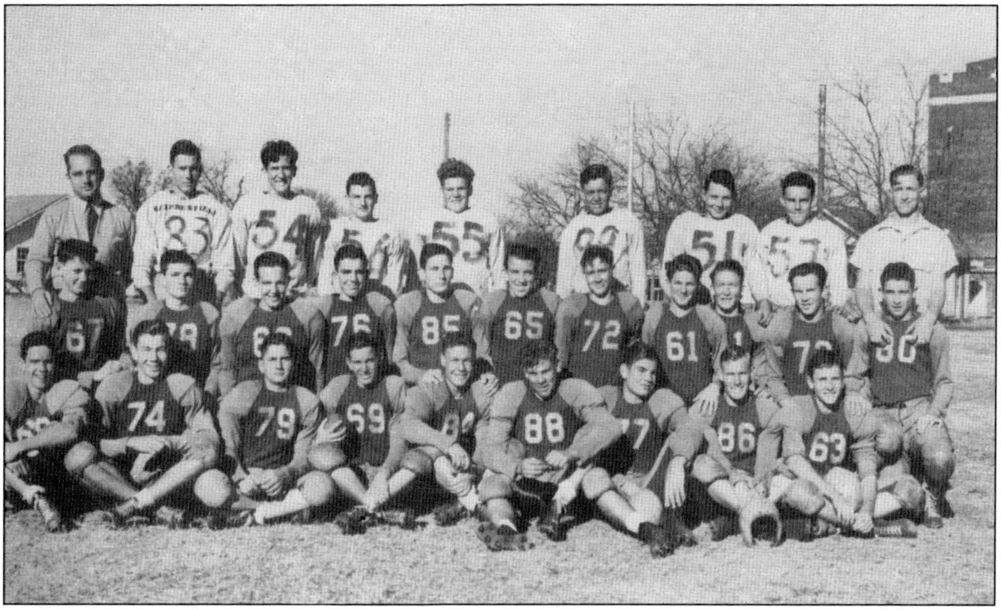

Marshall's 1942 team (above) went 9-1, with its only loss to the Breckenridge Buckaroos, who advanced to the playoffs. SHS remained at home. In the middle of World War II, E.E. "Flash" Walker replaced Marshall. Among the stars that year are, from left to right (below), (first row) unidentified, Billy "Pup" Willingham, Albert Cragwall, unidentified, unidentified, James "Bulldog" Willingham, and unidentified; and (second row) unidentified, Charles "Casey" Casstevens, Ralph "Bass" Poteet, and unidentified. Walker's 1943 team posted an admirable 7-2-0 record, but again the Jackets were denied, losing to Breckenridge, who won District 9-2A and advanced. Walker's Jackets did, however, soundly defeat future archrival Brownwood. That contest came on Thanksgiving Day, the traditional date of a season-ending rivalry matchup from 1922.

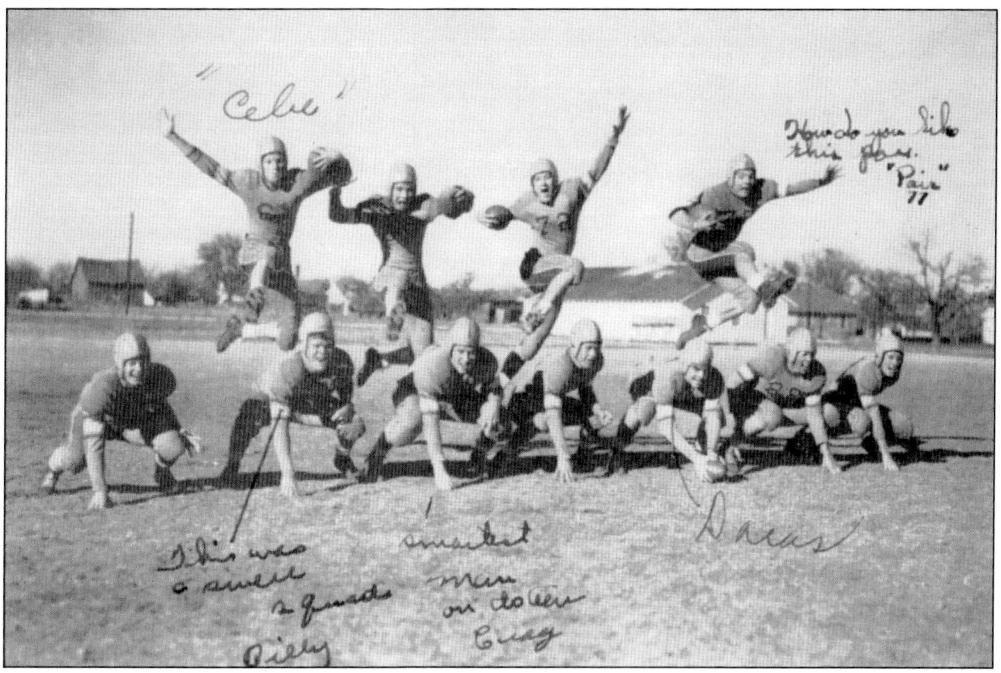

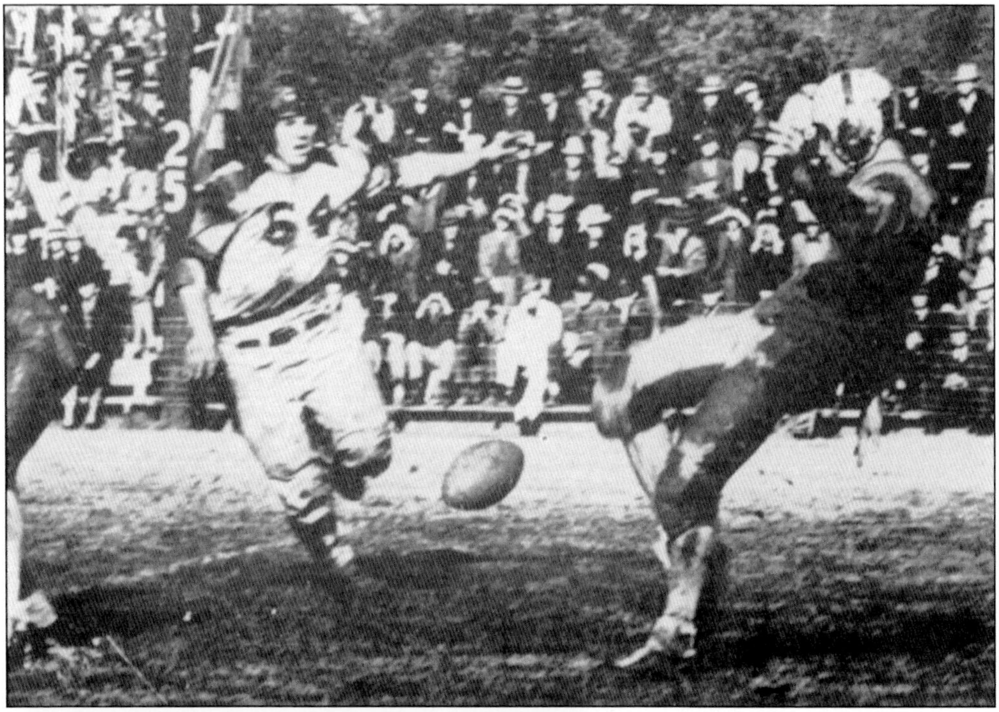

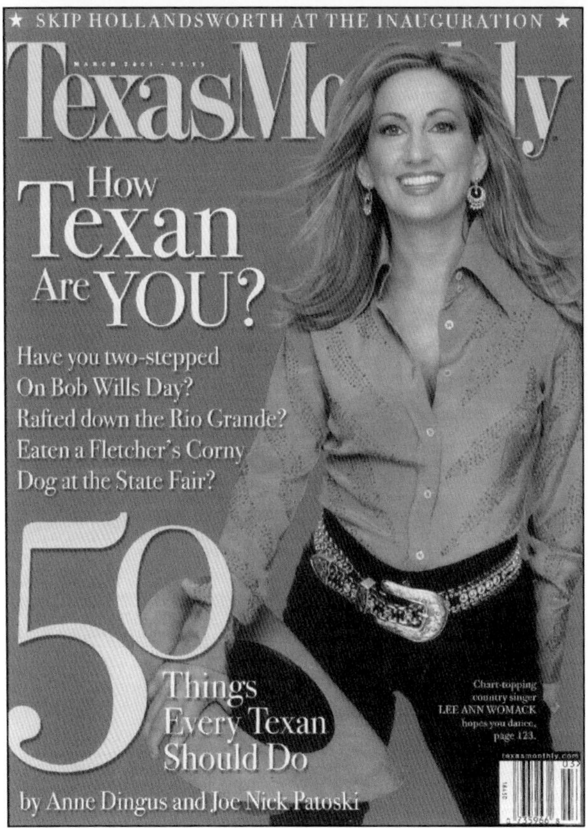

By the 1990s, Brownwood, not Breckenridge, had become Stephenville's chief opponent. SHS first played the Lions in 1937. Above, John A. Whitacre punts the ball in the 1940 Yellow Jacket–Lions contest that Stephenville won 19-6. Over the years, especially after Gordon Wood coached Brownwood to seven state championships between 1960 and 1981, "the game" evolved into one of the most intense Lone Star State rivalries. In the March 2001 *Texas Monthly*, Anne Dingus and Joe Nick Patoski included watching this contest on a list of "50 Things that Every Texan Should Do." The text that appeared in the Dingus-Patoski article declares, "this annual clash . . . exemplifies Friday night lights in all their glory. In these communities, football is both entertainment and obsession, thanks in no small part to each school's reputation for producing winners." (Left, *Texas Monthly*.)

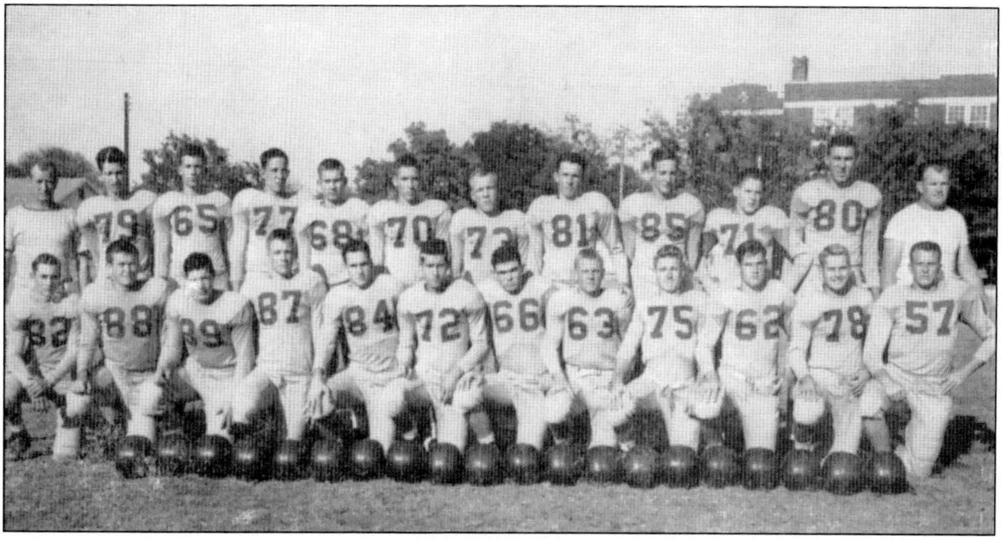

The year following the war's end, Mike Murphy came to SHS to coach (1946–1954). Much like Marshall before him, Murphy fielded some of the best teams in Texas. His 1948 Jackets (8-1-0) (above) again were denied by Breckenridge (who would win state in 1951, 1952, 1954, and 1958, and tie Cleburne 20-20 in the 1959 title game). Murphy enjoyed considerable success, thanks to a talented offense greatly aided by fullback L.C. Shuffield (below, second row, second from left), directed by Ray "Killer" Graves (second row, third from left), and inspired by the speedy lineman Wendell Lackey (first row, third from left). In 1951, Murphy led the Jackets to a second 8-1-0 season, with the team losing only to district foe Breckenridge, who advanced to win the state title.

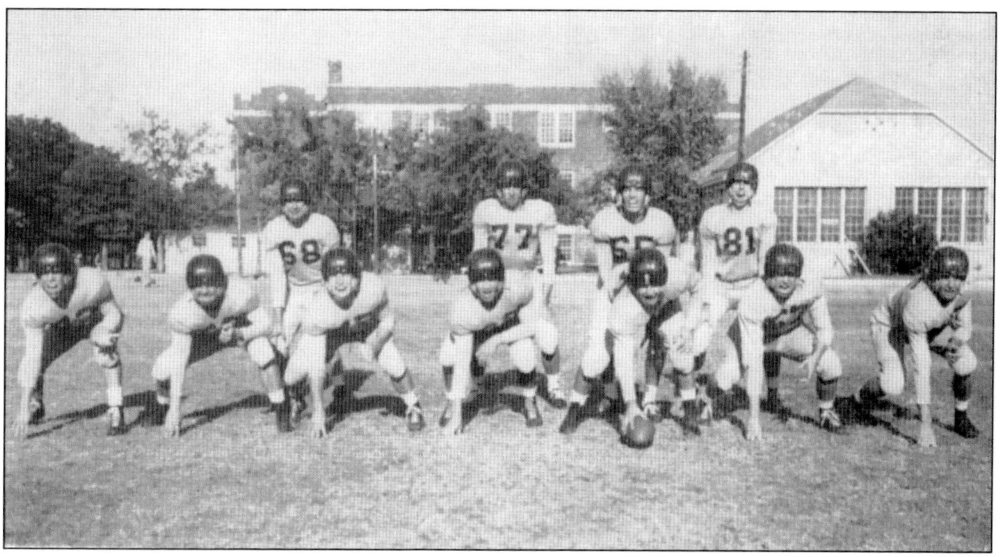

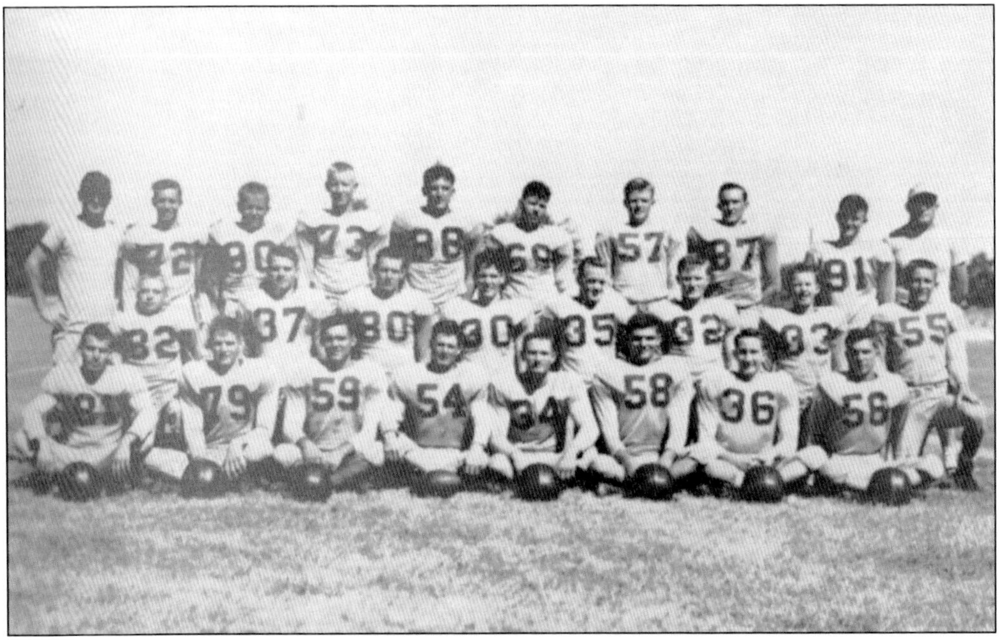

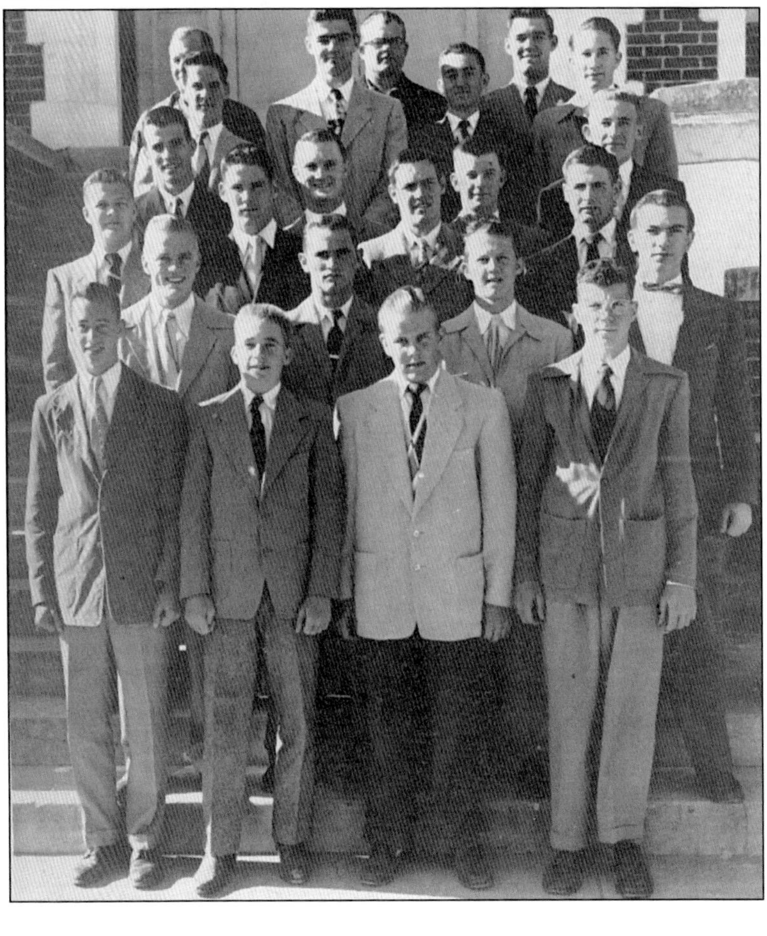

The following season, another Murphy team (above) went all the way to the 1952 3A Regional contest. In the final outing, the Jackets lost to Terrell High School, who later won the 1952 state title. Left, a smartly dressed 1952 team poses in celebration of district, bi-district, and regional appearances. In spite of fielding several excellent teams after 1952, it would be another 37 years before the Yellow Jackets would return to the playoffs.

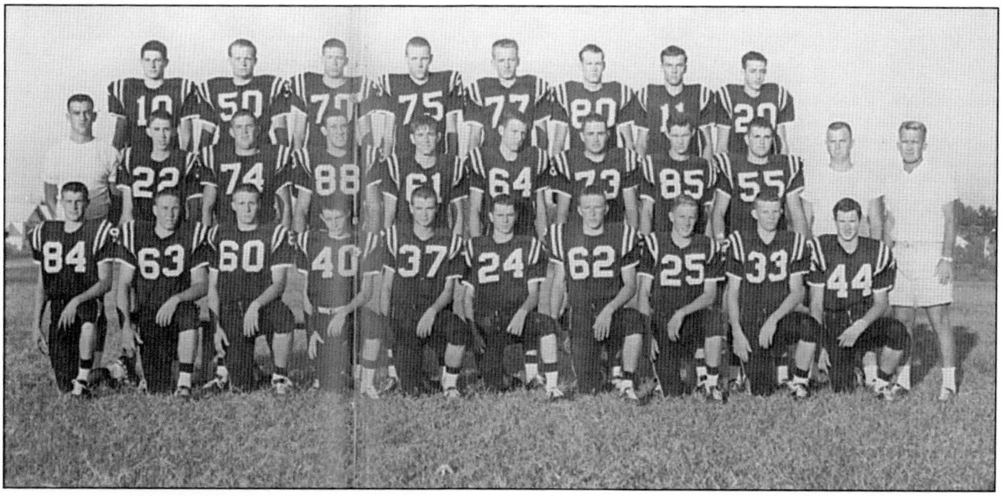

During the playoff drought, several Jacket teams still did well. Coach Kenneth Scott's 1963 team (above) went 7-3. Although the squad did not advance to the playoffs, the team beat Brownwood 12-6 and included future SHS Athletic hall of famers Steve Gunn and Van Evans, both juniors. Below, jubilant ends Donnie Laughlin (left) and Jug Little lead the way as teammates carry Scott off the field in celebration.

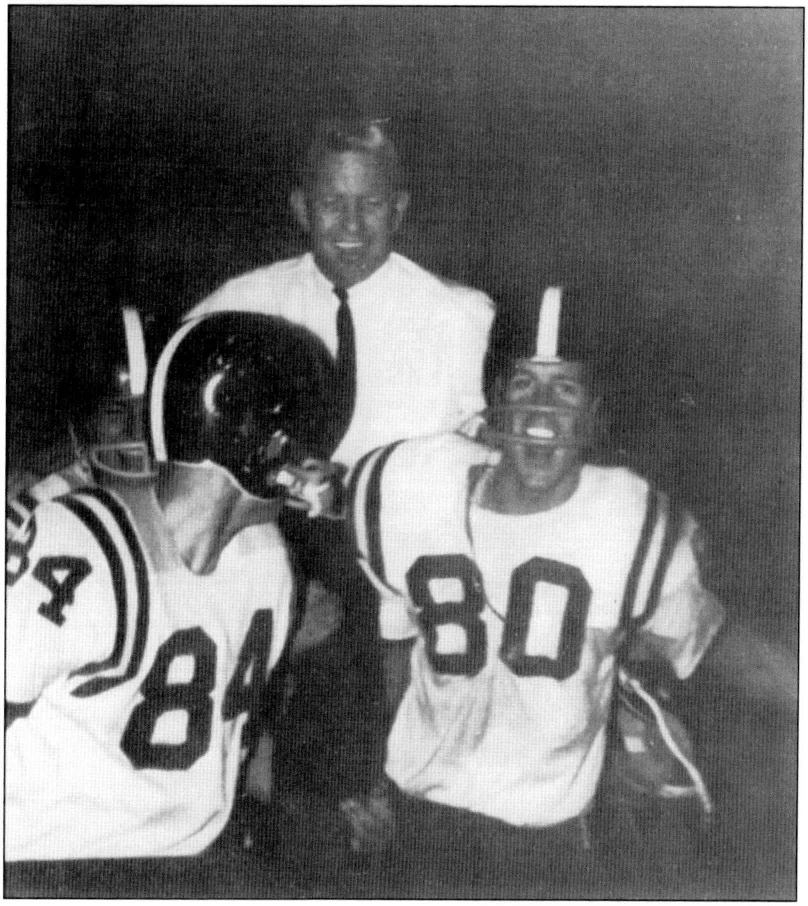

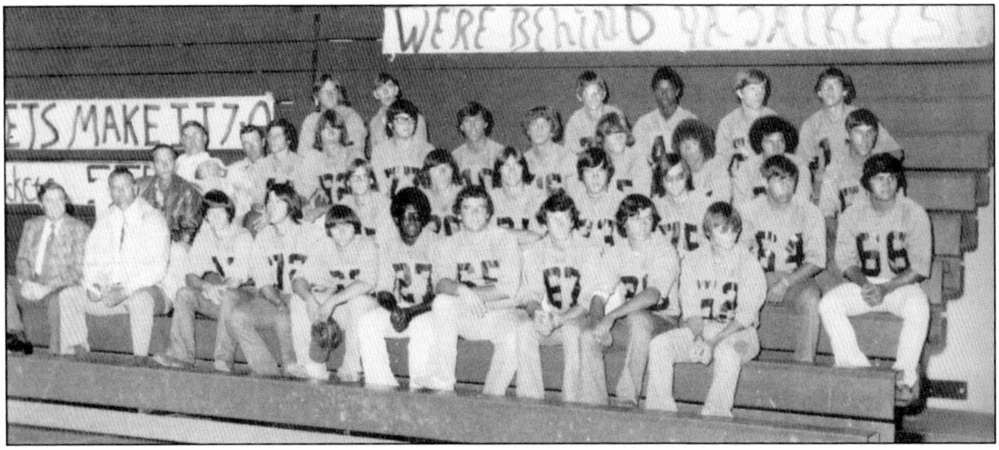

Above, coach Leon Manley's 1976 Jackets were 6-4. Among its ranks were future hall of famers Mark Manley and Ricky DeLoach. In 1980, Manley's team posted a 7-3 record and included future hall of famers Kyle Heffley, Tod Ryden, and Kobe Fornes. Below, the 1980 team breaks through the cheerleaders' banner on its way onto the field of play. Coach Joe Loudermilk's 1986 Yellow Jackets went 7-3. Future hall of famer Roy Graham was on this squad.

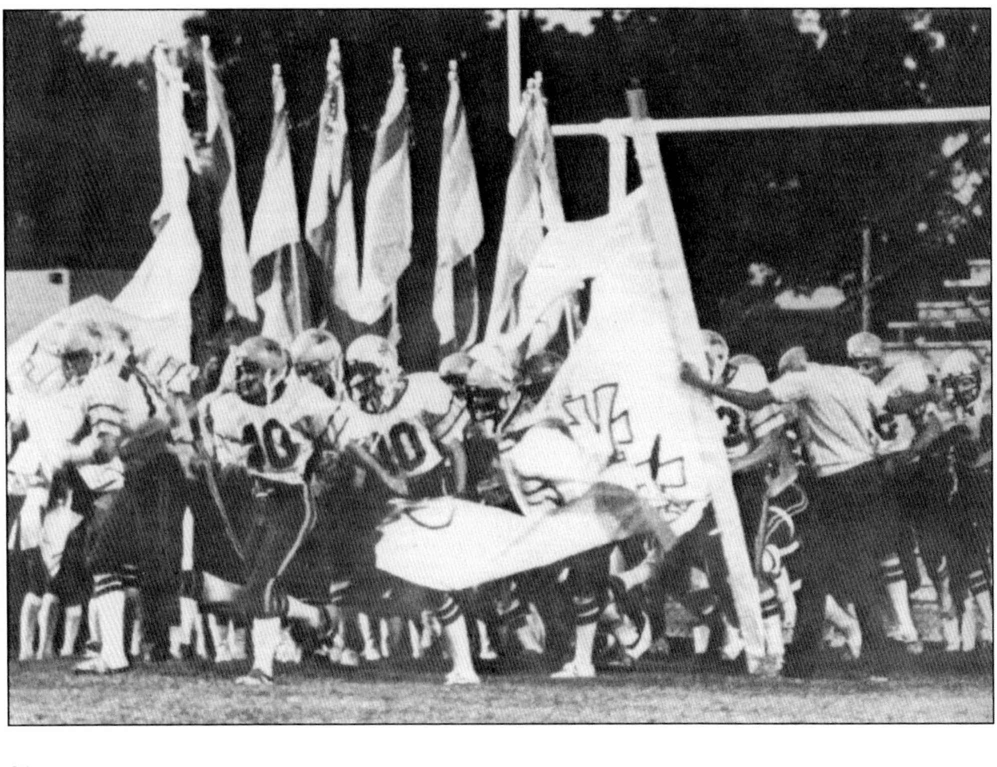

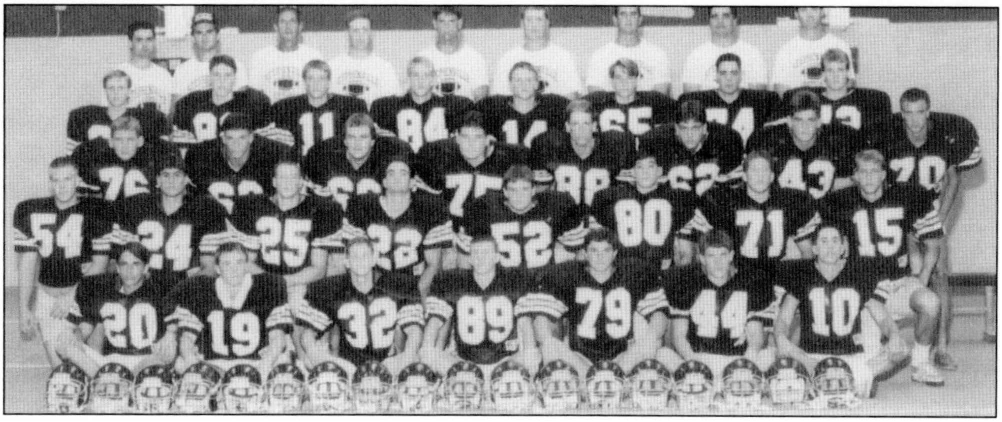

The playoff drought ended in 1989, when the Art Briles's Yellow Jackets (above) not only returned to postseason play but before a crowd of 4,689 at Baylor's Floyd Casey Stadium surprised pundits with a decisive 32-6 round-one win over sixth-ranked Belton. The following season at a heavily attended contest at Irving's Texas Stadium, the 1990 Jackets (below) made it farther than any Stephenville team had ever gone, losing in the semifinal to eventual 4A state champion Wilmer-Hutchins. The Jackets had come a long way in terms of performance since 1920. The earliest teams, commonly numbering under 20 players, were dwarfed in size by teams like those pictured here, which had 31 and 36 players, respectively.

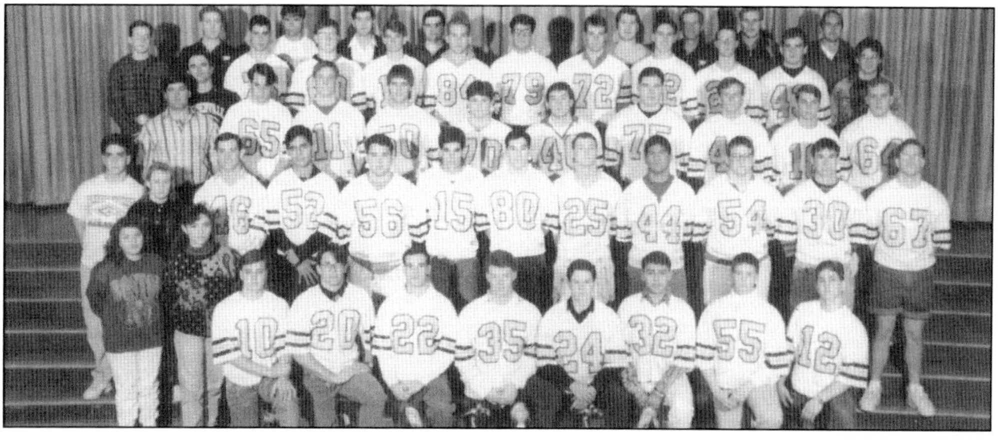

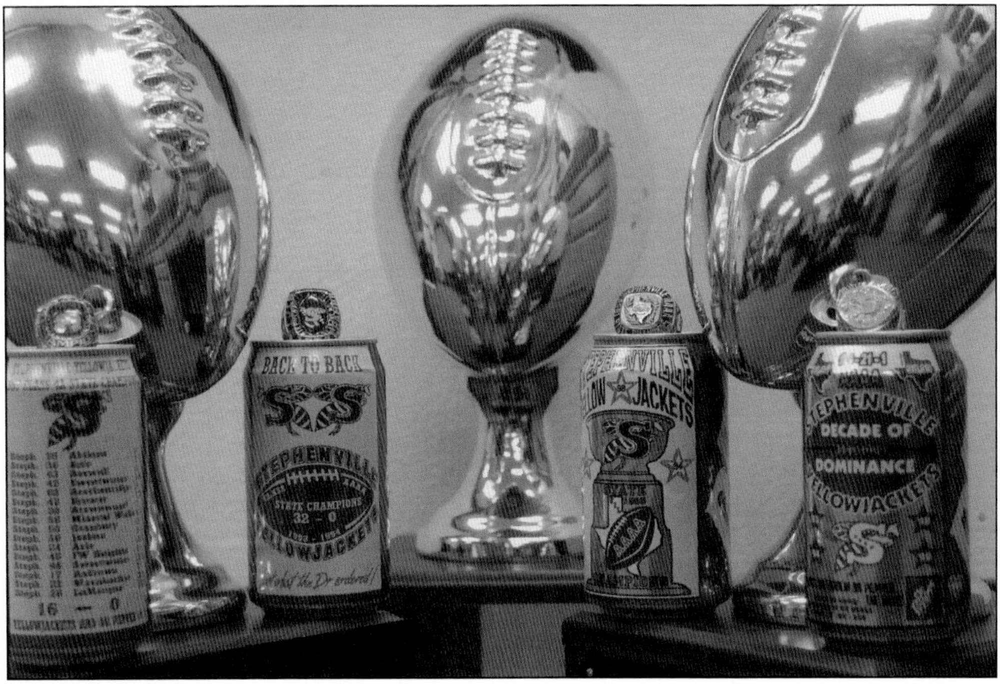

The pièce de résistance came, of course, in 1993, when SHS began a run that made the Jackets the acknowledged team of the 1990s. The Dublin Dr. Pepper facility commemorated Stephenville's four state-championship seasons with the special commemorative cans pictured above. Sitting atop each respective can are championship rings, which are awarded to both players and coaches. The cycle of success began when the 1993 Jacket team (below) defeated La Marque 26-13 at Austin's Memorial Stadium for its first state title. (Above, Debbie Cashell; below, Ellen Skipper.)

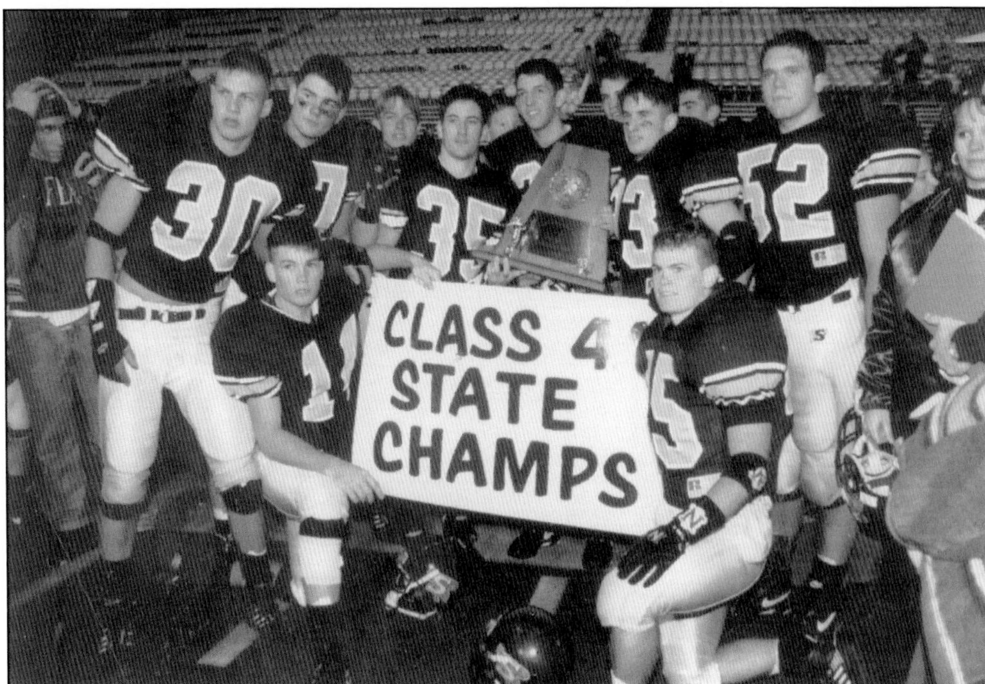

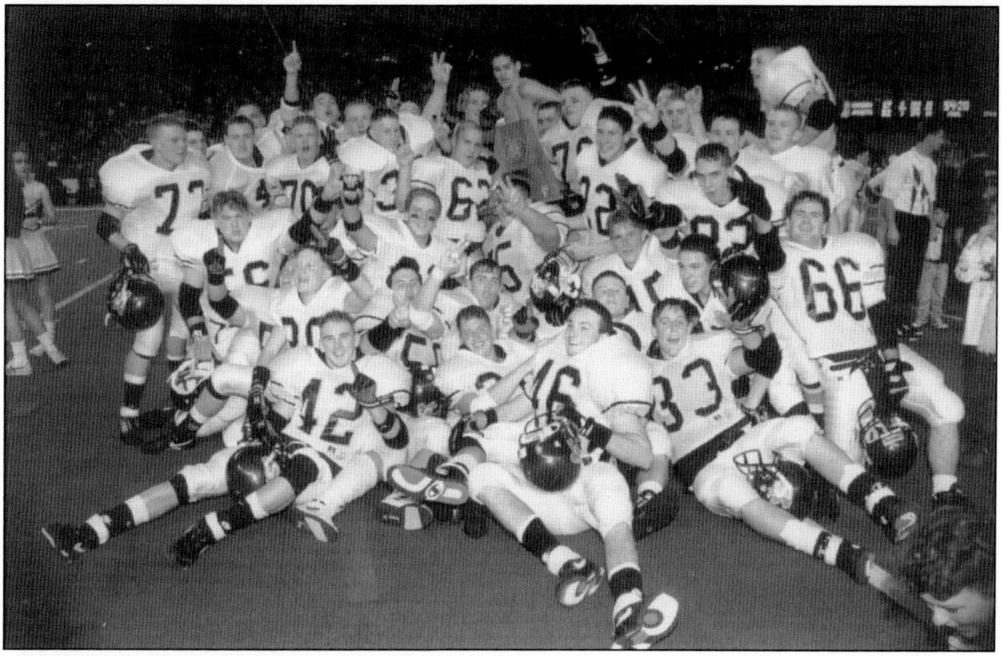

Building on a 16-game win streak, the National Sports News Service no. 8 nationally ranked 1994 team (above) doubled that total, capping off its 32nd straight victory with a 32-17 championship win, again over La Marque. Reminiscent of the phrase attributed to Los Angeles Dodgers baseball coach Leo Durocher, locals believed that the 1993 and 1994 teams caught "lightning in a bottle," capturing the powerful and illusive and displaying it before the world. Indeed, the Jackets of those two seasons did credit to Benjamin Franklin's kite and Leyden jar. After losing the season opener, the 1995 Jackets (below) continued their winning ways, advancing to the quarterfinals before falling to state finalist Denison in round four. (Above, Skipper.)

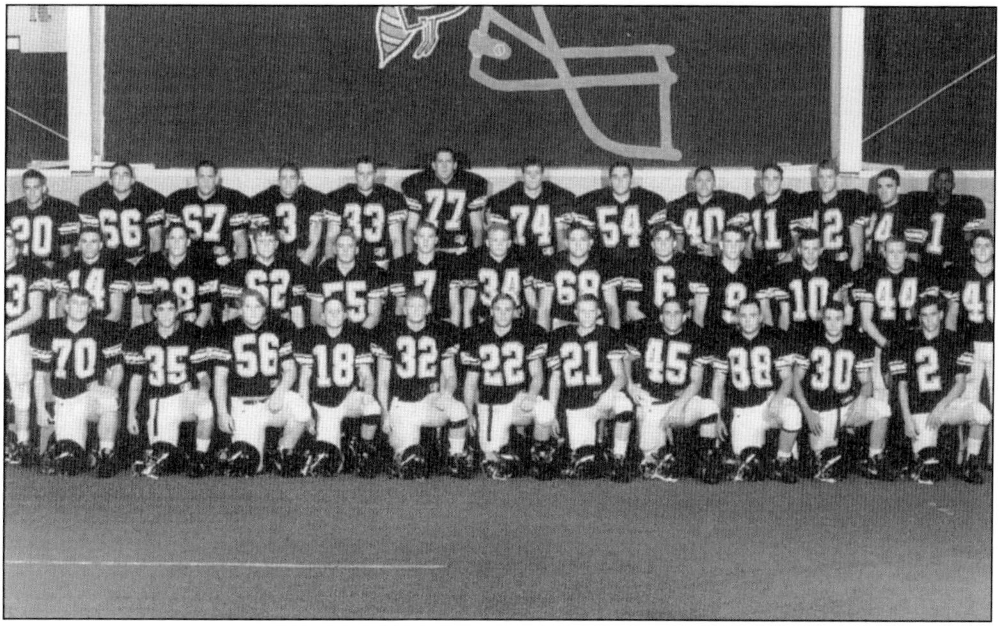

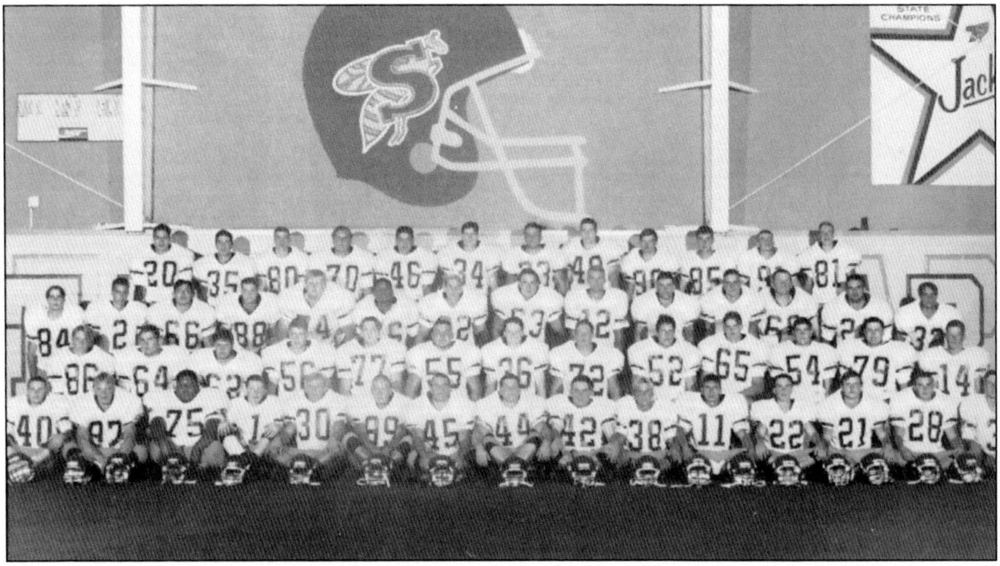

Likewise, the 1996 team (above) went to quarterfinals. The 1997 team advanced to Area. The Jackets returned to the state final (4A D-2) in 1998, meeting La Marque for a third time. During the interim (1995 through 1997), the Cougars won three consecutive state championships. In spite of confronting a team making its sixth straight title bid, the 1998 Jackets (below) used their high octane offense to post 34 points while the Stephenville "War Dog" defense limited the Cougars to a single touchdown and point after. (Below, Skipper.)

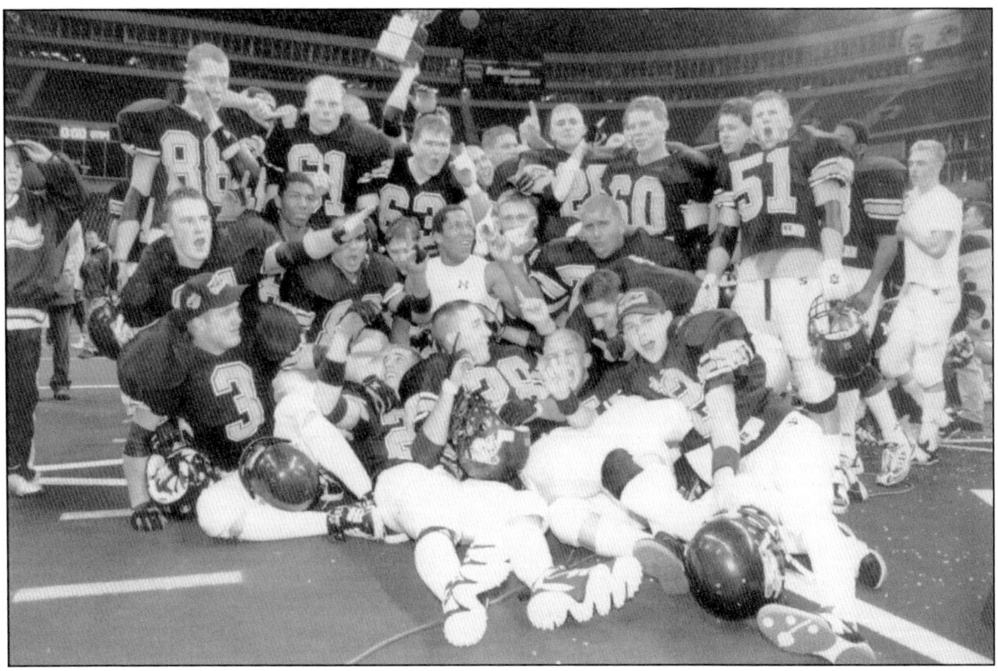

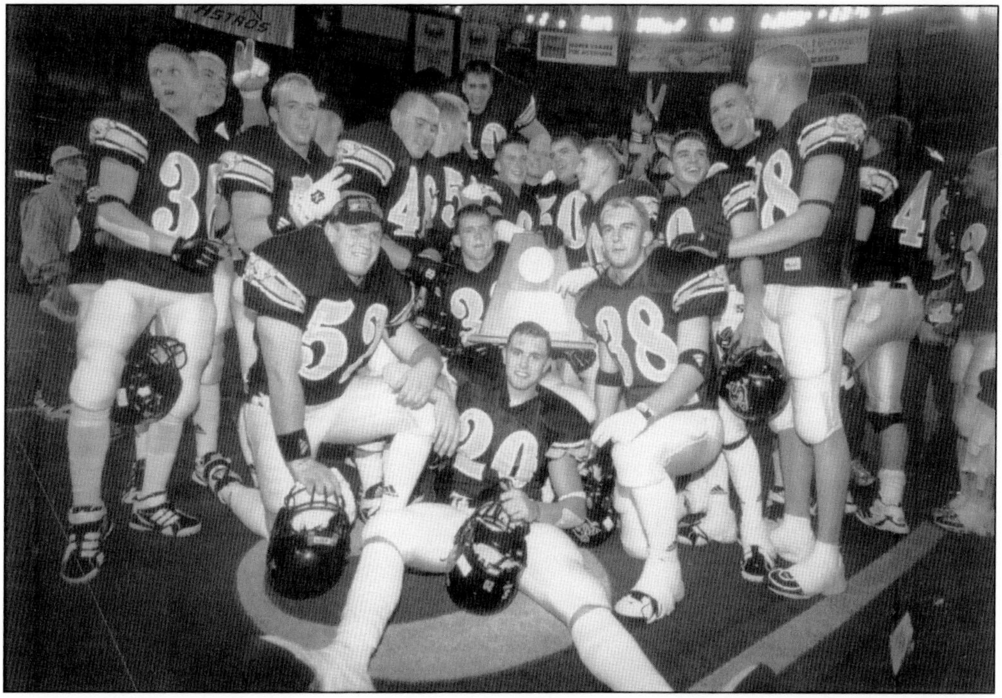

In a remarkable reprisal of the 1993–1994 back-to-back state championships, the no. 17 nationally ranked 1999 Jackets (above) posted a perfect undefeated season. This time, Stephenville met Port Neches-Groves at the Houston Astrodome. The 28-18 score obscures a lopsided contest in which Jacket quarterback Kendal Briles ran for three touchdowns and was 13 for 18, passing for 125 yards. *Fort Worth Star-Telegram* staff writer Jeff Caplan's Dec. 19 postgame analysis proclaims, "Yellow Jackets' '90s dominance official now." In 2005, the Jackets (below) were again undefeated until the semifinal, when they narrowly missed upsetting the Highland Park Scots who, one week later, became 4A Division-1 (D-1) state champions. (Above, Skipper.)

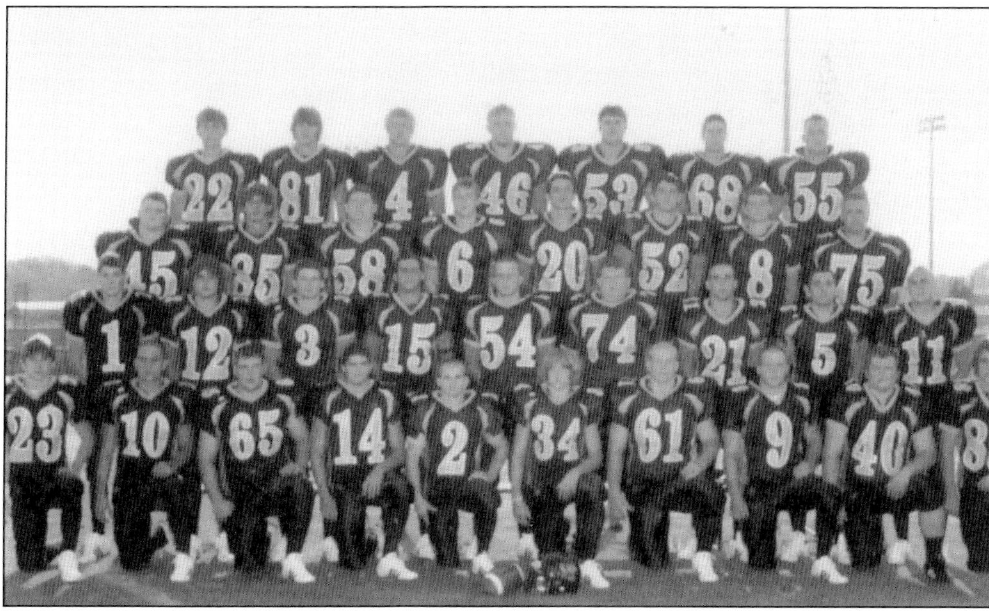

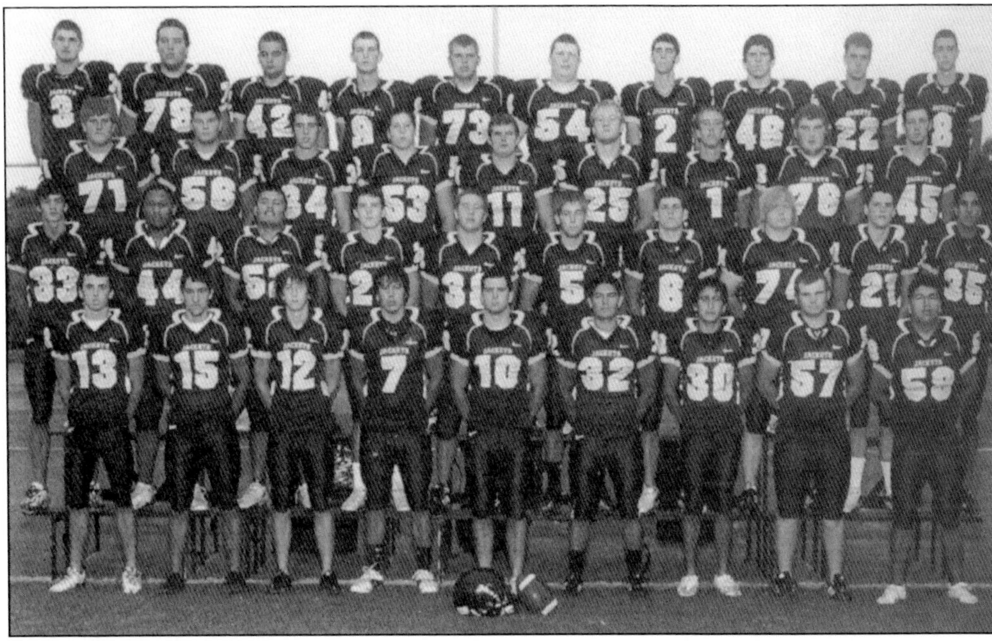

Thereafter, Stephenville's deepest playoff penetration came when the 2008 team (above) returned to the quarterfinals, this time against the Everman Bulldogs. After leading through much of the game, the Jackets came up short, losing 27-24. The 2010 team met Aledo in the quarterfinals at Baylor's Floyd Casey Stadium. With the Jackets leading 10-6 late in the third quarter, the nearest official ruled a Witt Westbrook catch (below) out-of-bounds. At the final gun, the Jackets trailed by 8, thus denied the opportunity to advance to the 4A D-2 Semifinal. The Stephenville-Aledo rivalry remains alive and well. It will be the substance of hard-fought contests for many years to come. (Below, Dr. Jeffrey K. Edwards.)

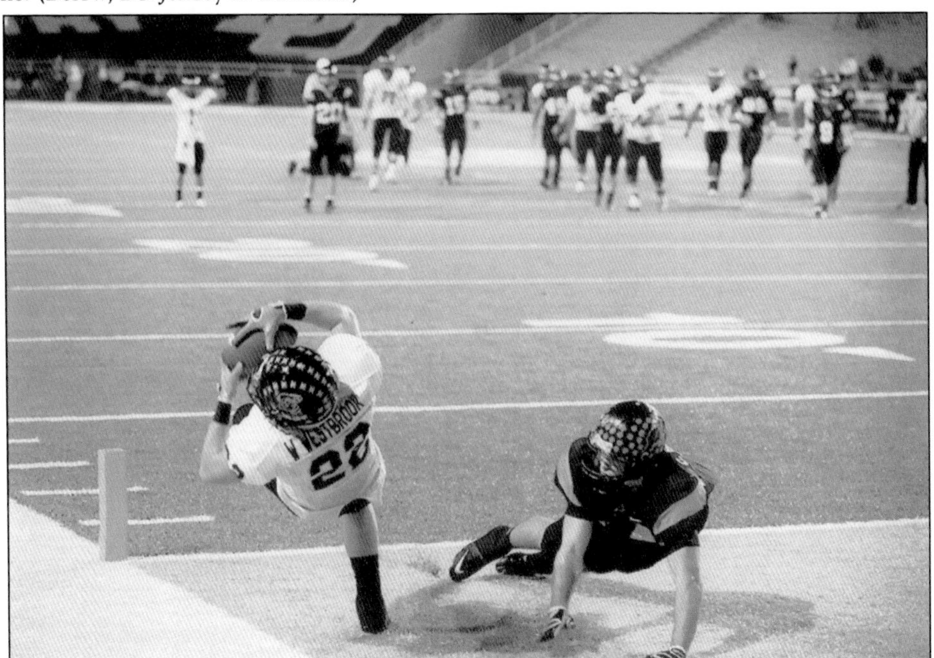

Three

QUARTERBACK HIGH

Writing for the *New York Times* in 1991, Roy McHugh christened Western Pennsylvania a "football factory," an "incubator for excellence," and the "cradle of quarterbacks." His claim had substance. George Blanda, Johnny Unitas, Len Dawson, Joe Namath, Joe Montana, Jim Kelly, and Dan Marino, to name only a few, originated from this area. Stephenville legitimately has a similar claim. On December 7, some 11 days before the 1999 4A D-2 Championship Game, *Dallas Morning News* sportswriter John Marshall appropriately dubbed SHS "Quarterback High."

This moniker probably would have surprised Stephenville's first football coaches. Like most early-20th-century American football teams, the Yellow Jackets passed infrequently. The early Jackets ran the single wing, a backfield alignment often considered the ancestor of the modern spread formation. That was then. The spread popular today in Texas schoolboy football did not appear at SHS until the arrival of Art Briles.

Coach Preston's 1920 quarterback (a position in the early years often referred to simply as "passer") was the fleet-of-foot, poetically nicknamed Lee "Bo" Poteet, the first in a long line of successful Jacket signal callers. Before Art Briles brought the spread to Stephenville, several SHS quarterbacks marched their offenses up and down the field, occasionally leading the team to playoff glory. Johnny "Zero" Dunn, Ray "Killer" Graves, Harry "Bubby" Braeuer, Jerry Flemmons, Gary Chandler, Kyle Heffley, and Matt Copeland were among the best. Nothing compared, however, to the succession of statistic-producing Briles-era field generals: Cody Ledbetter, Chris Harkey, Branndon Stewart, Glenn Odell, Jason Schwartzkopf, Kyle Dempsey, Kelan Luker, Kendal Briles, and Kevin Kolb.

In a setting where "tradition never graduates," the post-Briles string of gunslingers has rarely missed a stride. Successively, under the coaching administrations of Mike Copeland, Chad Morris, and Joseph Gillespie, the tradition of Quarterback High endured into 2000 and beyond. Familiar names like Kevin Kolb, Tie Lasater, Conner Elms, Jevan Snead, Kody Spano, Brad Picha, and Connor Washington have continued a legacy likely to persist.

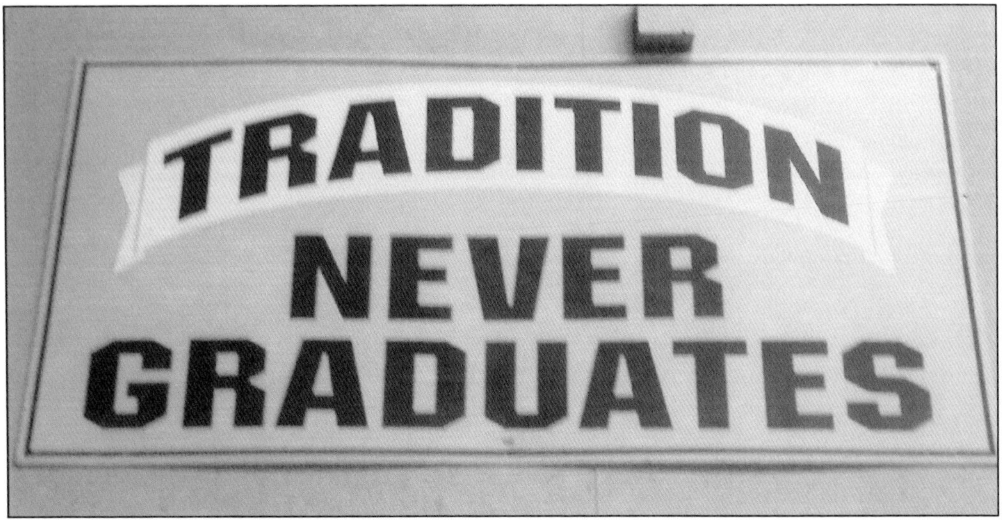

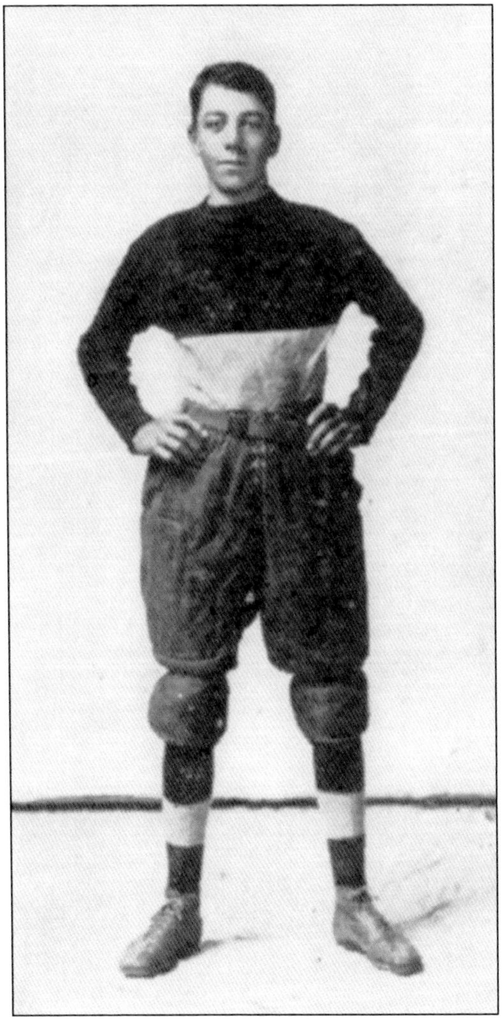

High on the northwest wall of today's SHS Green Room—an indoor workout facility attached to the weight room—a navy-blue-and-yellow sign proclaims, "Tradition Never Graduates" (above). Jacket quarterback greats are part of a continuing tradition dating from 1920. The 1921 yearbook described Lee "Bo" Poteet (left), SHS's first signal caller, as "our quarterback, fleet of foot and a player who uses his head." After the fifth consecutive win of the 1920 season, on November 5, the local *Tribune* identified "Poteet's broken field running" as one of "the features of the game." The November 30, 1923, *Stephenville Empire* quotes *Fort Worth Star-Telegram* sports editor Billy Bee, who identified Poteet as "the outstanding Star of the Yellow Jackets," one who played well on both sides of the ball. (Above, author.)

Perhaps the next most successful quarterback was the rugged, quick-thinking, 145-pound Charles "Chee Wee" Lockhart (right), who, as a junior, guided the undefeated 1936 Jacket team to the Class B Regional Championship. Lockhart also had a successful 1937 senior season, leading the Jackets to a 9-1-0 record. Shown in 1937 (below), he finds a gap in the defense and races downfield.

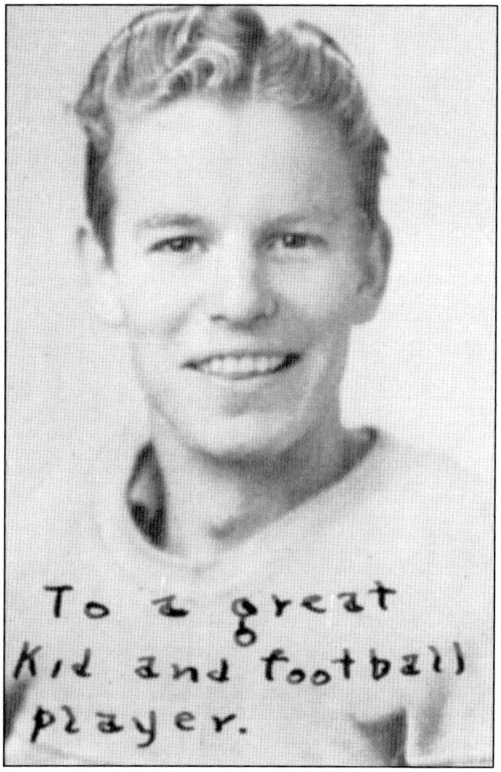

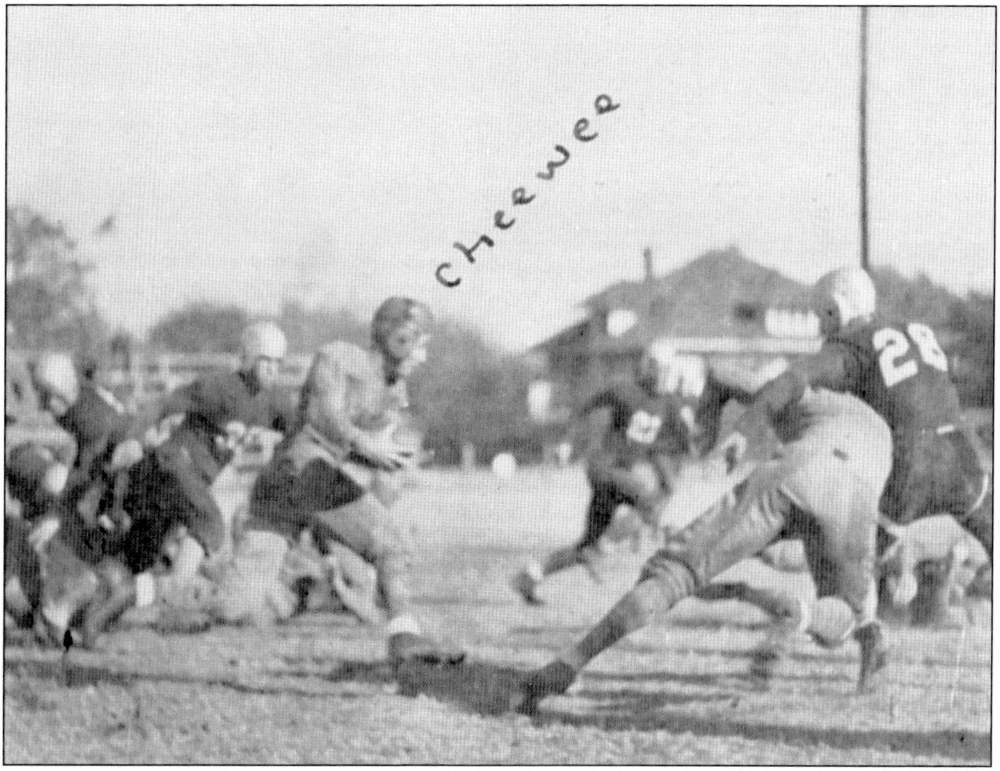

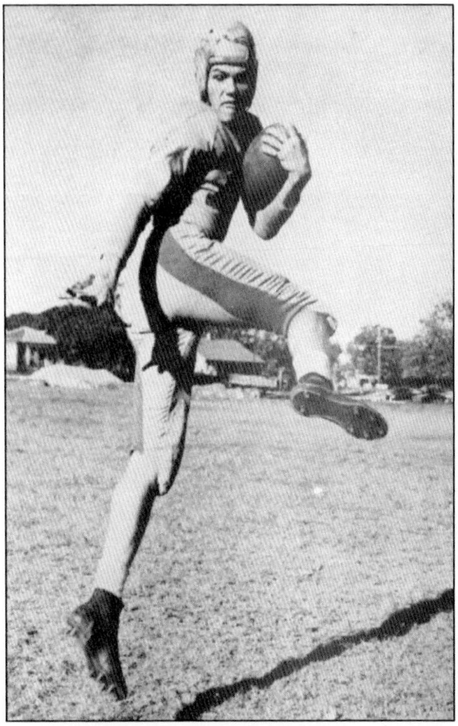

In 1945, junior quarterback Johnny Dunn (left) earned second team all-district honors for his broken field running (below). The following season, the yearbook editor wrote of his "side-stepping, swiveled-hipped" style that made Dunn the leading scorer in 1946 District 9-2A and honorable mention all-state. Dunn went on to Texas Christian University, where he lettered three years in football and four years in track. In 1992, Dunn received induction into the SHS Athletic Hall of Fame.

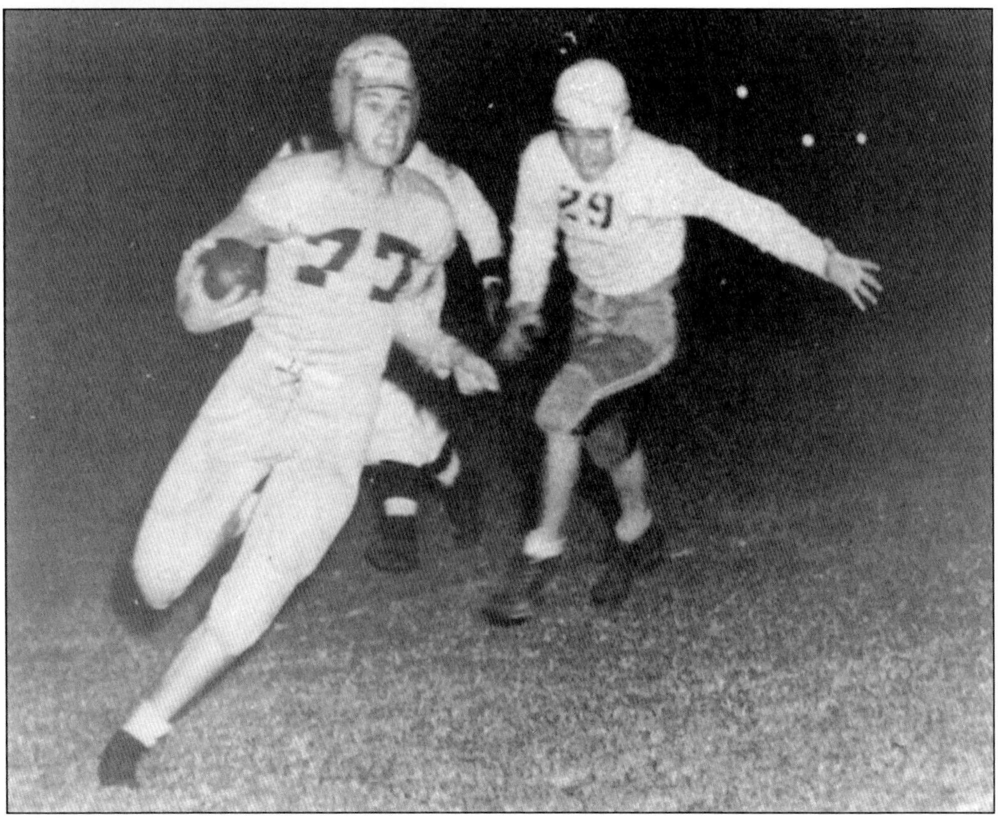

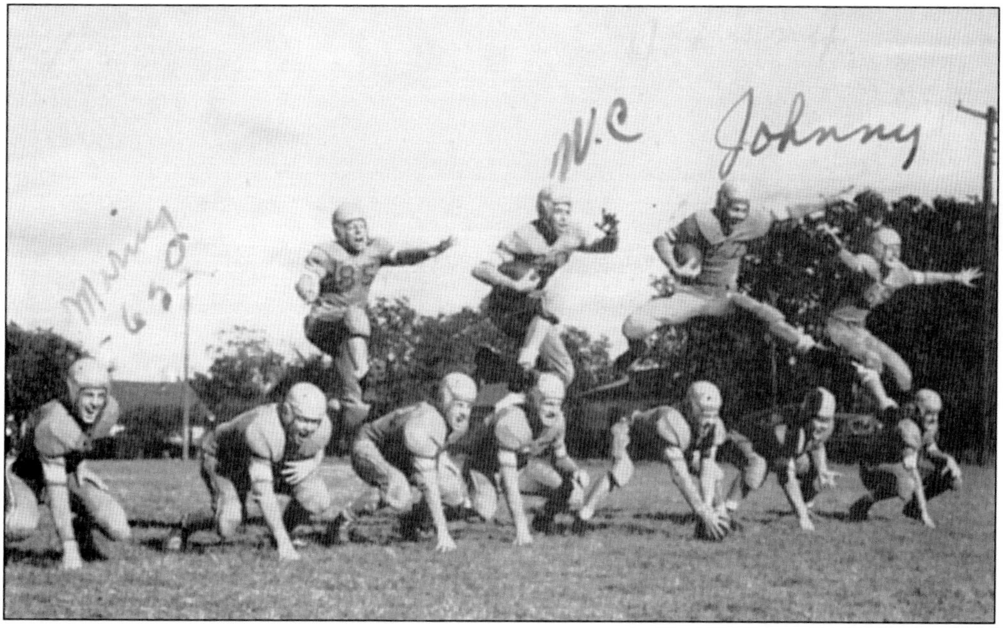

In addition to Dunn (above, third from left, jumping), three of his 1945 offensive linemen—Kenneth Scott, Danny Wolfe, and Billy Willingham (bottom row, third, fourth, and sixth from left)—are Jacket hall of famers today. Historically, the O-line has protected Stephenville quarterbacks well. As early as 1937, Stephenville fans called the offensive line the "Front Wall." By 2005, it became simply "The Wall." Pictured below after winning the November 26, 2005, quarterfinals are, from left to right, the following wall members, their coaches, and backfield: (first row) coach Kyle Spano, running back Eric Edwards, quarterback Jevan Snead, and coach Yancey Cashell; (second row) Travis Dirk, Bobby Boggs, Tanner Rainwater, Josh Clements, and Matt Parker. (Below, Debbie Cashell.)

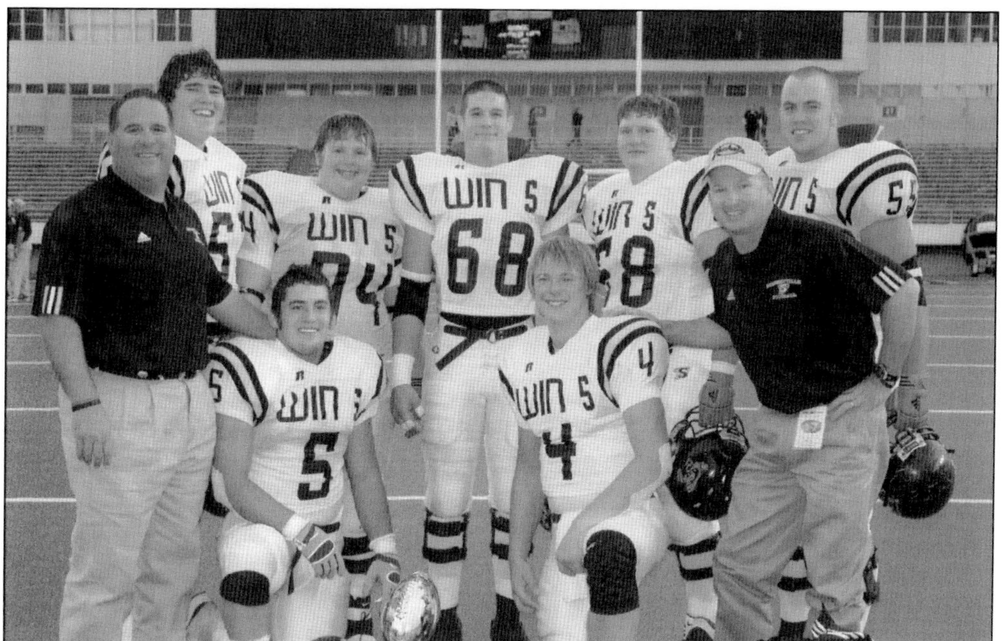

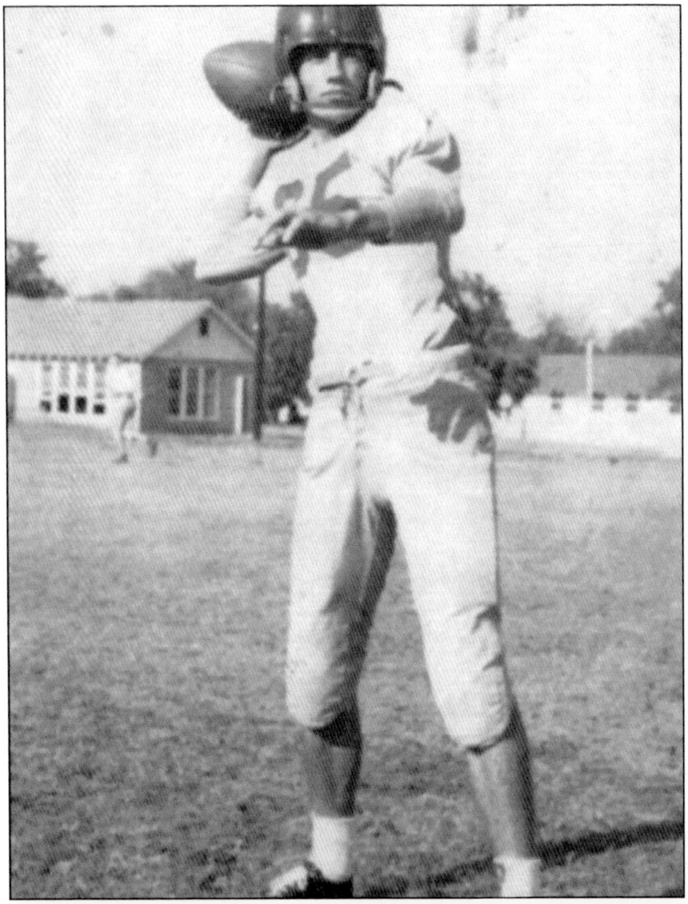

Dunn's successor was Ray Graves (left). In 1947, Graves ran the Jacket's "T" offensive formation. As a senior, he guided his teammates to an 8-1-0 second-place District 7-2A finish. Breckenridge denied SHS the opportunity for a playoff run. Graves nevertheless received all-state recognition for his running (below), bullet passes, and punting.

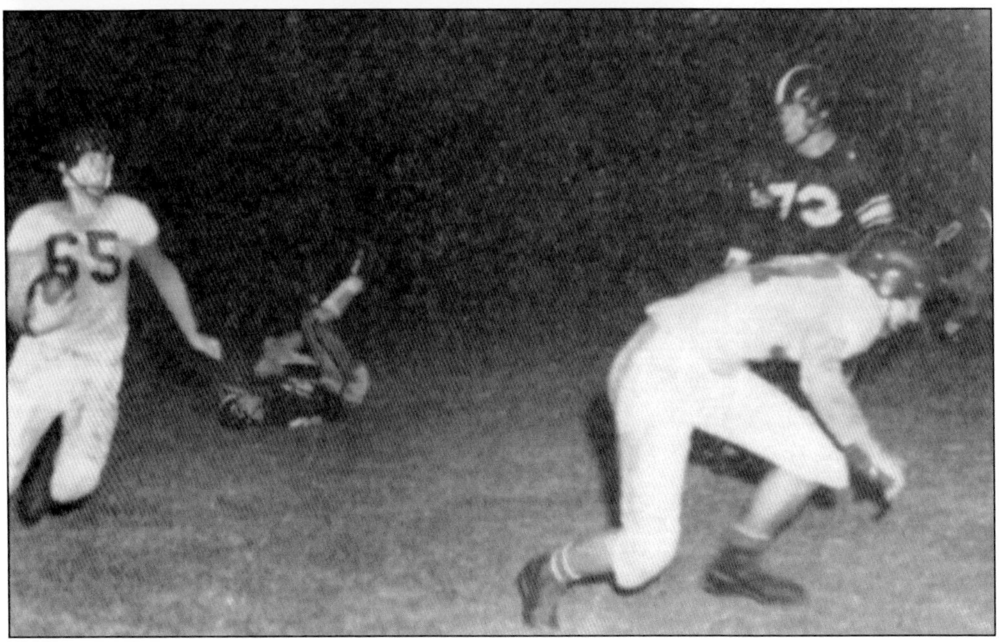

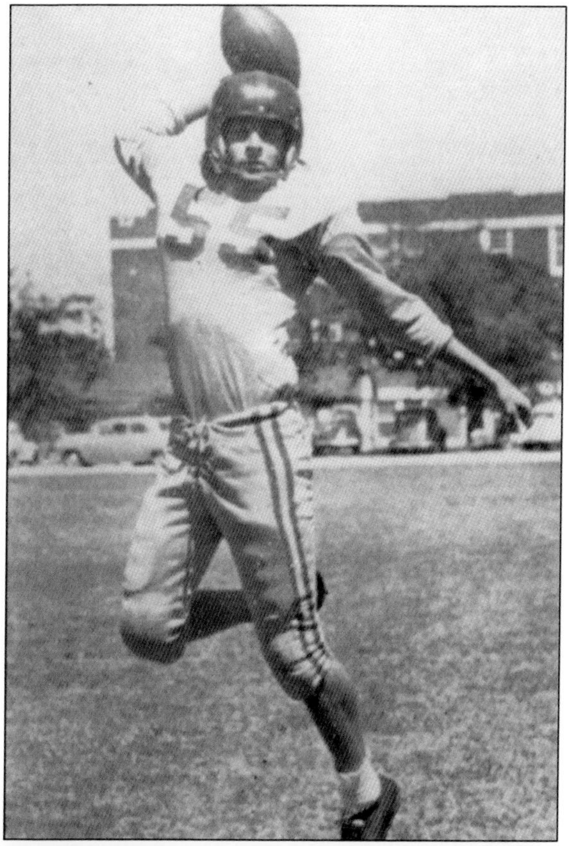

In 1952, Jerry Flemmons (right) contributed to the Yellow Jacket Regional appearance not as quarterback but as defensive end. Flemmons became the 1953 SHS field general and earned all-district honors for his long, accurate passes, his punts, and his backfield blocking. Below, he runs around the left side of the line against rival Brownwood.

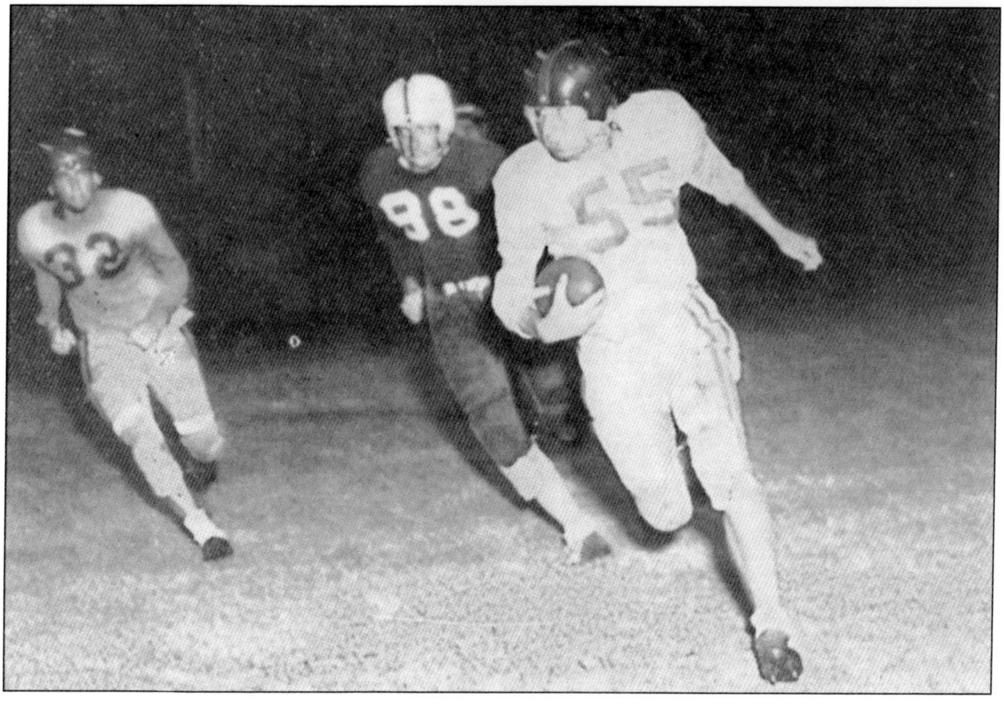

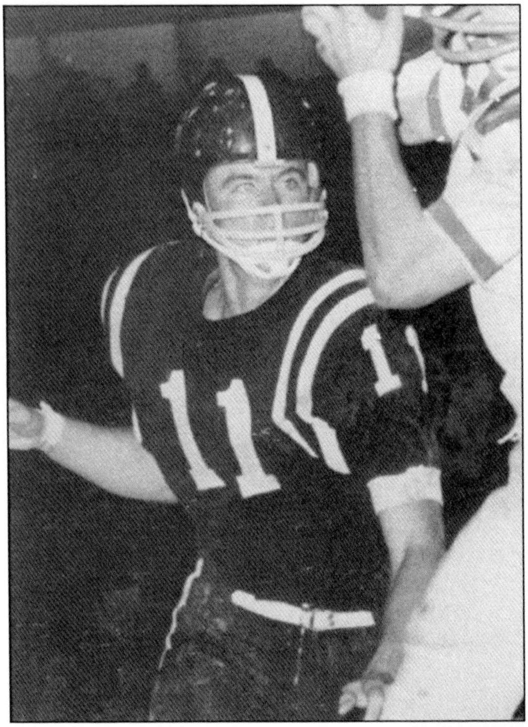

Hall of famer Gary Chandler (left) directed the Jacket offense, earning all-state honors in 1967. A full 23 years later, Cody Ledbetter (below) quarterbacked a Jacket team that made the high school's first semifinal appearance.

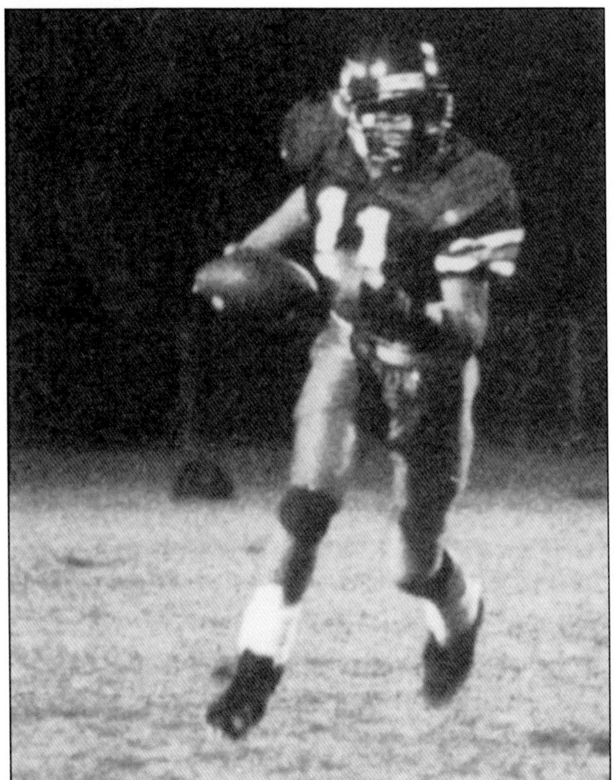

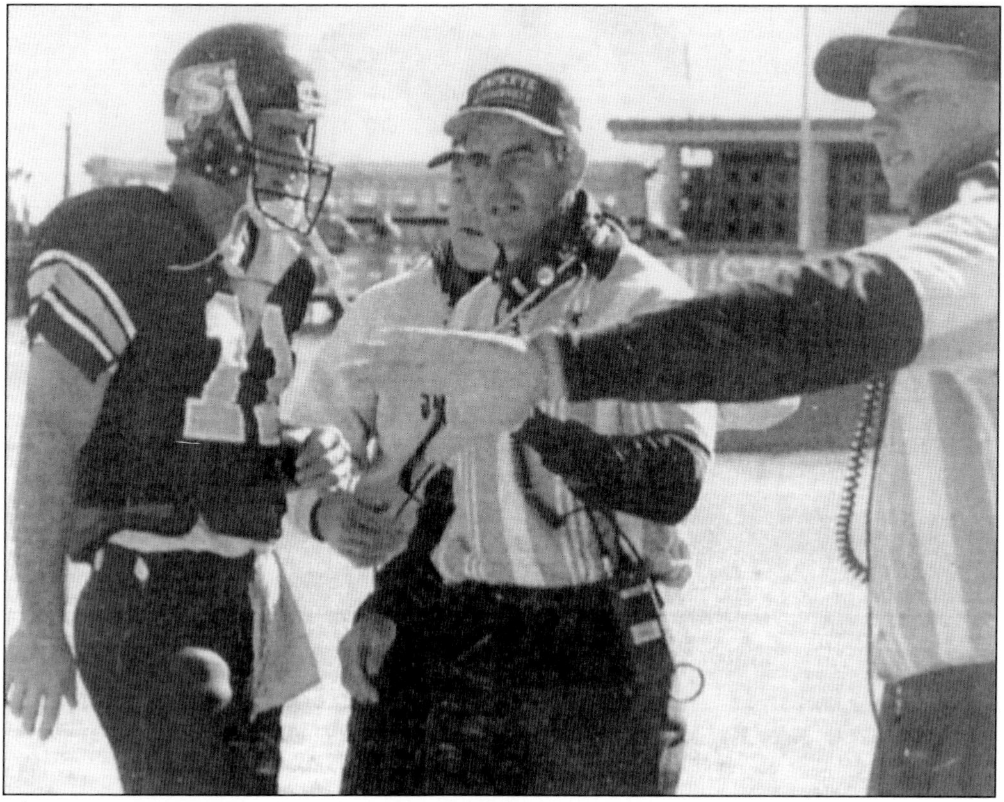

The greatest succession of Stephenville quarterbacks began in the 1990s. Leading the charge was Branndon Stewart (above, left on the sidelines with Coach Briles, middle). Stewart directed the SHS offense in 1992–1993. Below, in his finest hour as a Yellow Jacket, Stewart runs the ball against La Marque in the 1993 state final. (Above, *Fort Worth Star-Telegram*; below, Skipper.)

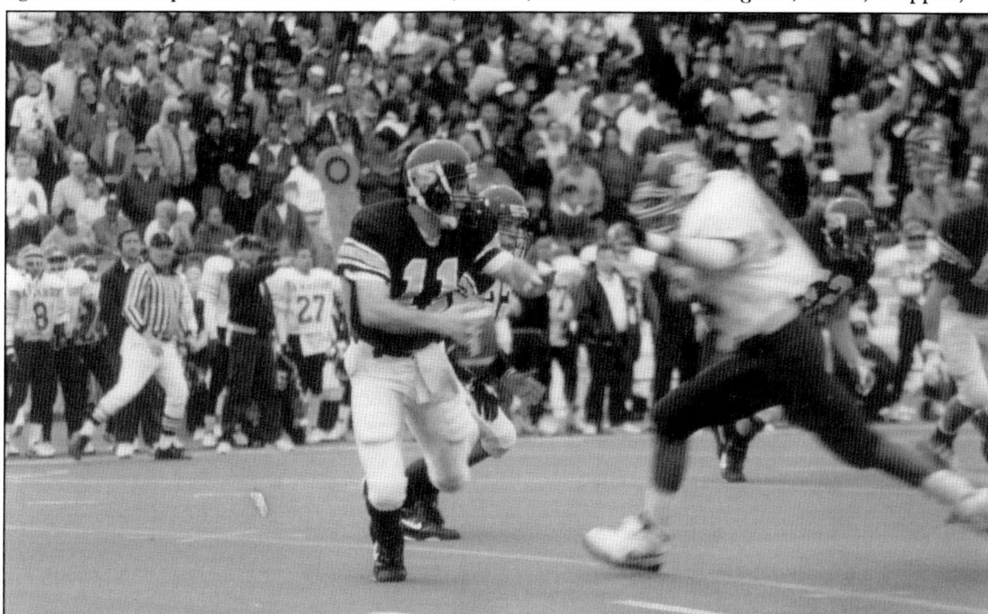

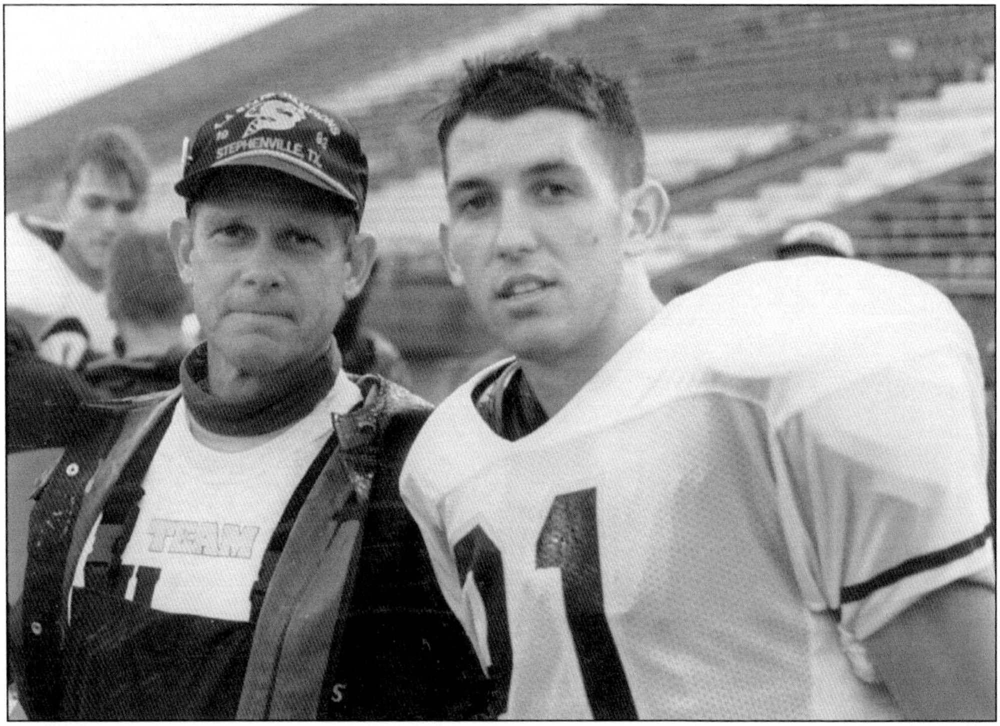

In 1994, senior Glenn Odell (above with his father, Mike) proved a worthy successor to Stewart. In leading SHS to the 1994 state title, Odell's 3,013 yards passing and 38 touchdowns were second on the class 4A all-time list. The Texas Sportswriter's Association named him 1994 Offensive Player of the Year. Below, Odell as a University of Houston Cougar poses with his high school quarterback coach Leon Greeson. (Both, Glenn Odell.)

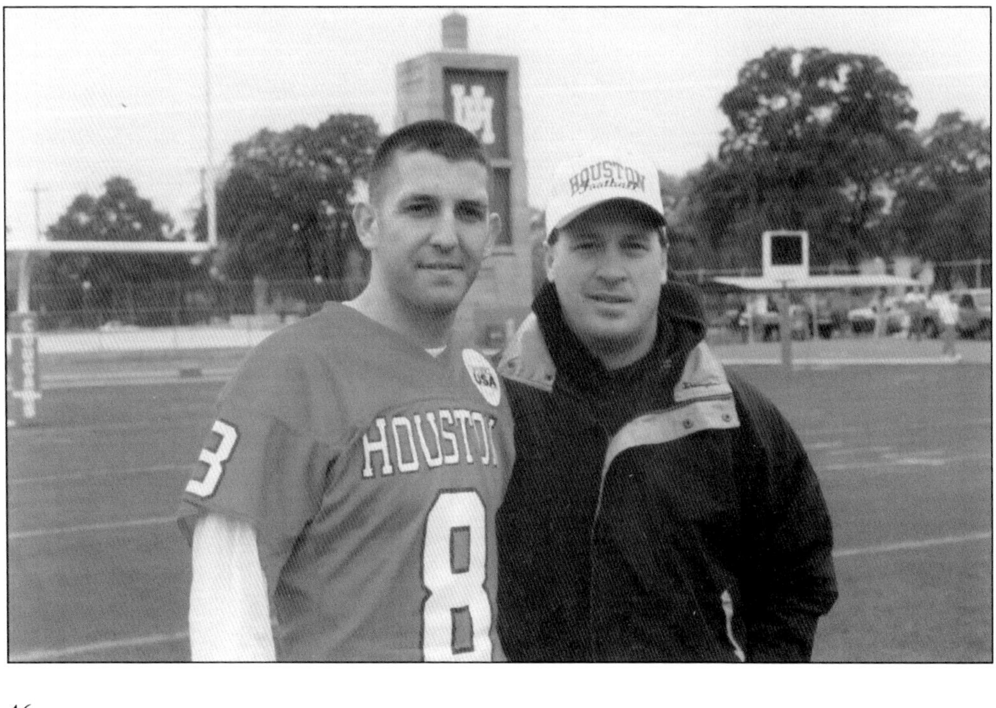

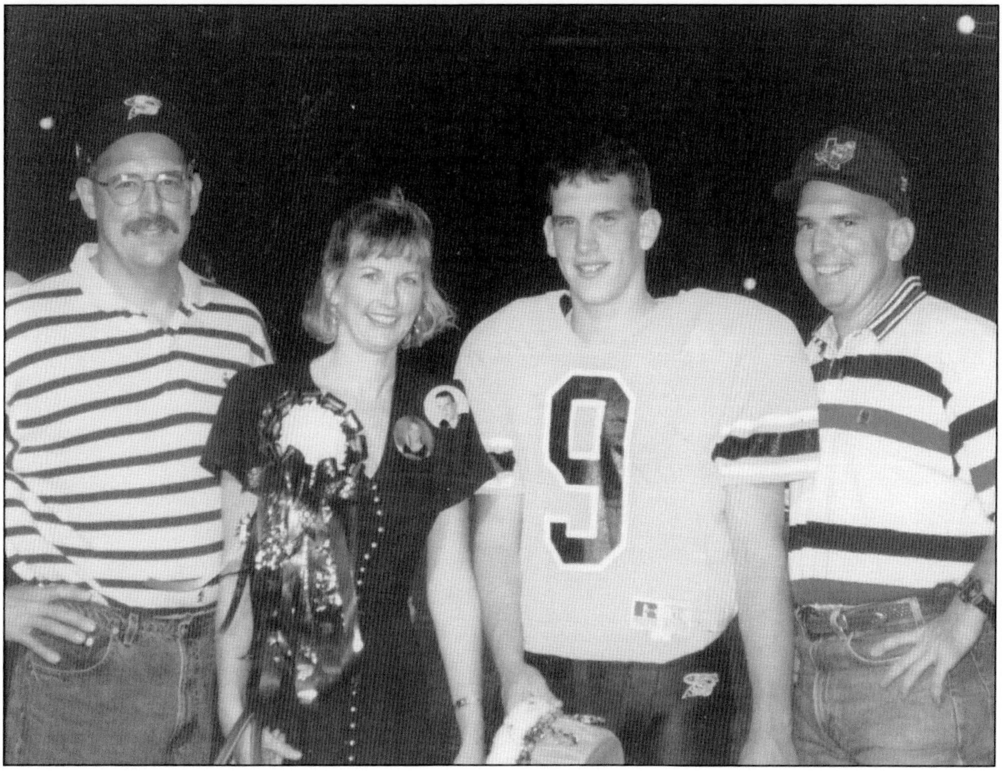

Jason Schwartzkopf was starting quarterback for the 1995 Jacket team, throwing for over 1,200 yards. Shown above on the field at the SHS Homecoming game, Schwartzkopf (no. 9) holds his homecoming king crown and is flanked by, from left to right, his father, Lee Schwartzkopf, mother, Lise, and uncle Chad Hicks. Kyle Dempsey, pictured below in the bi-district matchup against Fort Worth Arlington Heights, quarterbacked the 1996 Jackets and took them to a quarterfinal appearance. (Above, Lise Schwartzkopf; below, Skipper.)

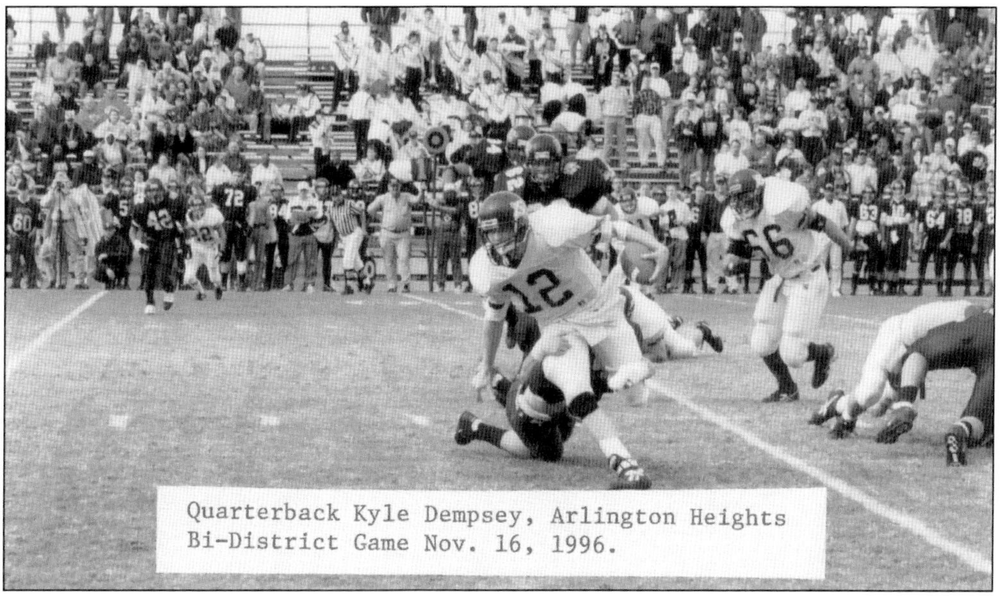

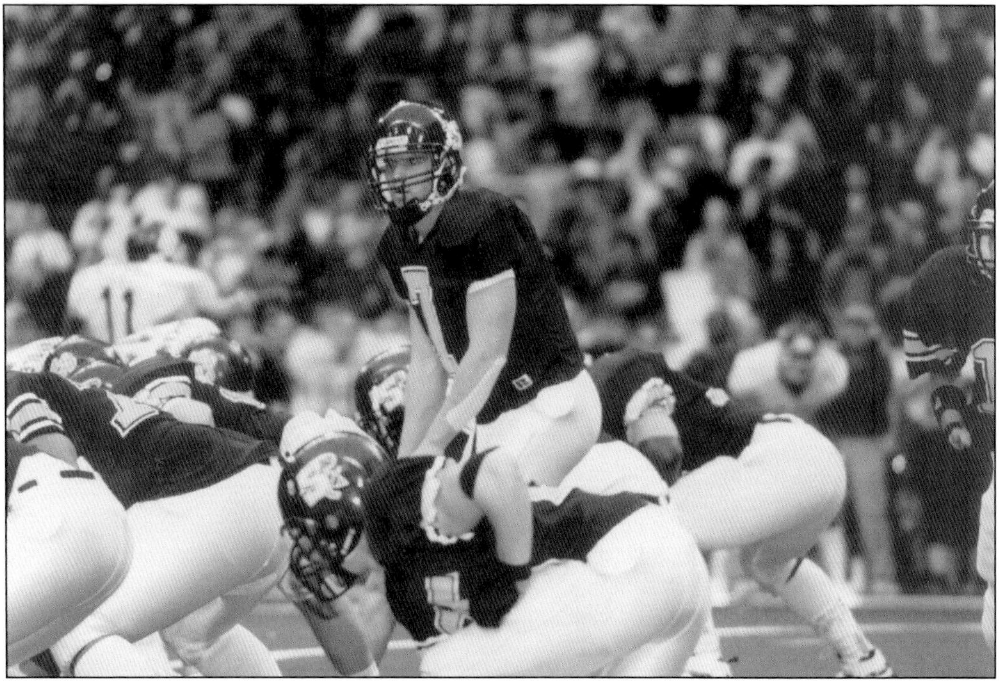

In 1998, Stephenville returned to the title game, this time under the leadership of quarterback Kelan Luker. Above, Luker prepares to take the snap during the Jackets win over a celebrated team from La Marque. Below, Luker appears with his mother, Diane Knight Luker, after the game. Today, Luker ranks no. 1 among Jacket quarterbacks in career and season passing yardage (8,297 and 4,697), career and season touchdowns (78 and 49), career attempts (708), and completions in a season (232). (Both, Skipper.)

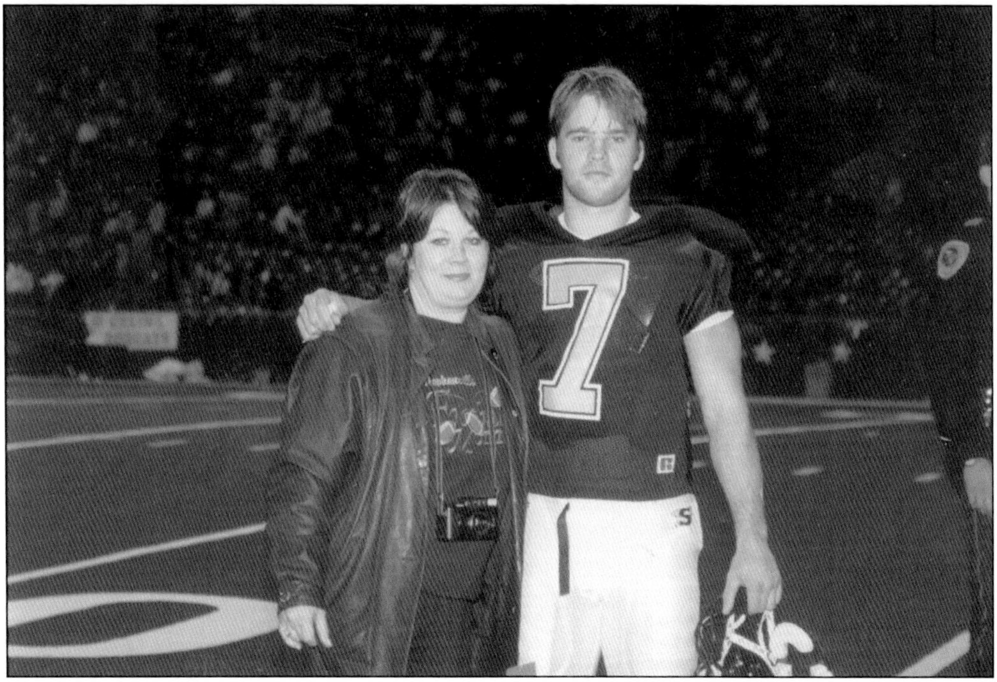

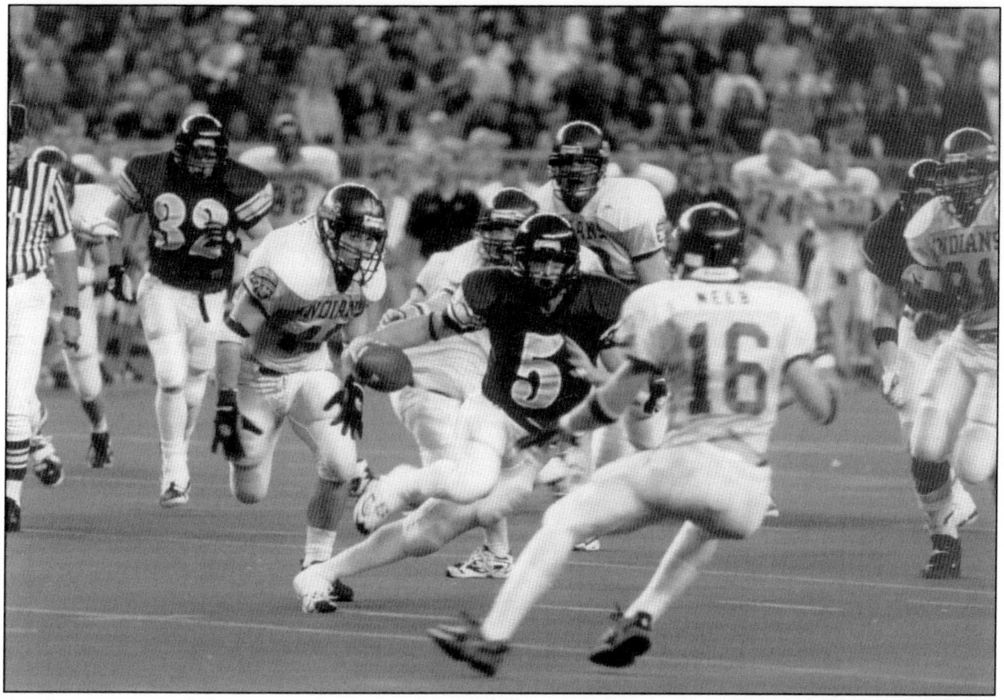

As Stewart passed the quarterback torch to Odell, Luker's successor was Kendal Briles, who led his 1999 Yellow Jacket teammates to an authoritative title win over Port Neches-Groves (above). Below, fellow students acknowledged his stellar performance, carrying him off the field at the victorious end of the contest. (Above, Skipper; below, *Fort Worth Star-Telegram*.)

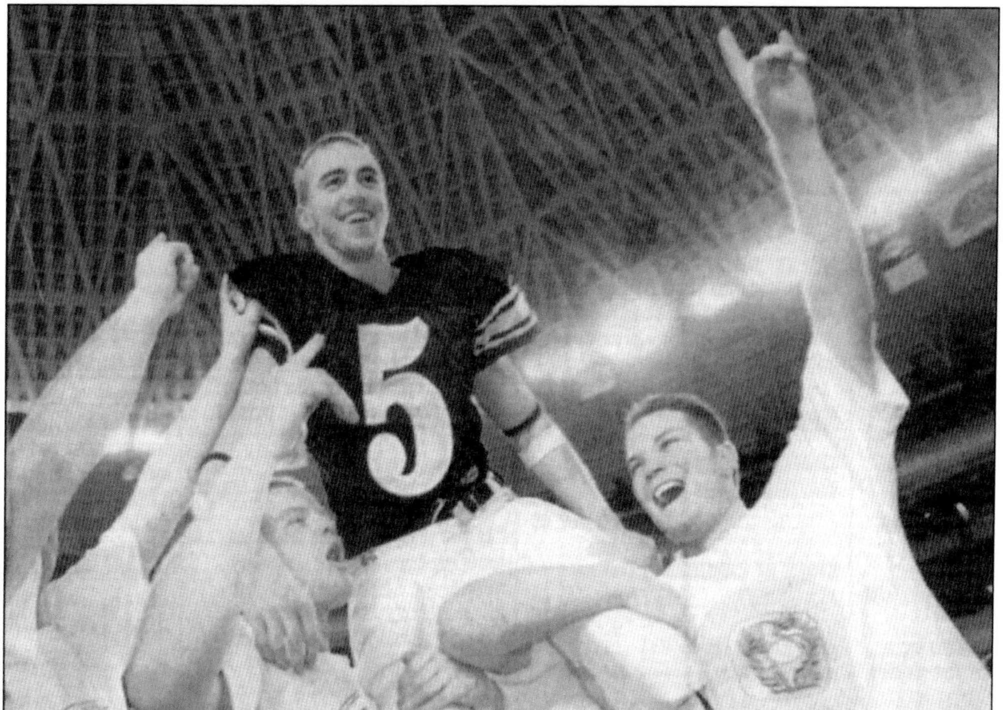

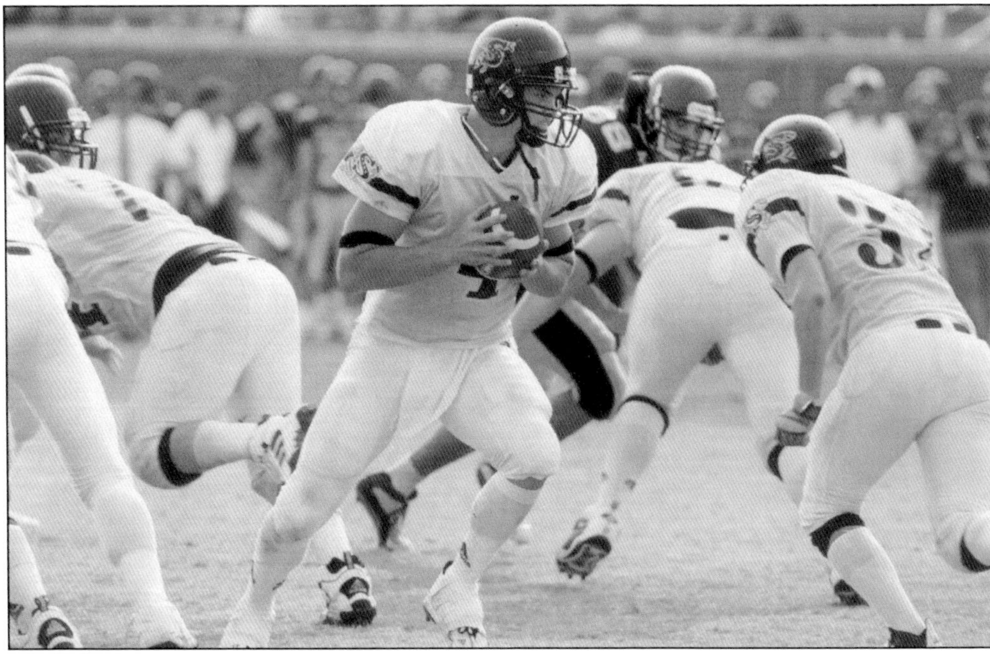

Kendal Briles's 1999 freshman understudy was Kevin Kolb. Above, Kolb leads the Jackets against the Highland Park Scots in the 2002 Tom Landry Classic at Southern Methodist University's (SMU) Gerald J. Ford Stadium, where the two teams combined for almost 1,000 yards total offense. Kolb began the 2000 season under center and, over his three seasons as starter, ranks third in Jacket passing yardage for a career (5,733), season (3,347), and game (434). He ranks second in completions in a single game (29). Kolb was a two-time District 8-4A Offensive MVP and honorable mention all-state. During his senior season, he passed for 3,357 yards and 29 touchdowns. Below, as a University of Houston Cougar, Kolb scrambles in a Conference USA contest. (Both, Skipper.)

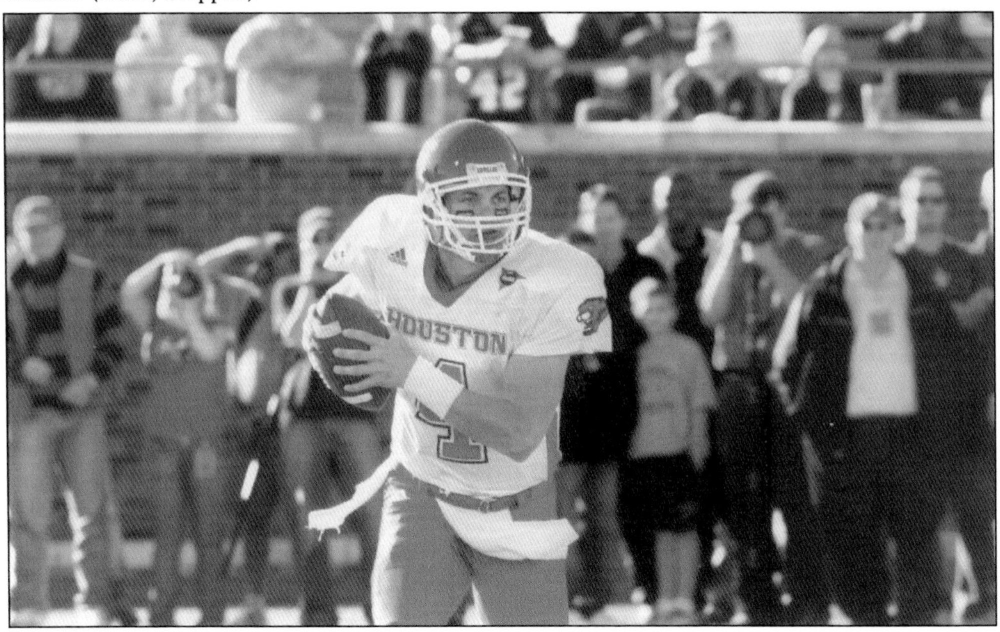

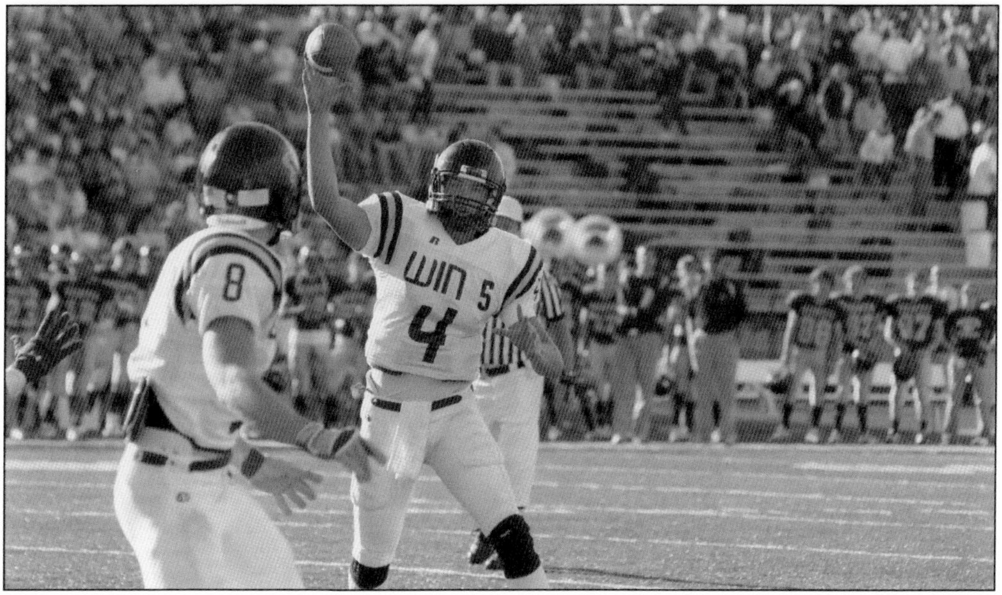

The next Yellow Jacket quarterback to lead his teammates on a deep playoff run was Jevan Snead. Above, Snead passes to his favorite target, no. 8 Brent McElfresh, in a closely fought December 3, 2005, semifinal contest against Highland Park. Among Snead's many honors, in 2005 he was among ESPN's Elite 11 premier high school quarterbacks and selected as a *Parade Magazine* and US Army High School All-American. Jacket quarterback Kody Spano, pictured below rushing for the winning touchdown against Aledo in 2007, took Stephenville to the playoffs two consecutive seasons (2006–2007). Spano later played football at Nebraska. (Above, Emily Hoke; below, Russell Huffman, *Stephenville Empire-Tribune*.)

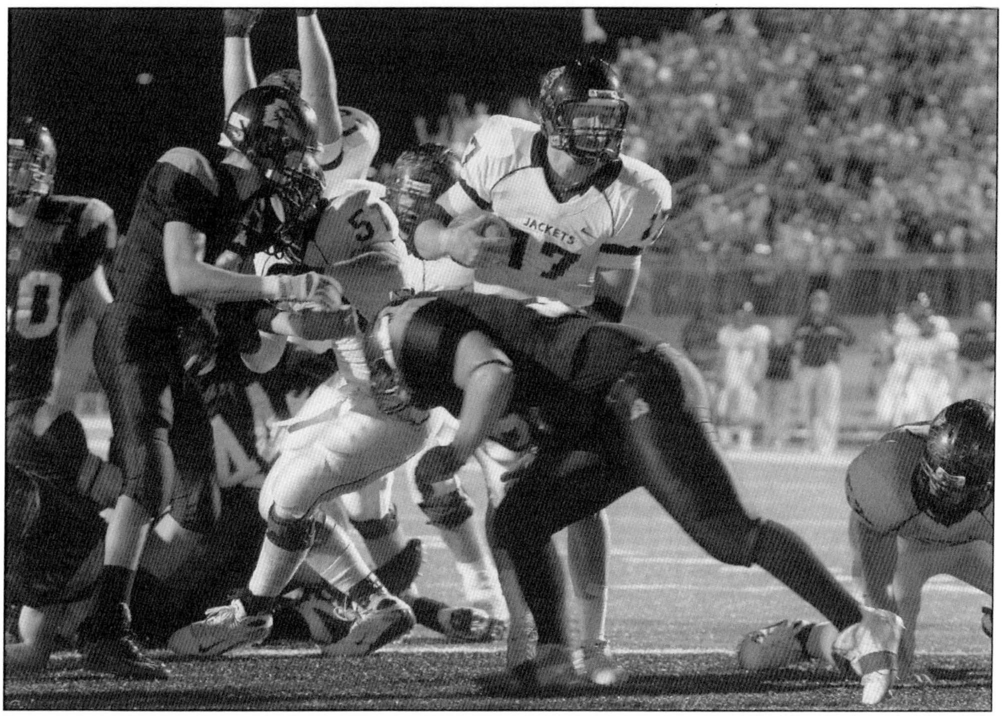

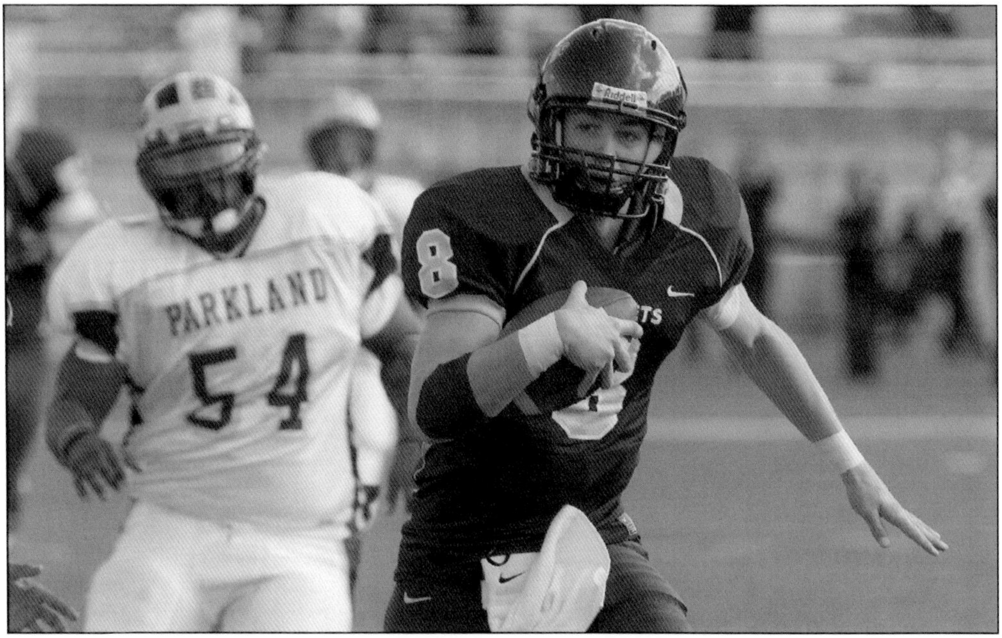

The 2007 departure of Yellow Jacket head coach Chad Morris introduced the Joseph Gillespie era at SHS. Senior quarterback Brad Picha, on a 2008 Area round run against El Paso Parkland (above), took the team to the quarterfinals. In 2009, sophomore Connor Washington (below) skillfully directed Stephenville through round two, and the following year, he led his team to the quarterfinals. In that game, he moves into the opening made for him by two honorable all-state linemen, center D.J. Vanden Berge (left) and guard Nicolas Perez (right). With one year left to play, Washington currently stands fifth on the SHS all-time passing list, with 4,886 career yards. His 2009 touchdown pass of 99 yards to Shylo Pankey against Arlington Seguin also is a school record. (Both, Huffman, *Stephenville Empire-Tribune*.)

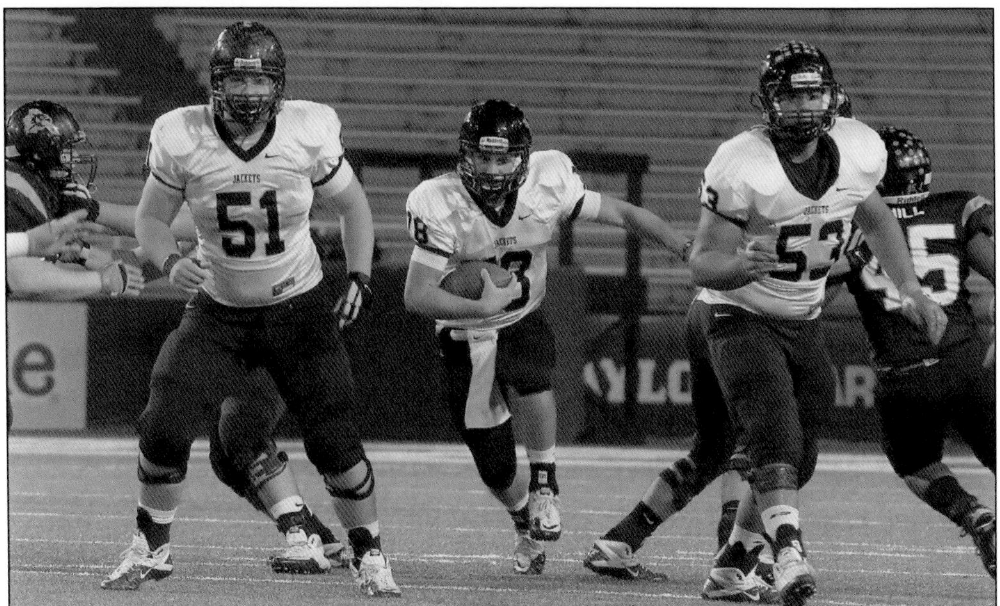

Four

Pigskin Pulpit

Ty Cashion is the author of *Pigskin Pulpit*, a one-of-a-kind sociological study of Texas high school football coaches from the 1930s through 1960s. The work speaks volumes about the Great Depression and World War II as a crucible shaping the coaching styles of an entire generation of mentors. Cashion suggests coaching provided a unique opportunity to imbue Texas youths with time-honored values—fair play, a work ethic, perseverance, courage under duress, being a team player, and becoming a part of something larger than one's own self.

Football coaches at SHS were part of this process, as were the administrators to whom those coaches answered. Included in *The 1946 9-AA Pigskin Review*, a May 10, 1947, letter from Stephenville Public Schools superintendent J.B. Merrell observes, "May we so keep the standards of District 9AA on such a high plane that good Christian men will continue to seek coaching positions in the District. . . . We say congratulations to the ones who have won and lost in the spirit of the 'Good Sport.' "

From the beginning, SHS coaches used football to turn boys into strong men able to weather difficult tests and adversities. Not surprisingly, the first two SHS coaches—Joe Preston (1920) and J.C. Dykes (1921–1923, 1925)—also filled the role of principal. The title *headmaster*, connoting responsibility to proffer moral direction and develop righteous character, most likely better describes the way both perceived their coaching roles. In his 1923 season-opening 21-0 win over Granbury, Dykes did not run up the score but gave "all the men a chance to get in the game," according to the October 12 *Stephenville Empire*. Both Preston and Dykes set honorable tones that subsequent coaches have continued.

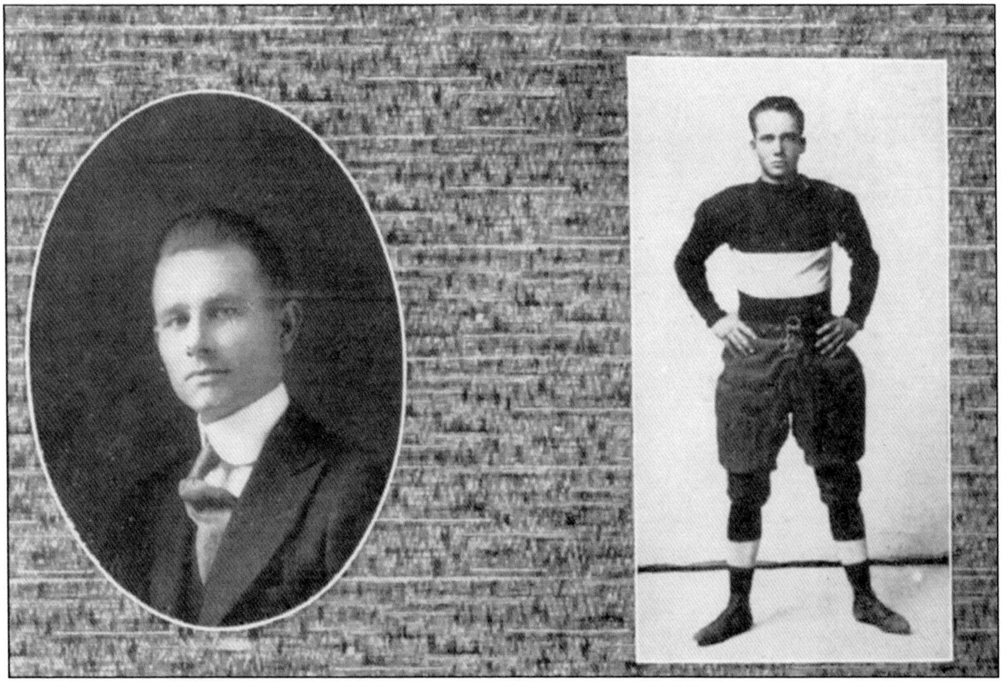

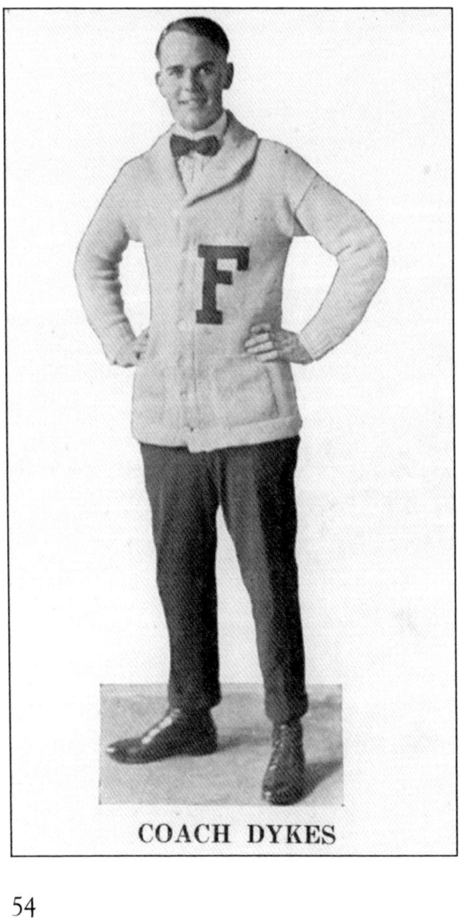

Principals Joe Preston (above) and J.C. Dykes (left) were Stephenville's first two football coaches. Preston went 5-2-0 the year he coached. Dykes coached longer and won more games (23-13-1), sometimes playing the same opponent twice in a single season. In 1921, his team played the first game against Breckenridge (a 20-0 loss) and even one against the Tarleton Scrubs. In 1922, SHS played the Jelly Beans, a "team composed of ex-college players," losing only 11-7. The yearbook comically notes that the contest was the "Has Wuzzers" over "Is Nowers." That same year, the tradition of an end-of-the-season Thanksgiving Day rivalry game began. Stephenville lost to Dublin 20-0.

In 1924, John Tarleton Agricultural College professor of veterinary science and animal production, "Doc" Verne Scott (right), coached alongside Dykes. Scott inherited almost an entire team of returning veterans. He used that experience to win the first Jacket district and bi-district titles ever, but was defeated in round two at Ranger's Nitro Park by the Cisco Loboes. In a father-and-son pattern that would continue through Yellow Jacket football history, coach Scott's son, Verne "Scotty" Scott Jr. (below), quarterbacked the 1941 Jacket team. (Right, Tarleton State University Dick Smith Library *Grassburr*.)

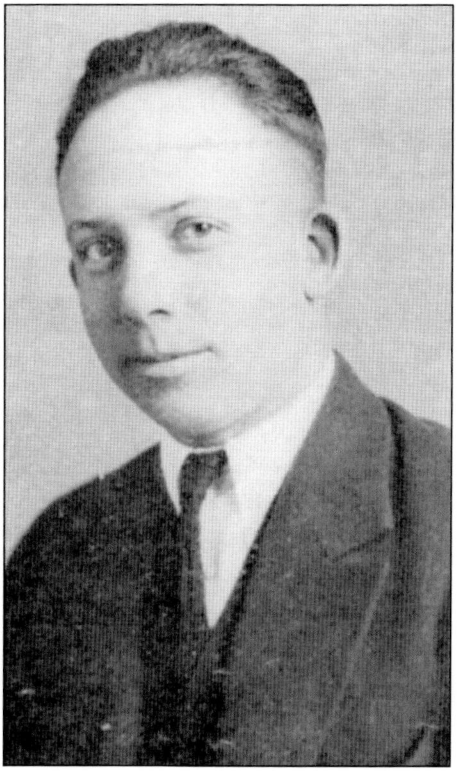

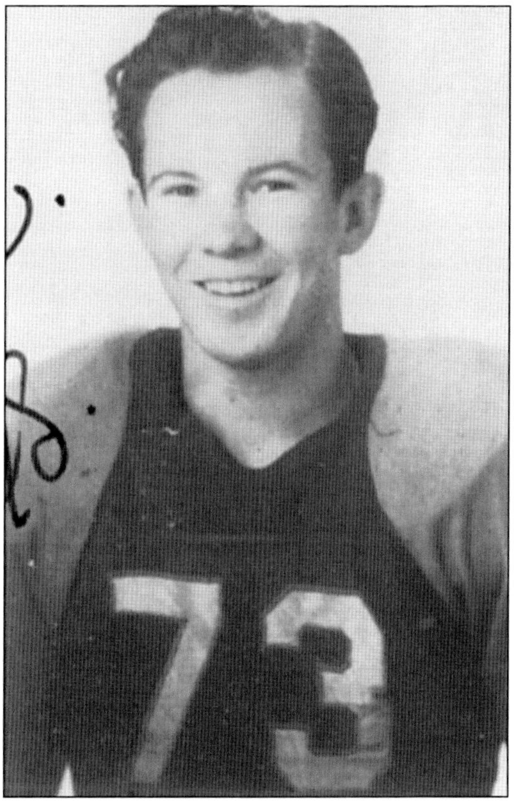

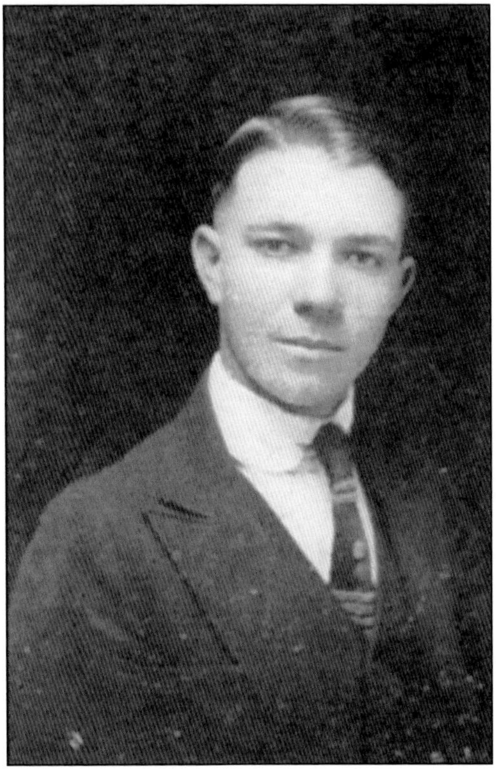

Coach Scott introduced SHS to the playoffs, but Joe Brown's teams (1926–1933) earned three district titles, establishing sustained momentum heretofore not experienced. On Brown's staff was Jim Mobley (left), an end on Preston's original 1920 team. Head coach for only two seasons (1936–1937), Mobley (below) had an 18-1-0 record and the highest win percentage—0.95—of any Jacket coach. He demanded sportsmanship from each and every player.

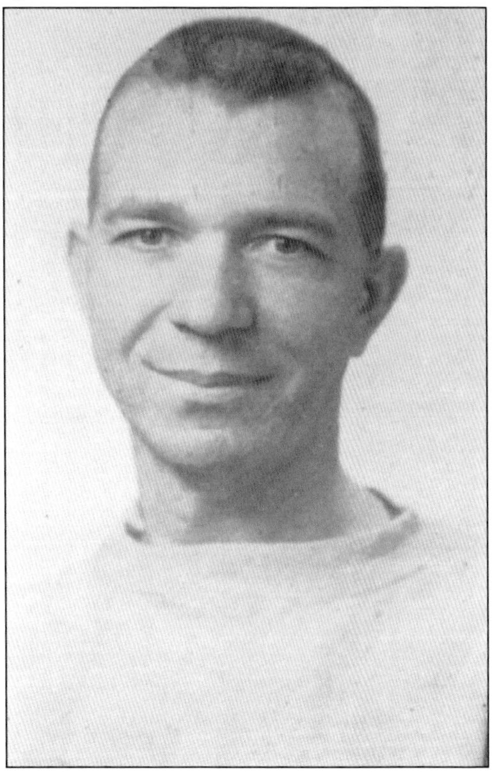

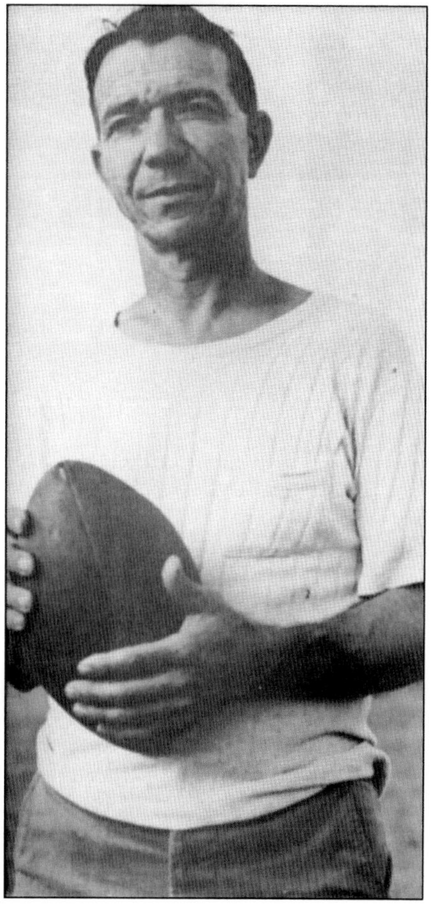

By 1946, Mobley (right) was back at SHS, primarily teaching the fundamentals to the B team and junior-high school students. A write-up in the December 4, 1936, *Empire-Tribune* notes that as a Yellow Jacket player in 1920, "Mobley was one of the most deadly tackles in Texas. The men he played with commonly referred to his dexterity, saying that when he 'tackled they stay tackled.' " Later, Mobley's son (below) played offensive right end. In 1952, Jim Jr. and his teammates advanced to round three.

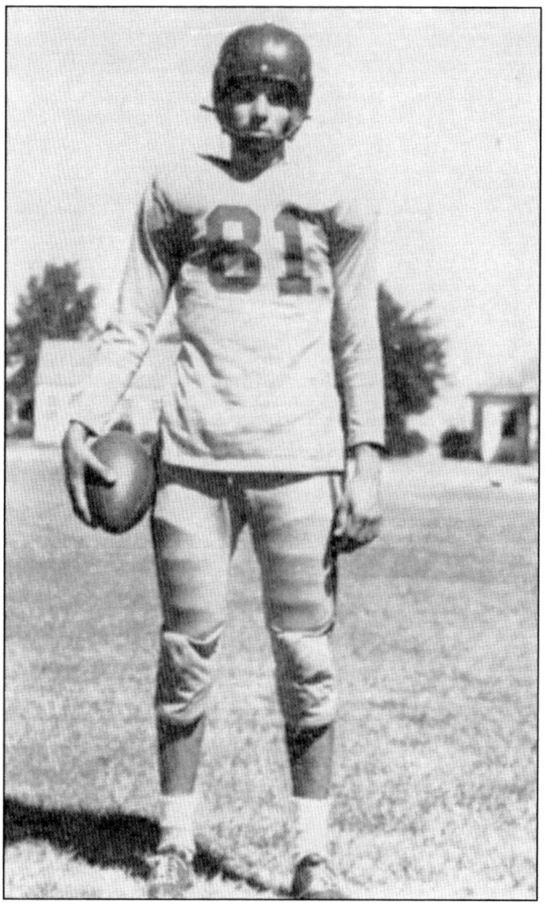

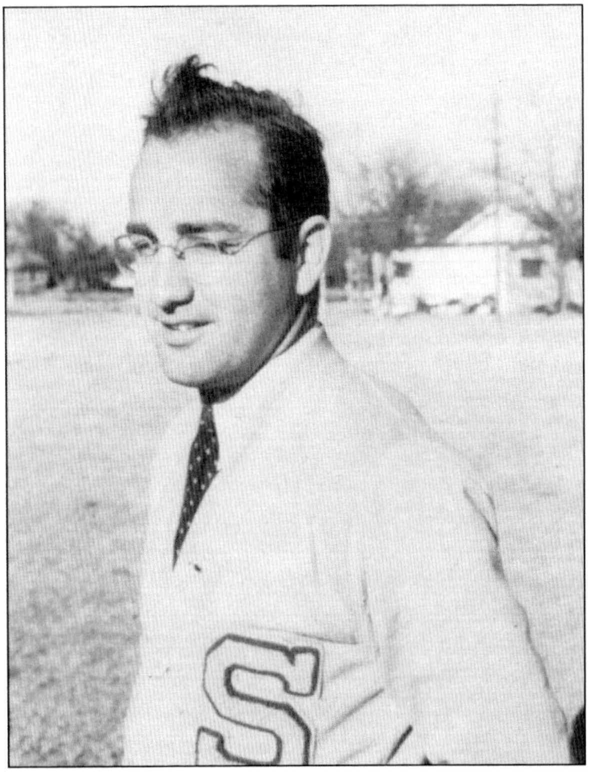

Mobley's replacement in 1938 was Jimmy Marshall (left). In five years, Marshall posted a 27-17-2 record, earning one District 9-2A championship and a trip to the 1940 playoffs. That year, the Jackets beat perennial foe Breckenridge 26-6 and went undefeated through the regular season. In 1942, Marshall had a 9-1-0 record. The one loss was to Breckenridge, who advanced to bi-district while Stephenville remained home. In 1943, E.E. "Flash" Walker (below) became head coach. His Jackets were 7-2-0, losing only to Fort Worth North Side and Breckenridge.

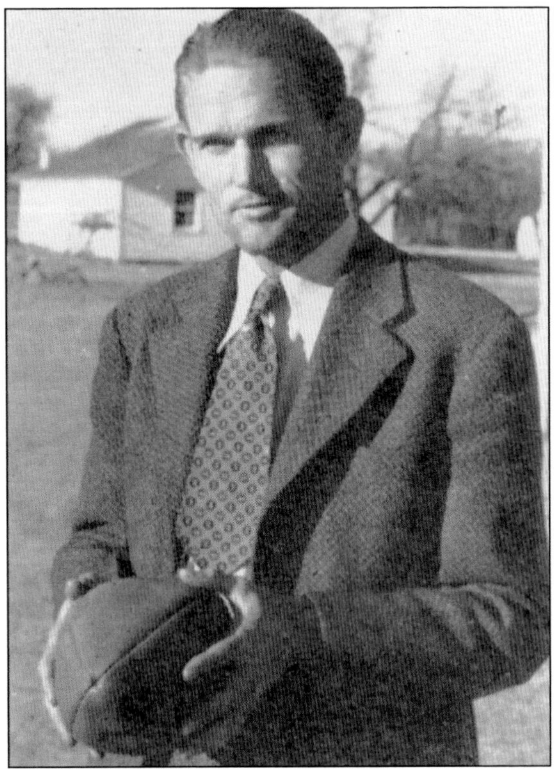

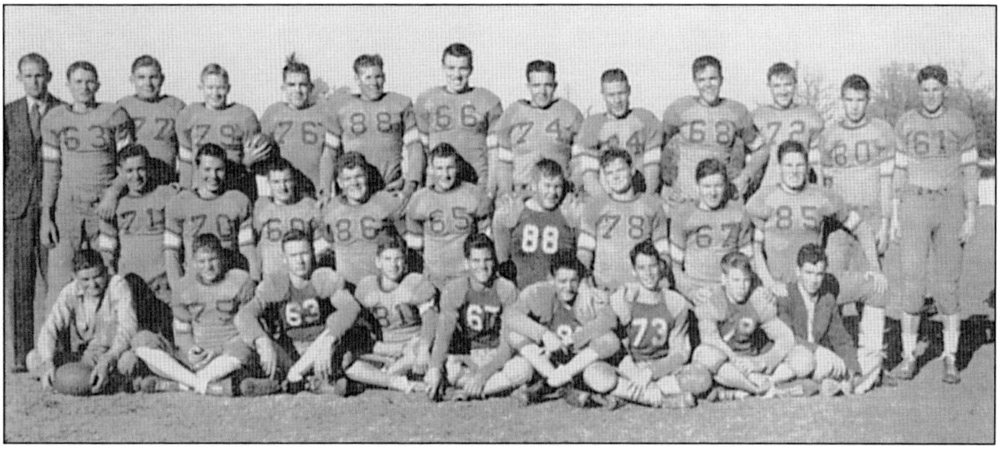

Although his team did not qualify for the playoffs, Walker's Yellow Jackets (above) included six future hall of famers. They are, from left to right, as follows: (first row), Johnny Dunn (fourth); (second row) Billy "Pup" Willingham (fourth) and Danny Wolfe (ninth); (third row) James "Bulldog" Willingham (sixth), Albert "Crag" Cragwall (seventh), and Charles "Casey" Casstevens (twelfth). In 1944, H.H. Hassler (below) took the reins. If his career record lacked luster, the 1945 yearbook identified the following lofty quality in his coaching style: "He came also to build boys into men who could play well in the game of life." During Hassler's tenure, the Jackets played the Mighty Mites of Fort Worth's Masonic Home, the championship team celebrated in Jim Dent's book *Twelve Mighty Orphans*, to a 12-12 tie.

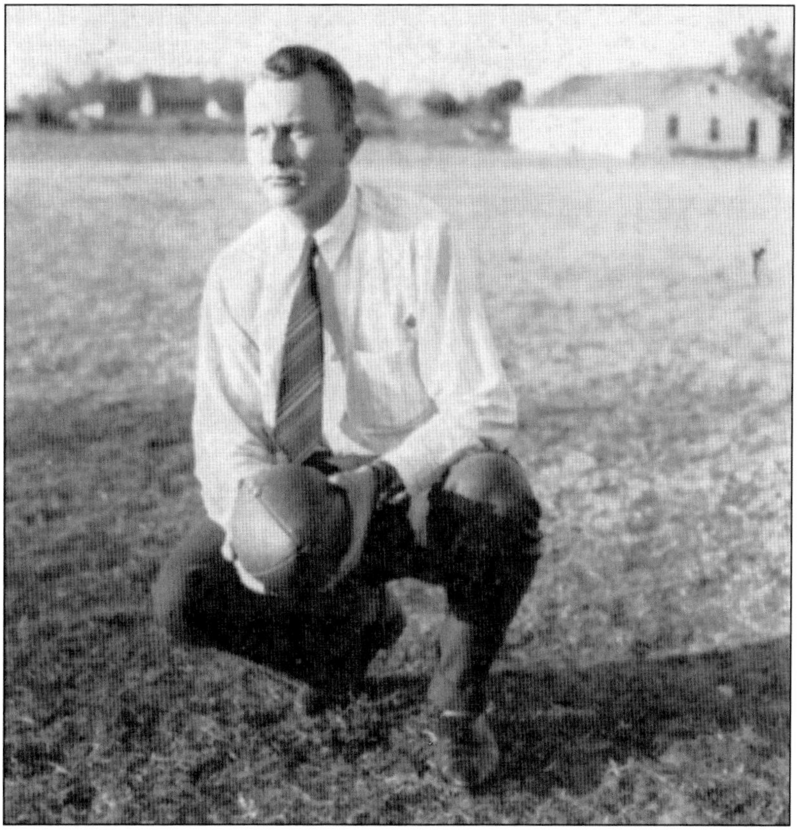

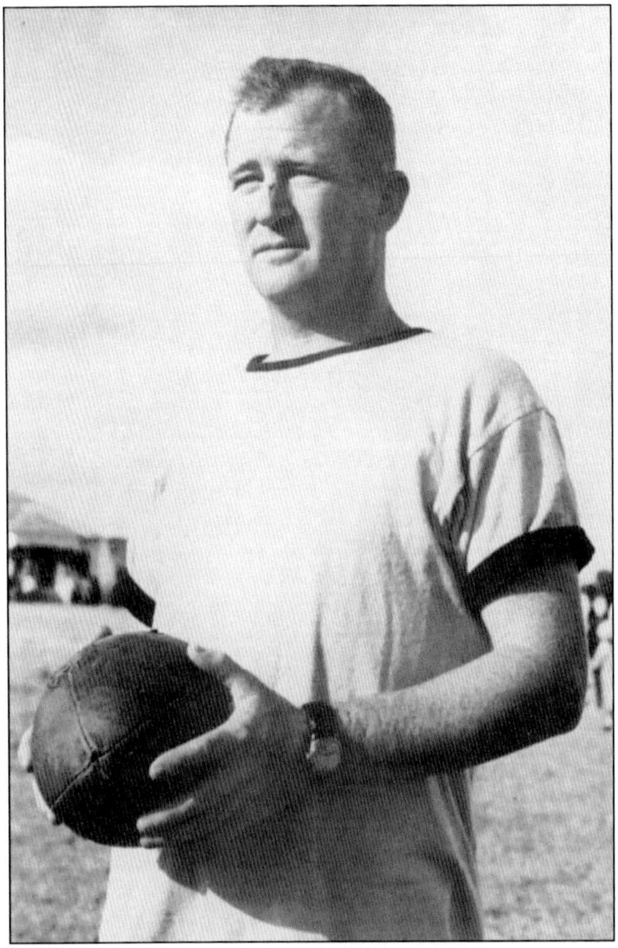

As World War II concluded, Mike Murphy (left) began an eight-year tenure (1946–1954) producing a 48-35-6 record that included one district title and two near misses (1948 and 1951). His 1947 offense (below) included hall of famers Kenneth Scott (first row, second from left) and Ray Graves (second row, far left).

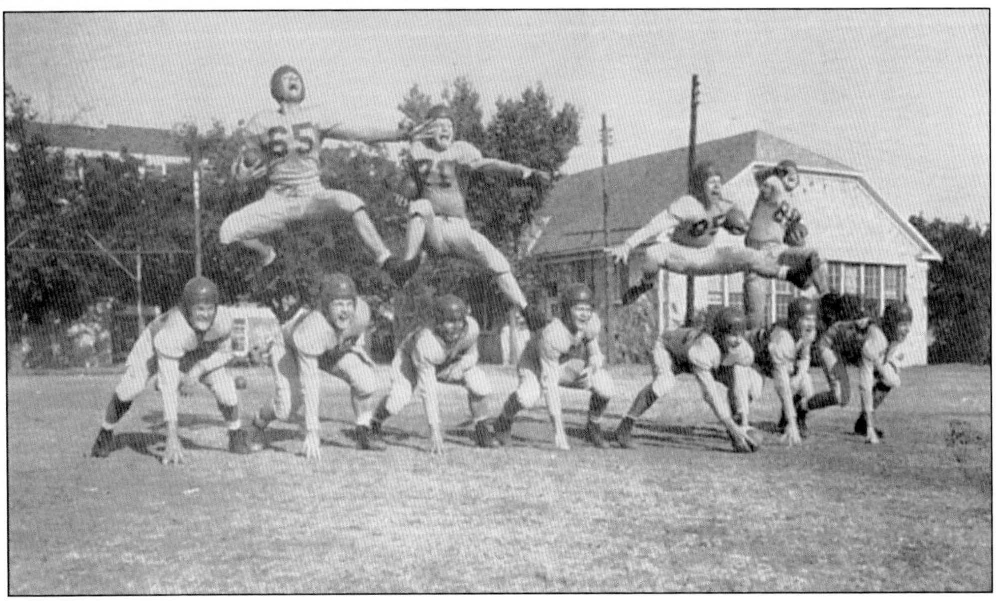

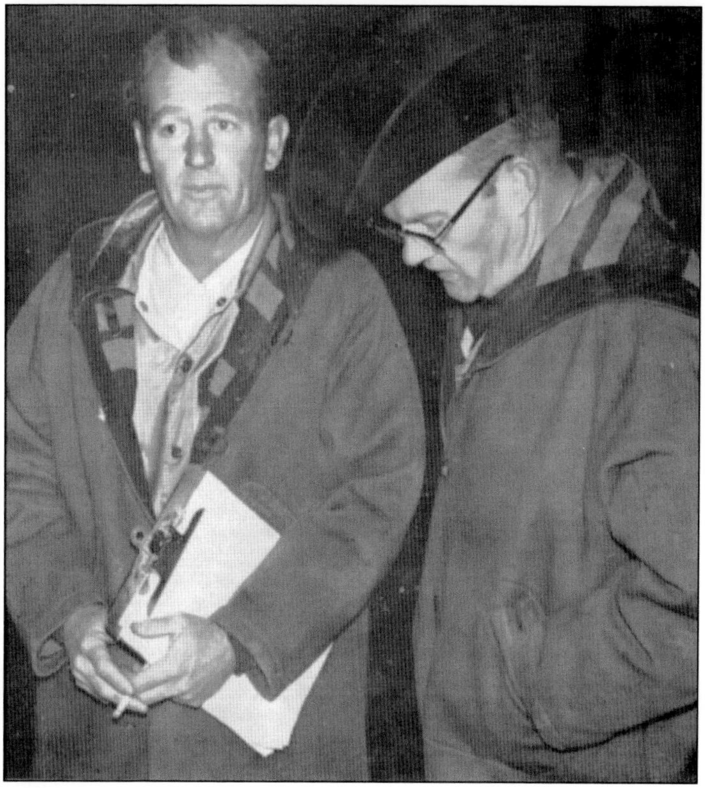

In 1948, Murphy (above, left) made an invaluable addition to his staff—Arnold Johnson (above, right). Johnson (below) was a standout 175-pound nose tackle on the 1936 and 1937 teams (as well as state champion in 1938 in the 220-yard hurdles). Logically, he coached the Jacket line. The 1953 yearbook observed that Johnson's "stalwart moral character has been an inspiration to us throughout the time he has been our assistant mentor." In 1952, the Murphy-Johnson duo took the team to regional.

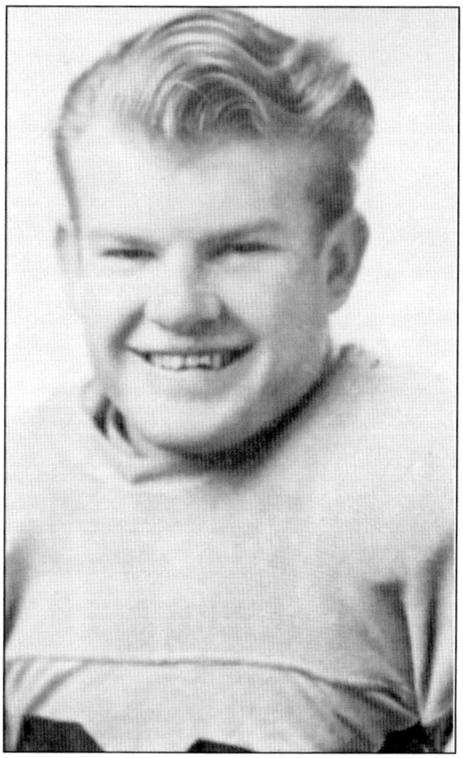

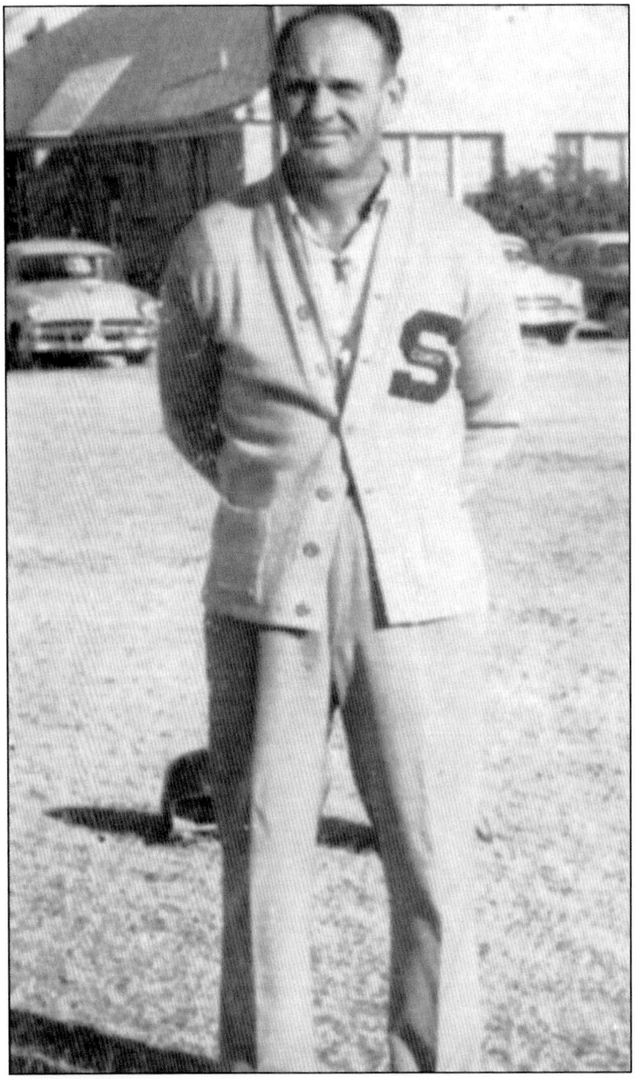

Scott McCall (left) arrived in 1955. As a schoolboy, he played tailback and linebacker for Masonic Home. A tough, irrepressible competitor, McCall was the best player for the Mighty Mites. He and the 1932 team earned Masonic Home's first trip to the state championship, playing Corsicana to a scoreless tie. McCall's 1956 Yellow Jackets (below) went 7-2-1.

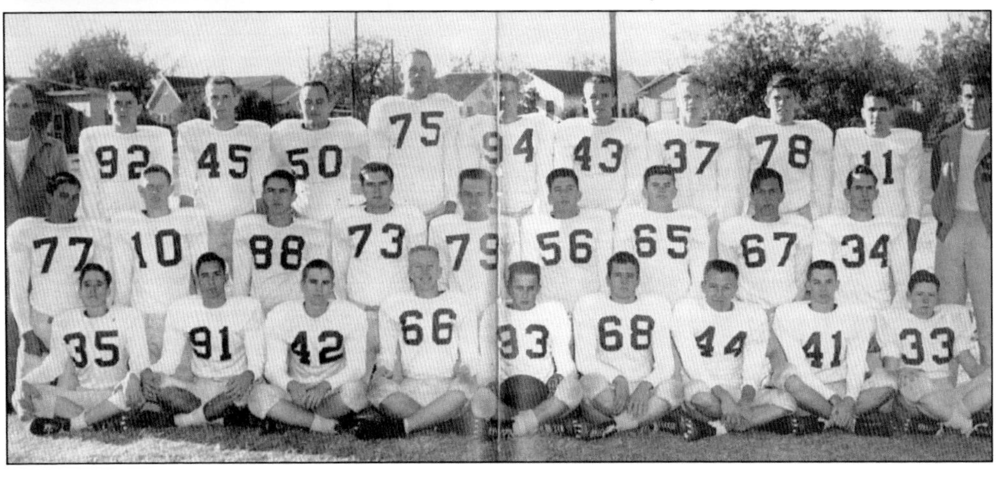

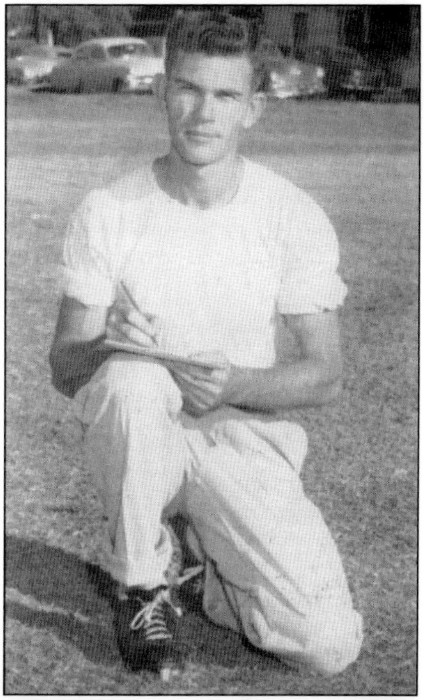

McCall brought former Yellow Jacket standout Johnny Dunn (right) onto his 1956 coaching staff. In 1962, another Jacket football star returned to the SHS. Kenneth Scott (below) became head coach for eight seasons (1962–1966 and 1971–1972).

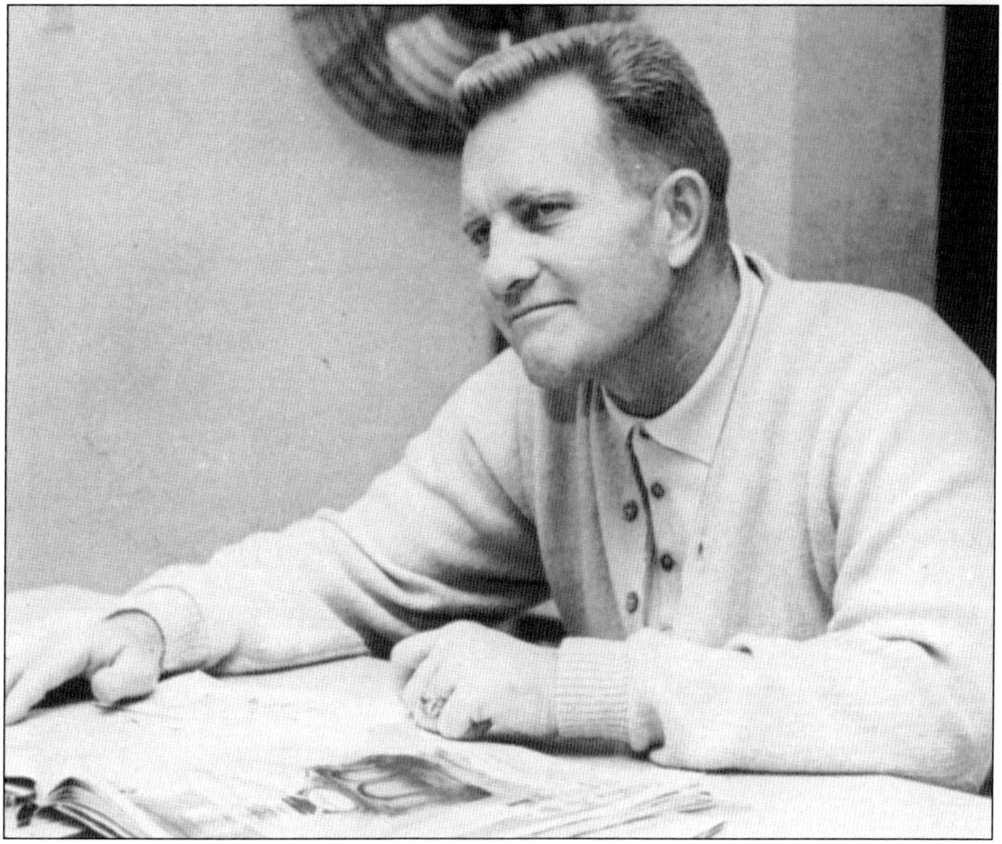

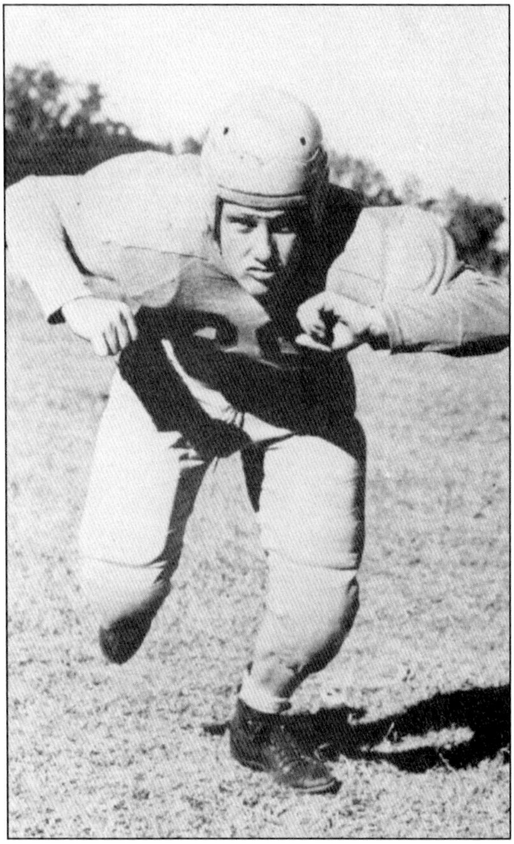

As a Jacket player, Scott (left) wreaked havoc as a defensive lineman. He played first-string tackle for three straight seasons and was known for bone-crushing hits. In 1946, Scott was first team all-district and honorable mention all-state. He coached five future hall of famers, including all-state 1967 linebacker Tri-Captain guard Michael Watkins (below), who later became team captain and MVP at Texas Tech.

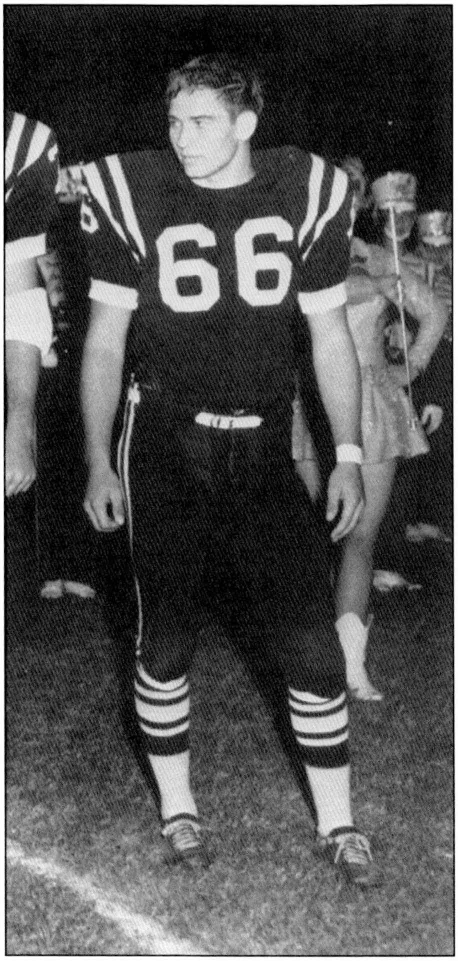

In the mid-1960s, another Scott standout was three-year letterman Steve Gunn. Gunn was all-district and all-state and received all-American recognition in several football magazines. Right, Gunn and the Jackets play against Duncanville in 1964. After high school, Gunn played four years at Texas Christian University (TCU). Below, Gunn is flanked by TCU teammates Don Neeley (left) and James Vanderslice at a 1967 home game in which the Horned Frogs shutout the no. 1 nationally ranked Texas Tech offense. (Below, Kathy Hamer, TCU yearbook.)

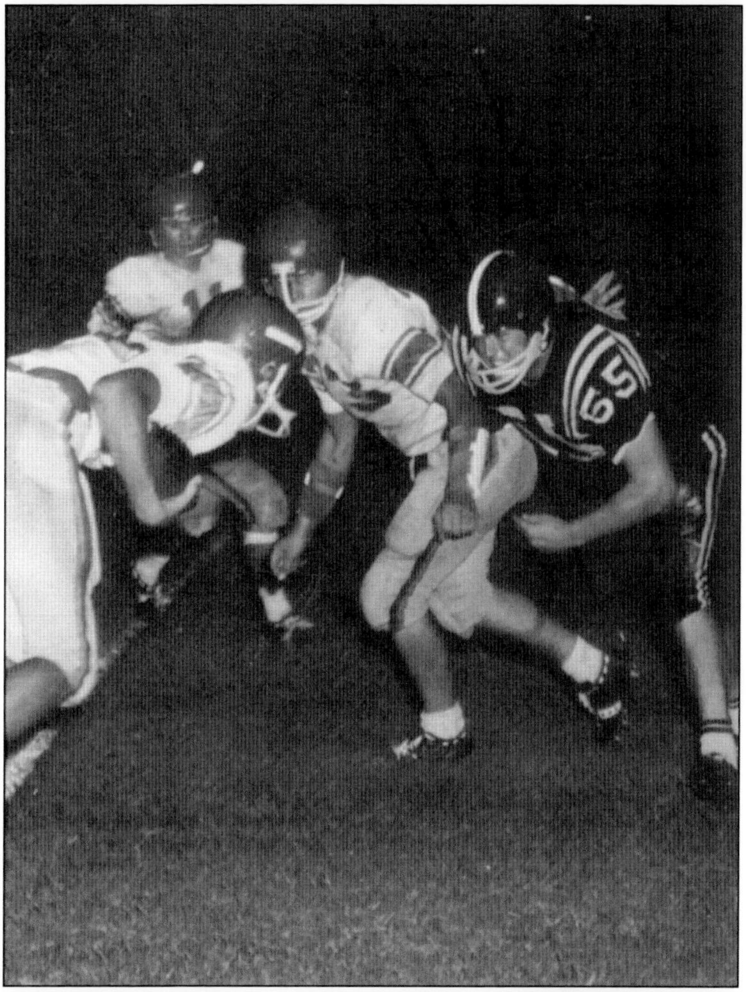

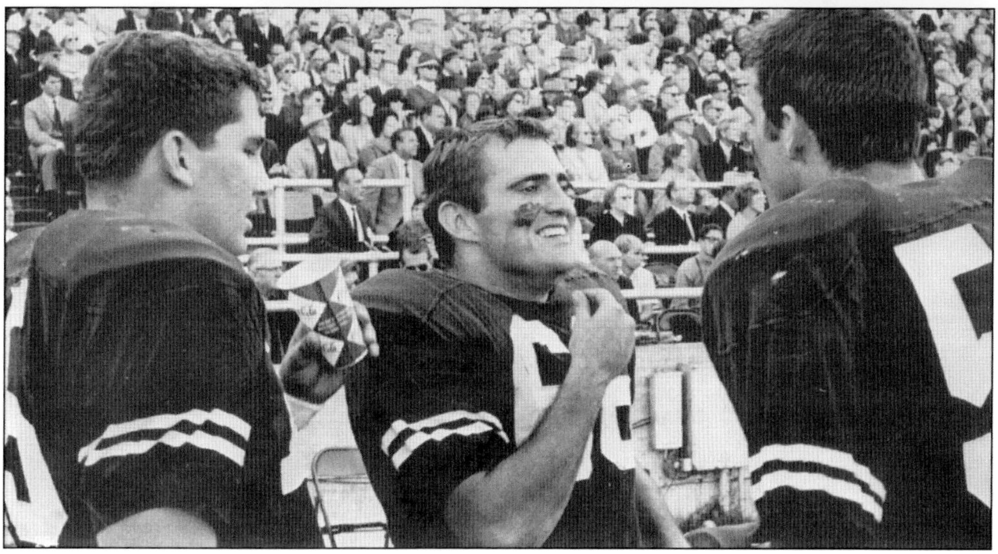

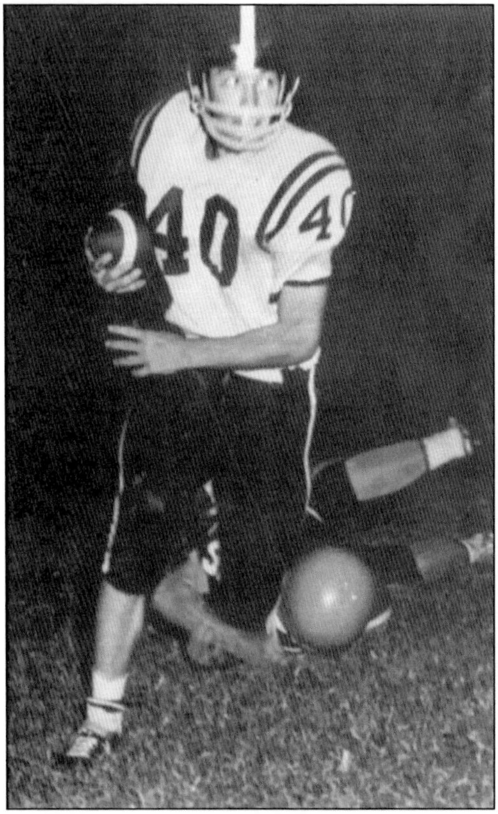

Other Scott protégés included quarterback Gary Chandler and all-district three-year letterman Van Evans. At left, in 1964, Evans makes a good run. After high school, Evans played two seasons for West Point. One of Scott's offensive team captains was Dale Brock (below), who later attended Tarleton State, where he played as an offensive and defensive starter his freshman and sophomore years.

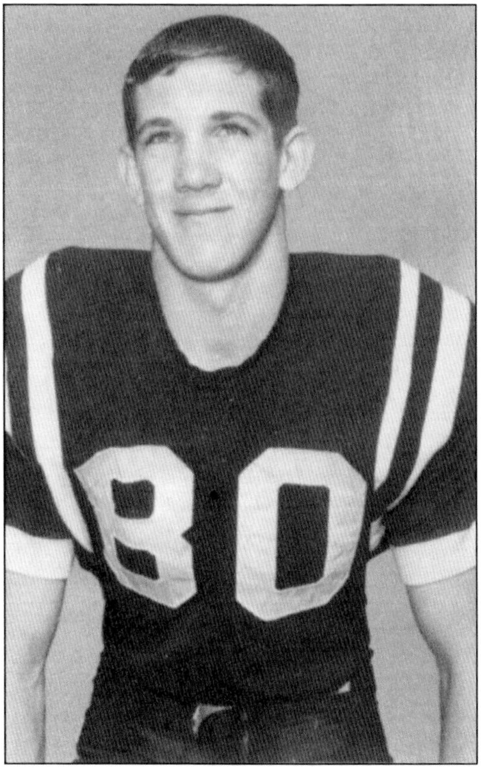

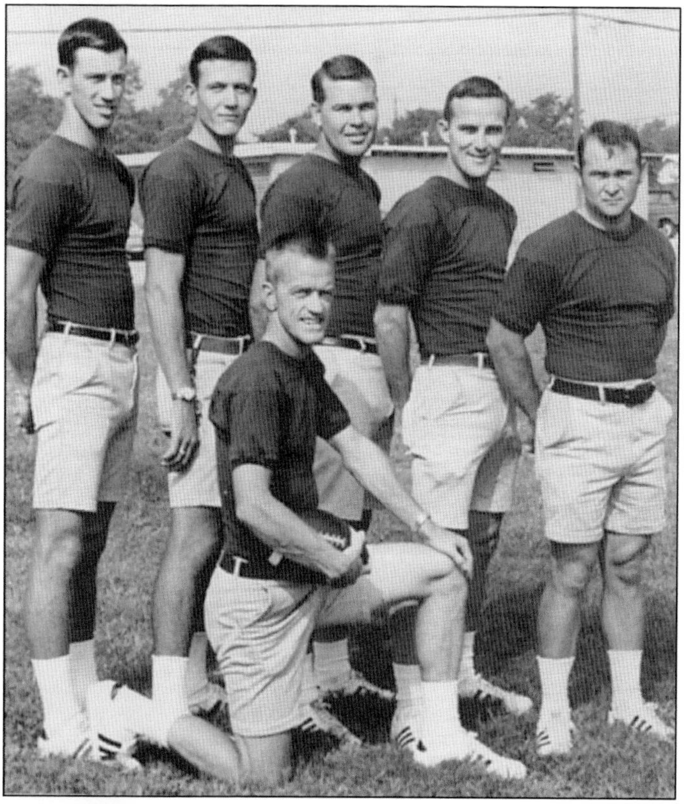

In 1969, Sam Taylor, who coached the Stephenville Honey Bees to the 1968 3A State Basketball title, began a two-and-a-half-year tenure as SHS athletic director and head football coach. The 1969 coaching staff includes, from left to right, Danny Potts, Mike Copeland, Taylor (kneeling), Ralph Garrett, Larry Aldridge, and Don Berry. Like others before him, Taylor was returning to his high school football home. Taylor played on Mike Murphy's 1951 Jacket team (8-1-0). The 1952 yearbook made special note that in the 40-21 SHS victory over Cleburne, Taylor (below) "performed well with his running and scored two touchdowns."

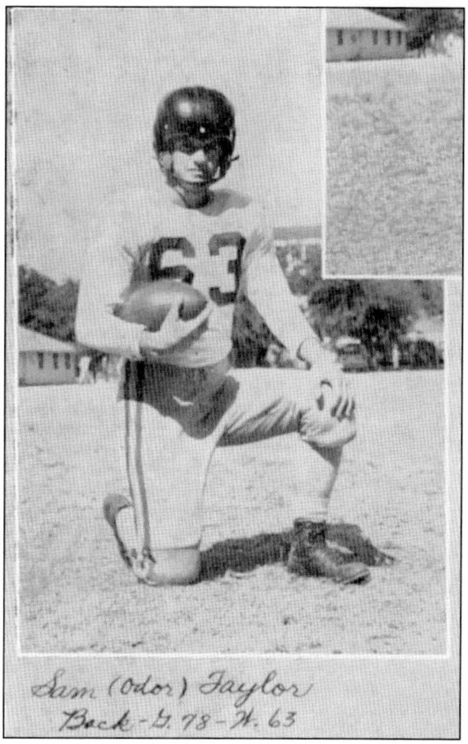

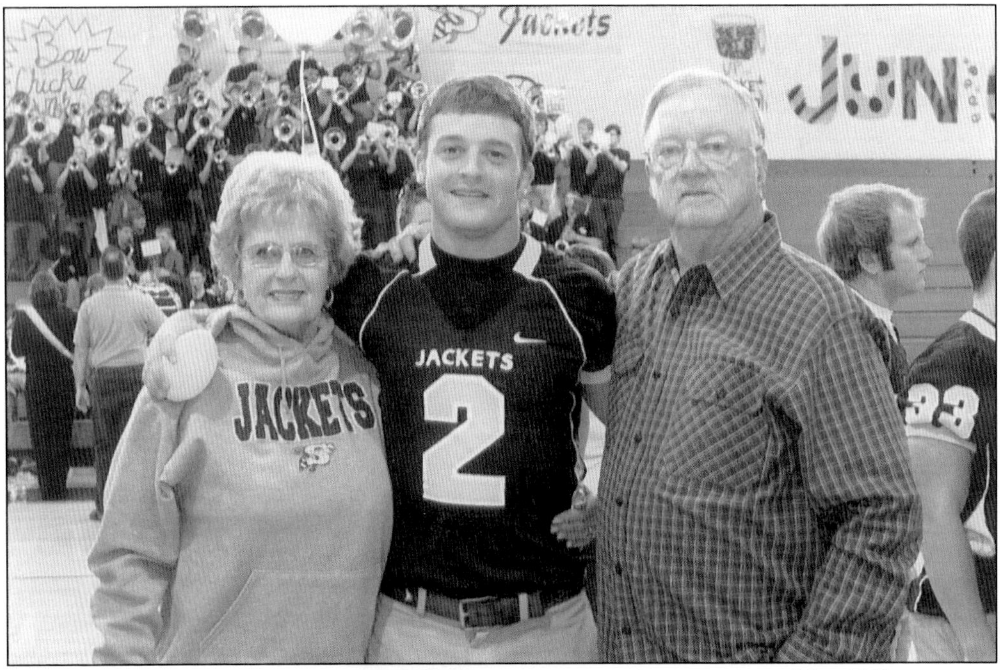

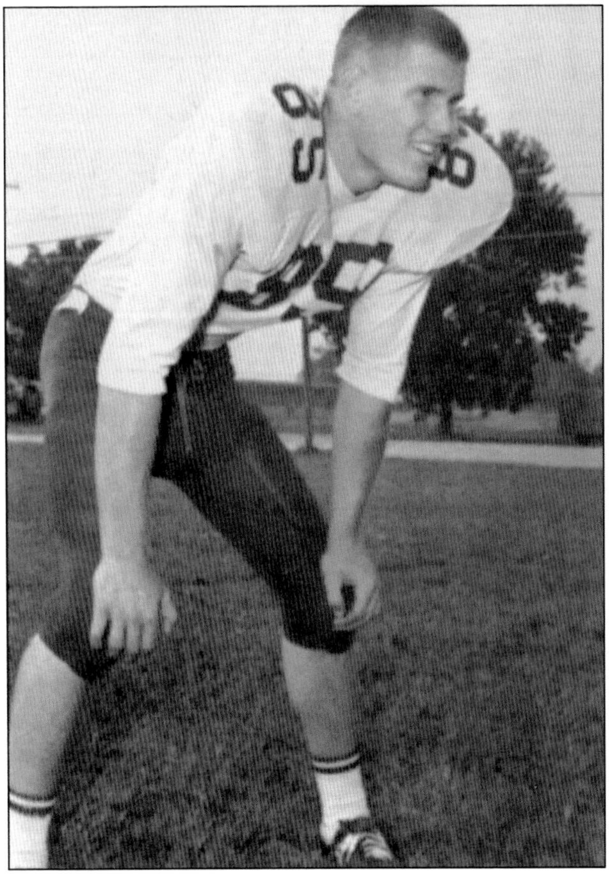

As a member of the 1952 team, Taylor was a 155-pound fullback with "lots of drive and determination. He played almost every position on the line and in the backfield. Sam was a great runner." Taylor passed the football gene on to his son Sam, who set a Texas single-game reception record in a 1980 Dublin versus Ranger contest with 22 catches. Coach Taylor's football skills went also to his grandson Trey, shown above at a pep rally and flanked by grandmother Joy and Coach Taylor. Trey was Stephenville's first four-year two-sport letterman (football and basketball). He was also MVP in both and played on the 2005 Jacket Semifinal team. A full 35 years before, Trey's grandfather coached all-state linebacker and future TCU football player Danny Brown (left). At SHS, Brown was a three-year letterman, all-district, all-area, and all-state. (Above, Sam Taylor.)

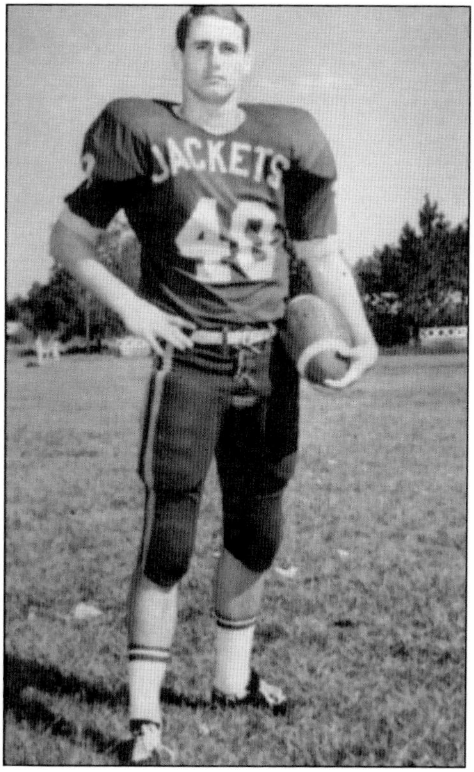

Like his grandson Trey, one of coach Taylor's athletes, Mike Wood (right), was also a four-year letterman. Wood received all-state honors his senior year and later played for Tarleton State University. In 1973, Leon Manley began a nine-year tenure as head football coach. Manley (kneeling) appears below with his 1976 coaching staff. They are, from left to right, Mike Copeland, Mike Woods, and Ray Ator. Before becoming high school principal in 1985, Manley had the pleasure of coaching both of his sons, Scott and Mark, to SHS Athletic Hall of Fame careers.

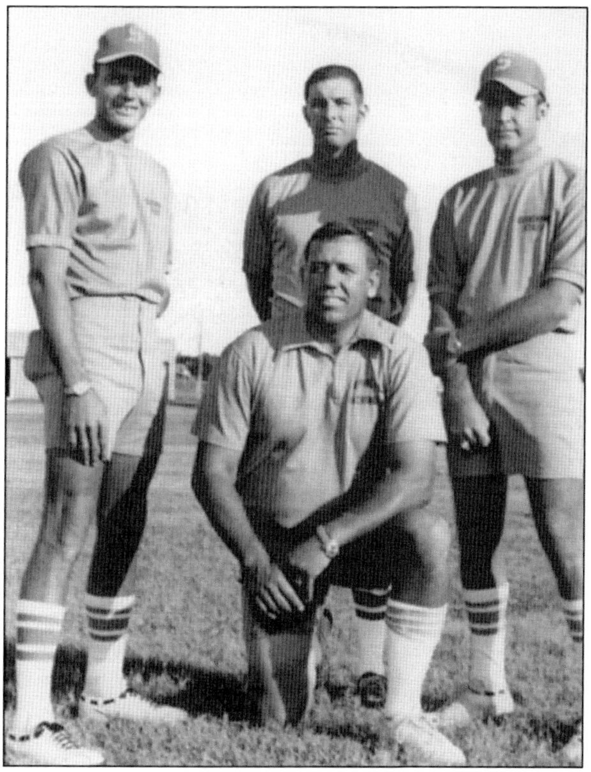

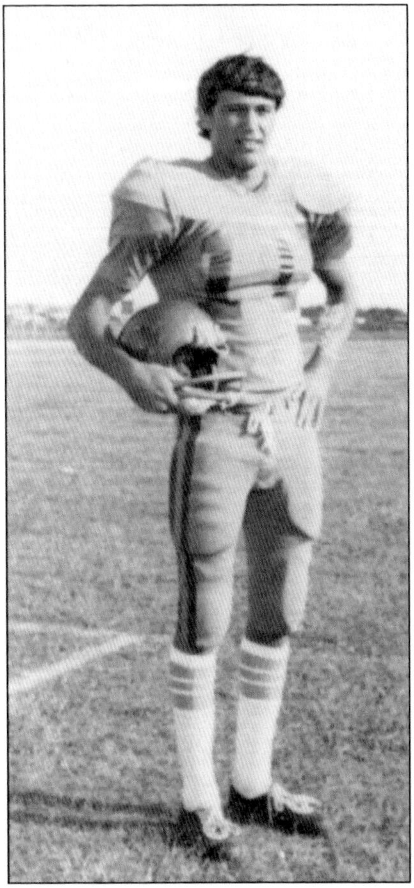

Mark Manley (left) was all-district in football and also selected to the *Abilene Reporter-News* All-Area team. He played college ball at West Texas State University (WTSU) where he was All-Missouri Valley Conference and Academic All-Conference. Scott Manley (below) was a 1979 All-District linebacker, Cross Timbers Defensive Player of the Year, second team all-state, and later a three-year letterman and team captain (1983) where his brother played, WTSU.

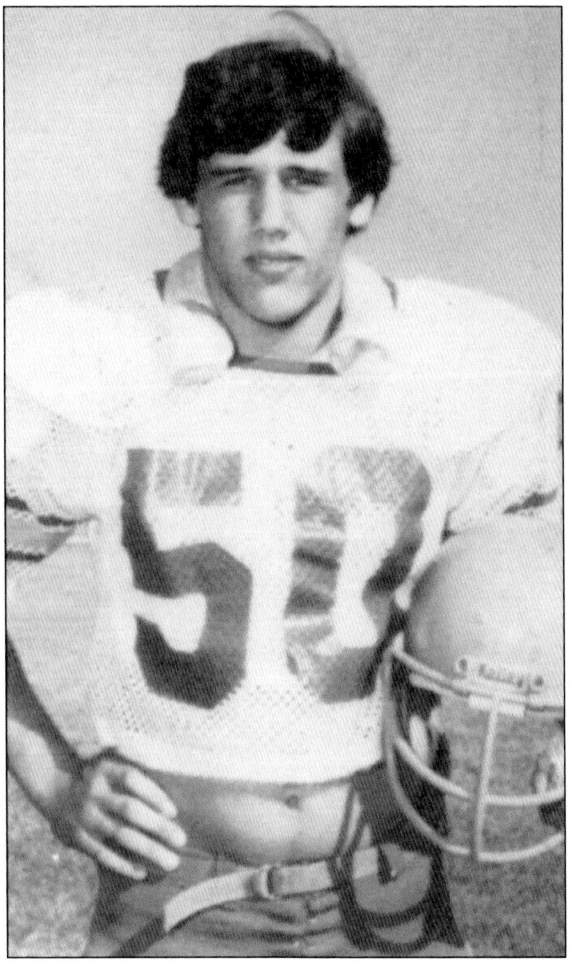

Manley's coaching successes were not limited to family. He mentored all-district quarterback L. Klye Heffley (right), the only five-sport letterman in SHS history (football, baseball, basketball, track, and golf). Heffley later played defensive back and shortstop for Princeton University. Manley also coached linebacker and tight end Rick DeLoach (below), a Jacket four-sport letterman who was all-district and all-area in football. The Chicago Cubs drafted DeLoach to play baseball, and he joined the Professional Golfers' Association in 1985.

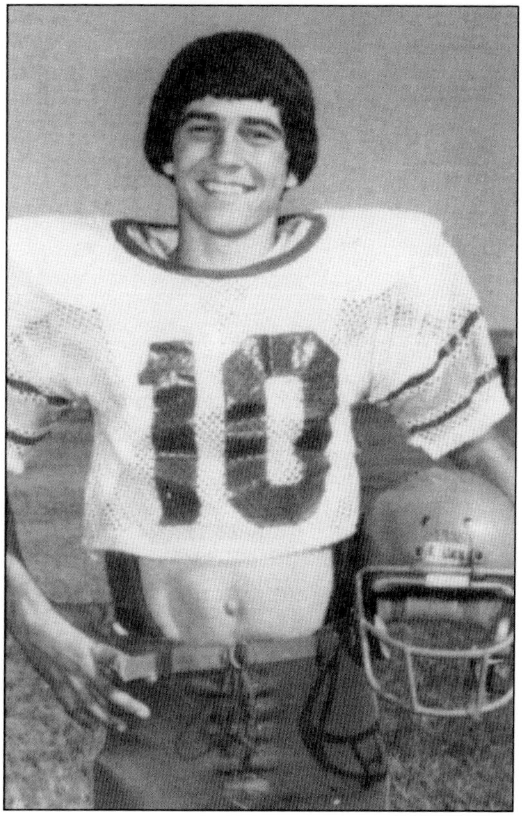

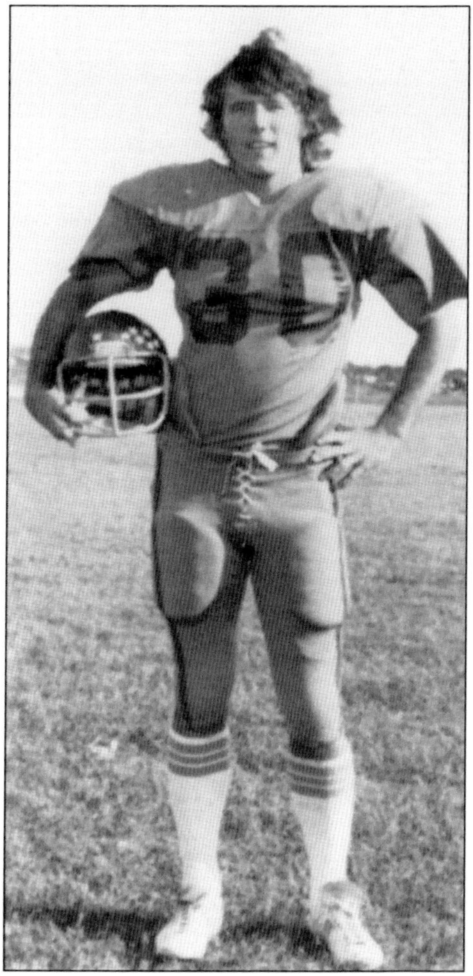

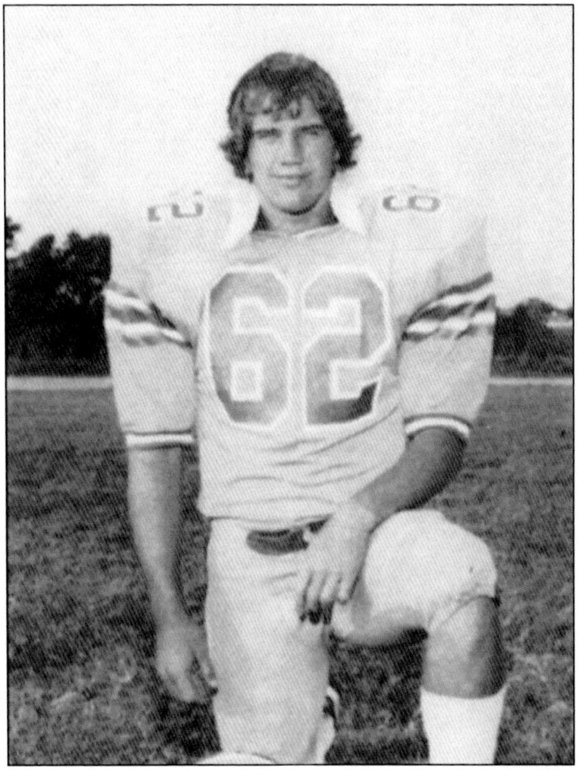

Two other hall of famers—Tod Ryden (left) and Kobe Fornes (below)—were Manley understudies. Ryden, a three-year letterman at linebacker and kicker, later attended Texas Tech. Fornes was a three-year starter at cornerback and tailback as well as a starter for Baylor University at fullback and tight end.

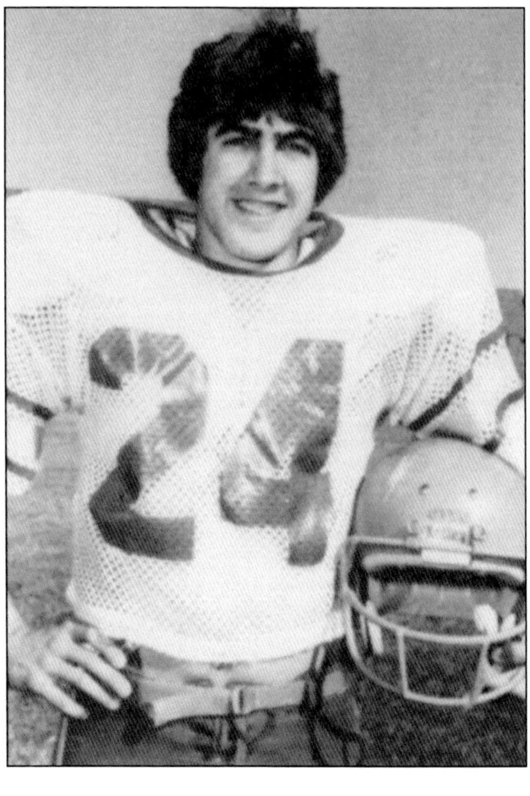

Fornes was also coached by Joe Loudermilk (1982–1987), as was hall of famer Roy Graham. Right, Graham stands by his hall of fame plaque at SHS. Graham was all-district football two years on both offense and defense. He later played on two Tarleton teams that went to the national playoffs. Below, Roy's brother Keith Graham, also in the hall of fame, played under coach Art Briles. Graham was an AP All-State defensive back who received a scholarship to Abilene Christian University. (Right, Thompson.)

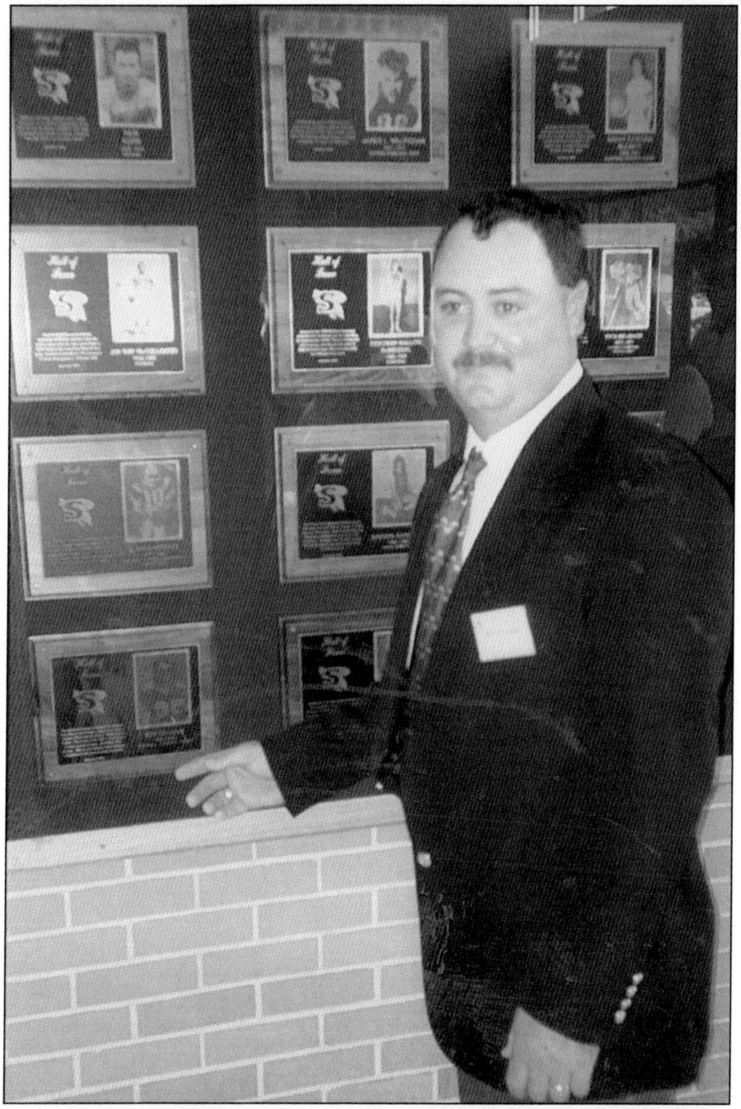

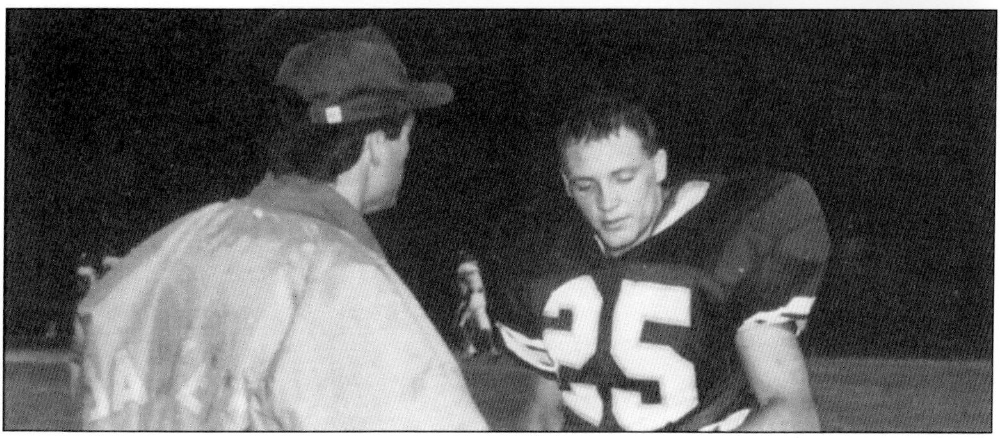

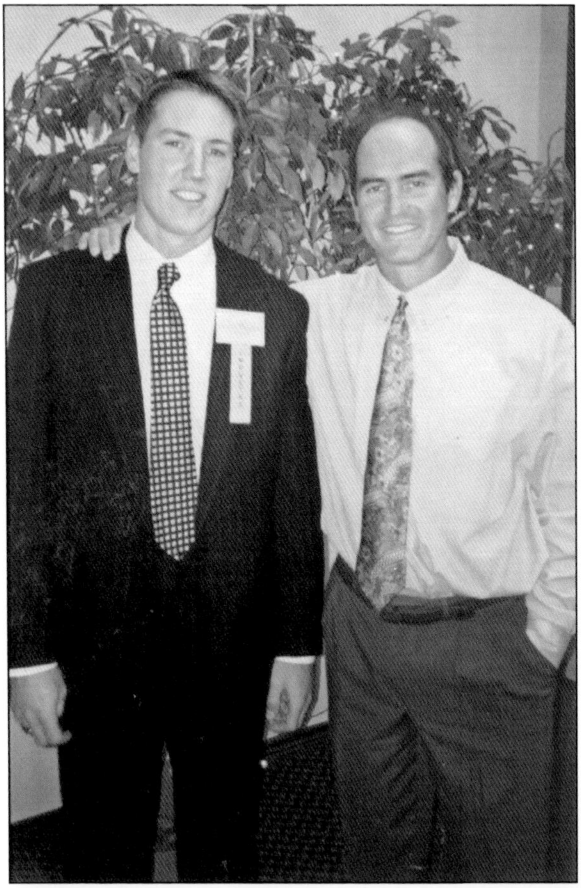

At left, Jason Poston (left), with his coach Art Briles, was an AP All-State wide receiver and kicker. Both the *Fort Worth Star-Telegram* and *Abilene Reporter-News* selected Poston as Offensive Player of the Year. He later played for Tyler Junior College in both the Championship and Shrine Bowls. Below is hall of fame kicking coach Bob Cervetto with his son Kellen. The latter played fullback–running back on the 2003 and 2004 teams and was District 8-4A Co–Most Valuable Player of the Year his senior season. (Left, Thompson; below, Bob Cervetto.)

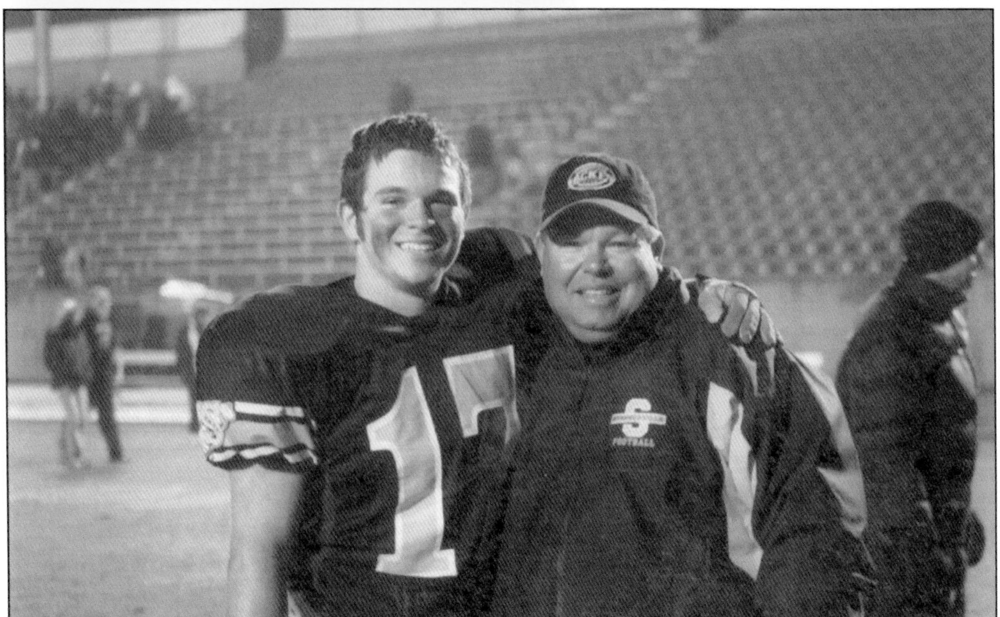

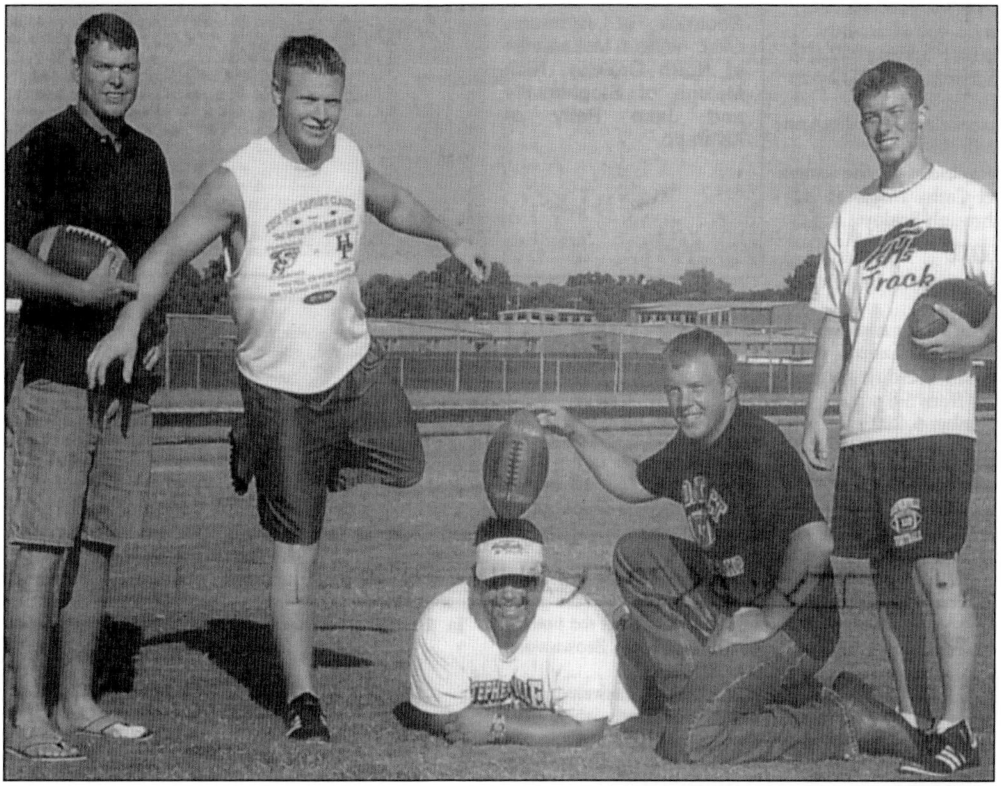

SHS kicking coach since 1981, Cervetto (on ground) appears above with four of his kickers. They are, from left to right, Chris Evatt, Eban Nelson (all-state, 2000), J.W. "Mr. Automatic" Boren (all-state, 1998), and Jamie Guin. At Tarleton, Boren set 13 school records and four Lone Star Conference records, was TSU's all-time leading scorer, all-conference all four years at TSU, all-American his sophomore and senior years, and was among the Lone Star Conference's Top 75 Players in 75 Years. Both Boren and Evatt (also a receiver and backup quarterback) were on the 1998 state champion team. Evatt punted effectively for both Hardin Simmons and TSU. Among Cervetto's other 45-Yard Club protégées are four more all-staters—Jason Poston, Brad Couch, Ben Bell, German Chavarria—and Garrett Schouten, Alex Fichera, and Josh Neaves. Right, Charlie Riola holds for 2008 All-State first team kicker Chavarria. (Both, Bud Jones and Huffmann, *Stephenville Empire-Tribune*.)

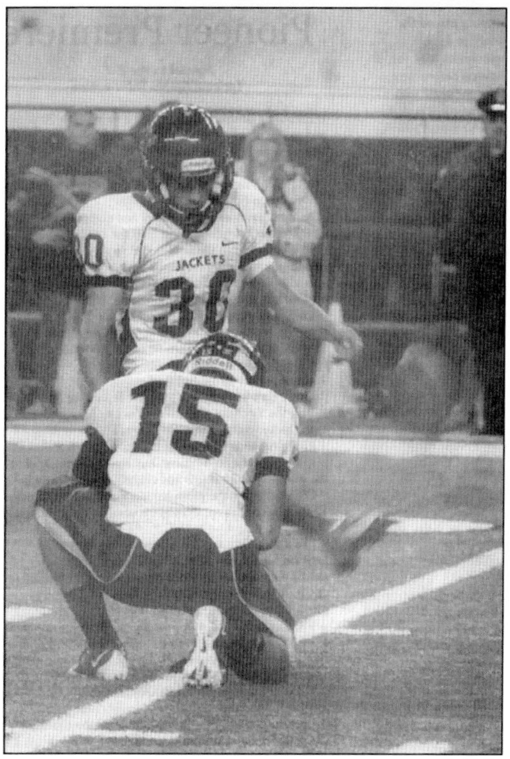

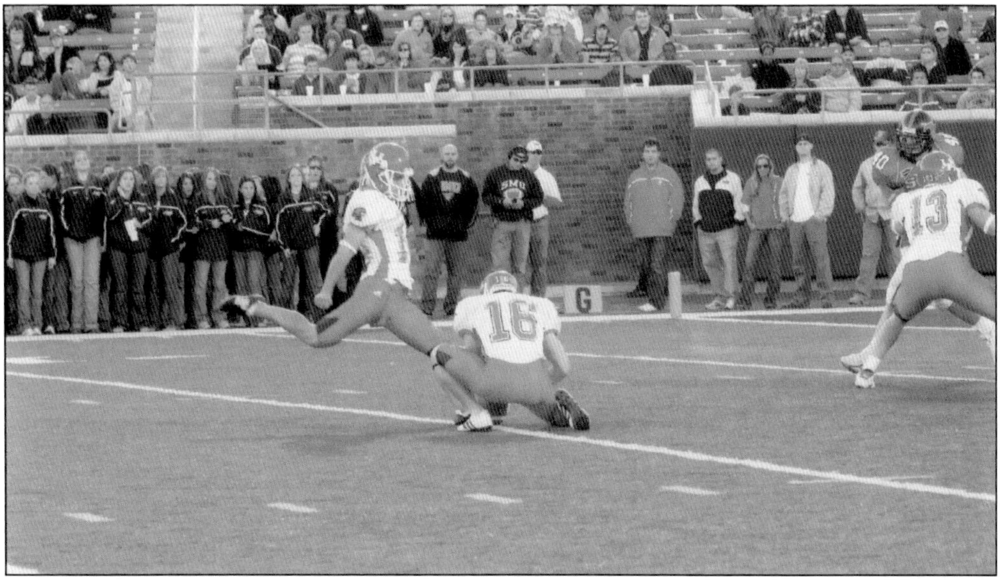

Ben Bell (above) later kicked for University of Houston (2005–2007, 2009). In 1988, SISD superintendent Ben Gilbert made one of the most influential SISD hires ever. Art Briles was literally on the way to assume head coaching duties elsewhere when Gilbert persuaded him to take the Stephenville job. Thus began a new era in Yellow Jacket football. In his inaugural meeting with the seventh graders of 1988, Briles declared, "The mean and lean days are over, it is time to get cocky and stocky." His words proved prophetic. From 1988 to 1999, Briles's career record was an unprecedented 136-29-2, with seven district titles, 11 playoff seasons, and four state championships. Briles (below, at Irving's Texas Stadium in 1998) first proved that Stephenville could win. Then, he instilled within his players—and just as importantly, within the community—the habit of winning. (Both, Skipper.)

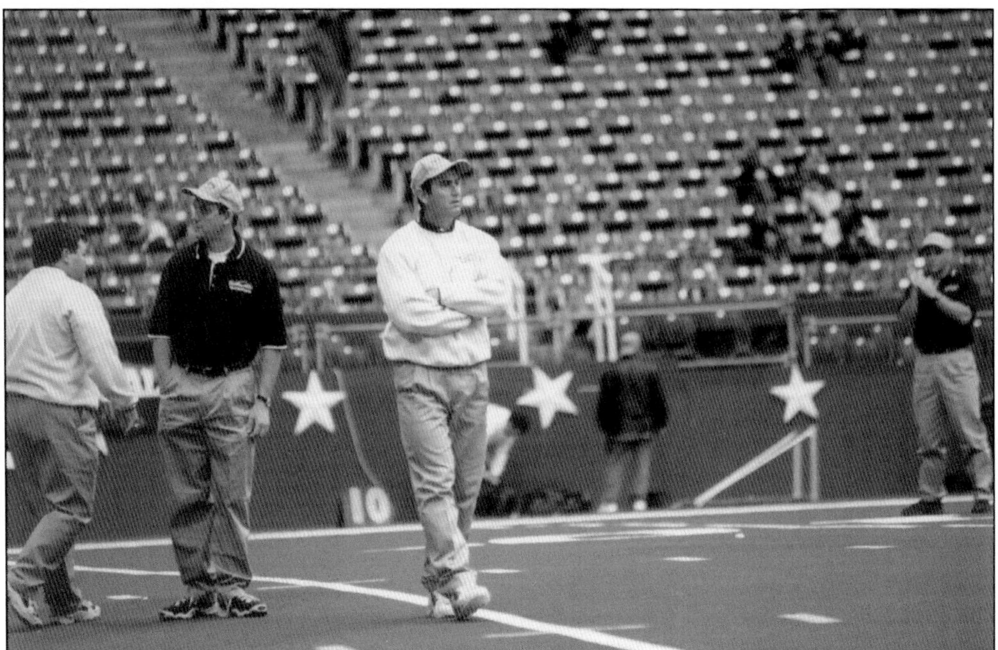

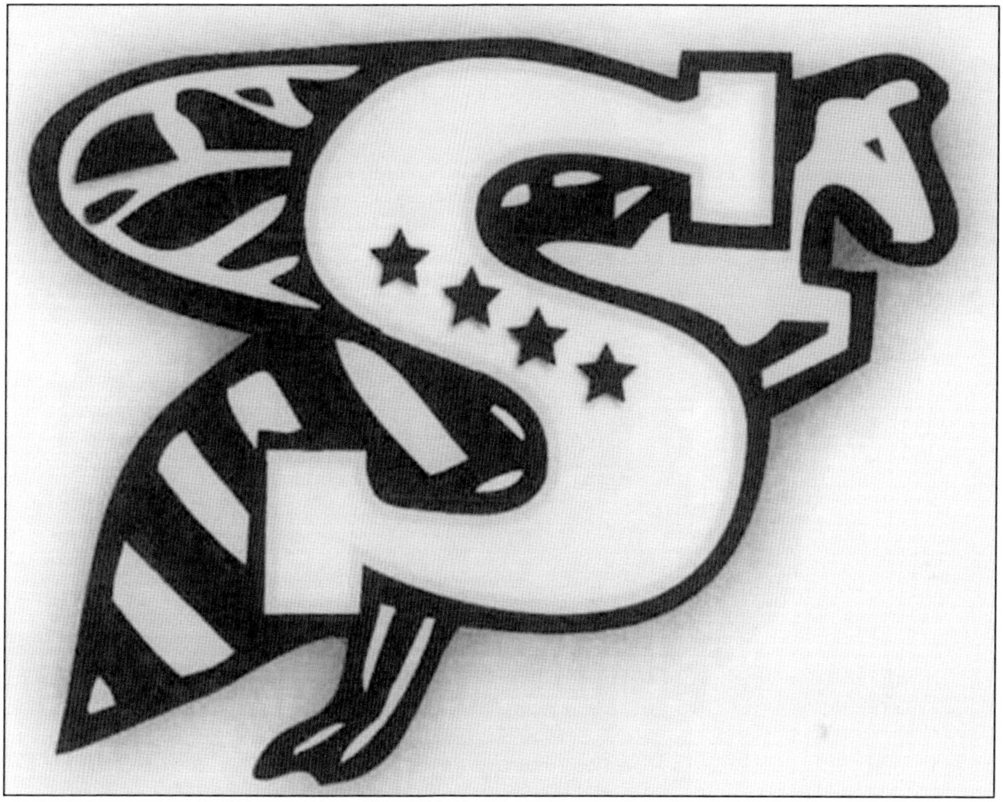

That habit required the recasting of the SHS logo (above). Following the 1999 season, four stars graced the S, reminding players, coaches, and community of the four Jacket state titles. Shown below with his son Kendal immediately prior to the 1999 4A D-2 state title game, Art Briles became one in a long list of Stephenville coaches who mentored a son both at home and on the field. (Below, *Fort Worth Star-Telegram*.)

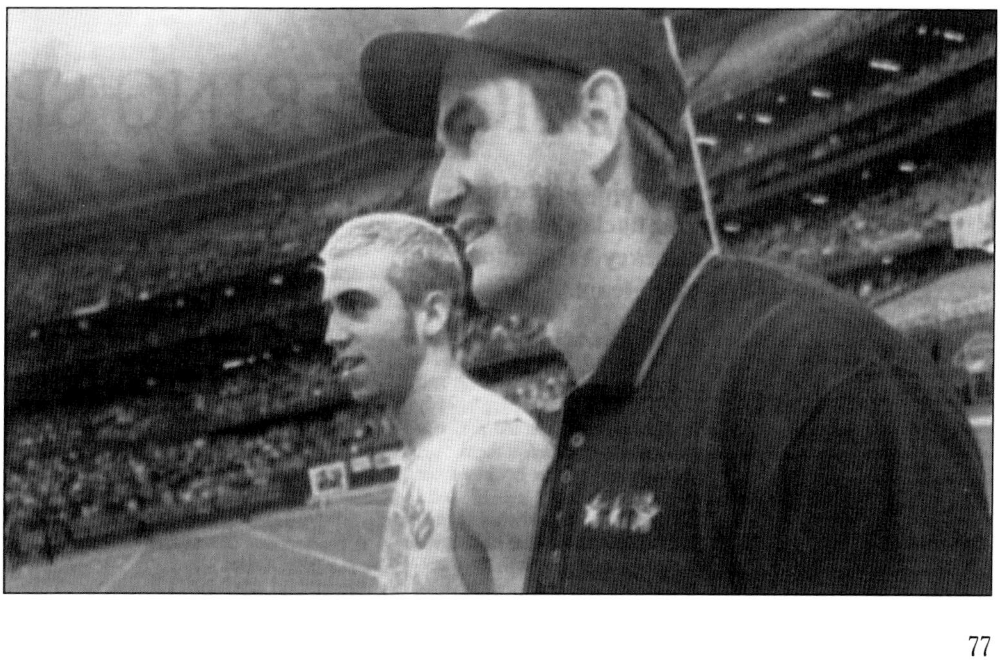

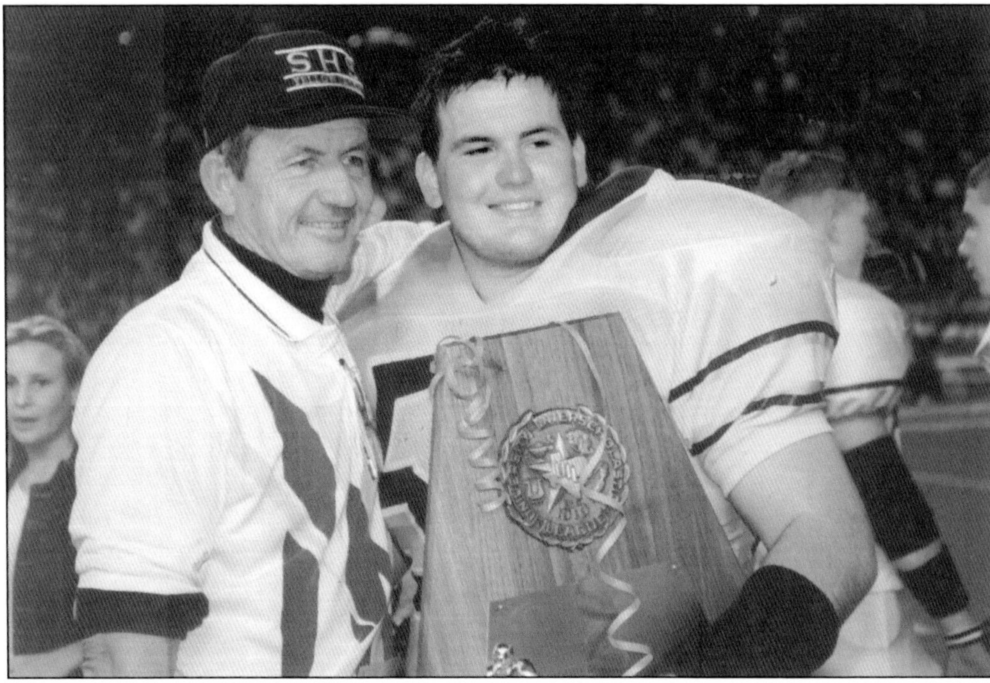

Briles left Stephenville at the end of the 1999 season to become running back coach at Texas Tech. Longtime SHS coach and teacher Mike Copeland stepped in to direct the program. From 2000 to 2002, he enjoyed a 26-9-0 record, including a 2002 district title and three trips to the playoffs. Above, Copeland appears with his son Mitch, all-state lineman in 1993 and 1994 and 4A Defensive Player of the Year in 1994. Coach Copeland took a five-year retirement at the end of the 2002 season, only to return to coaching in 2008. Before Copeland's coaching resurrection, SISD honored his contributions to the youth of Stephenville, naming the high school athletic complex below in his honor. (Above, Skipper; below, author.)

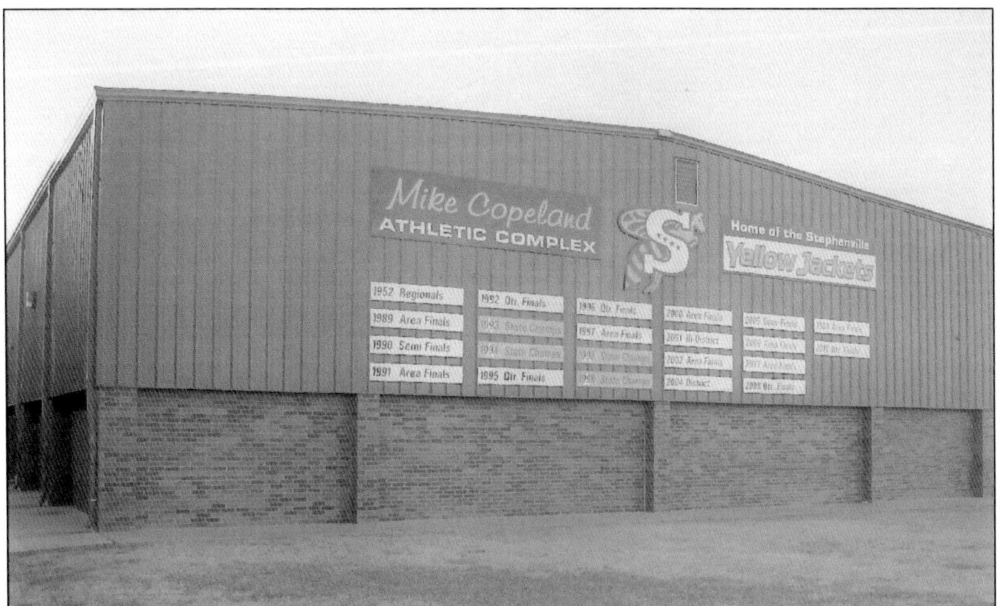

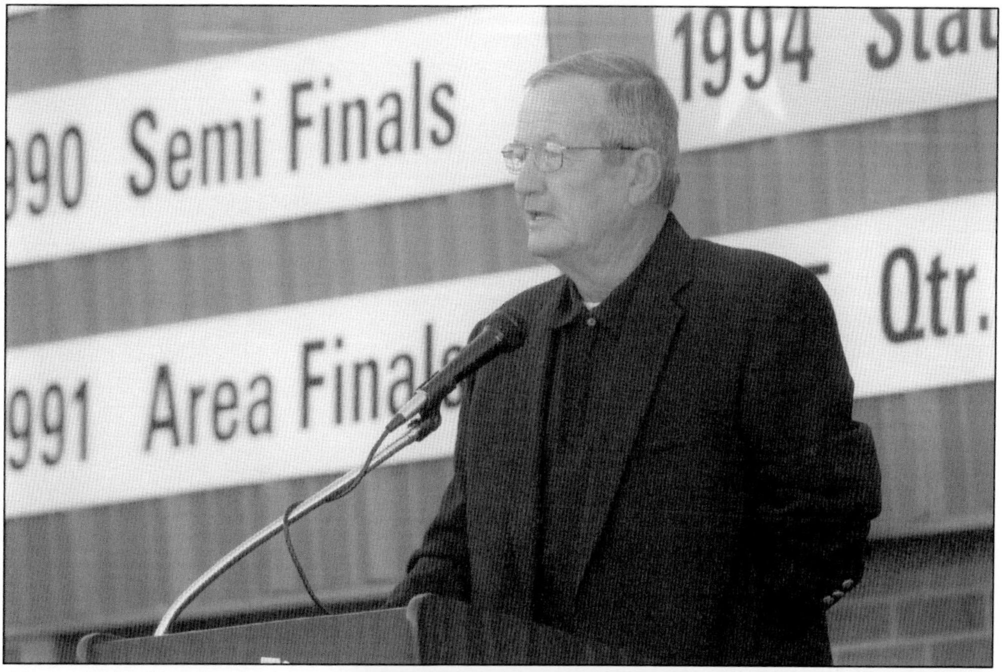

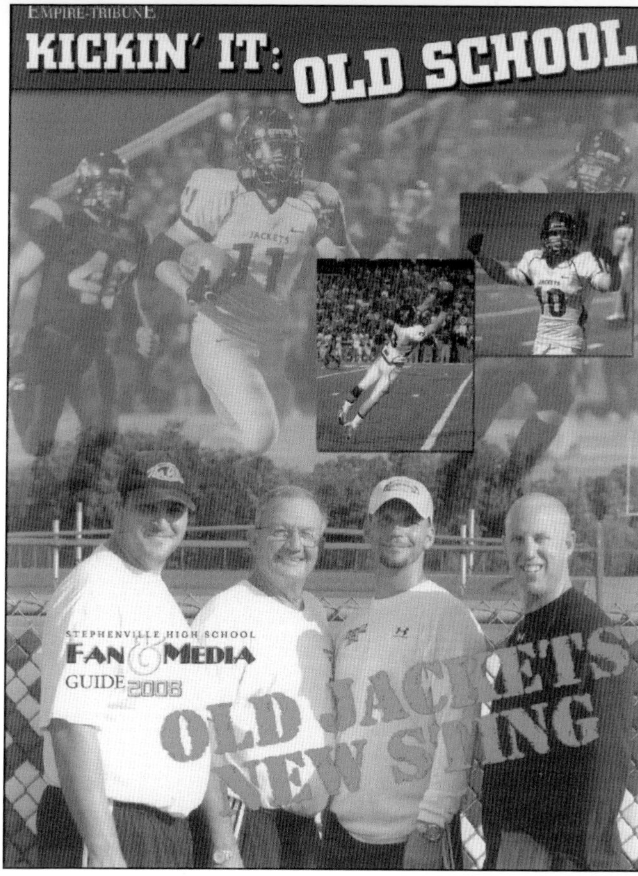

Above, Mike Copeland speaks at the athletic complex dedication ceremony. When Copeland rejoined the coaching staff in 2008, he did not return without familiar faces. The cover of the *Fan & Media Guide 2008* (right) includes, from left to right, Curtis Lowery of the 1993–1994 state champion teams and later a standout lineman at Texas Tech; Copeland; newly appointed head coach Joseph Gillespie; and Jeffrey Thompson, also of the 1993–1994 state champion teams. (Above, Debbie Cashell; right, *Stephenville Empire-Tribune*.)

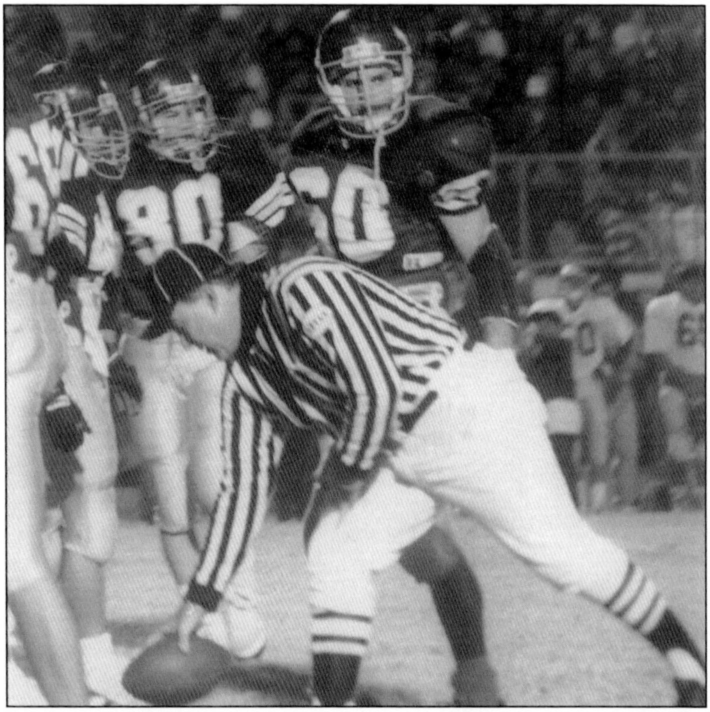

At left, Joseph Gillespie (center) is another former Jacket who returned to SHS to coach. He was a member of the 1989 team that upset heavily favored Belton in the bi-district round. In 2008, Gillespie received the nod, becoming athletic director and head football coach. In three years at the helm (2008–2010), Gillespie has captured one District 8-4A title (below) and has gone to the playoffs every season, including two quarterfinals appearances in 2008 and 2010. (Left, Joseph Gillespie; below, Kathy Slemmons.)

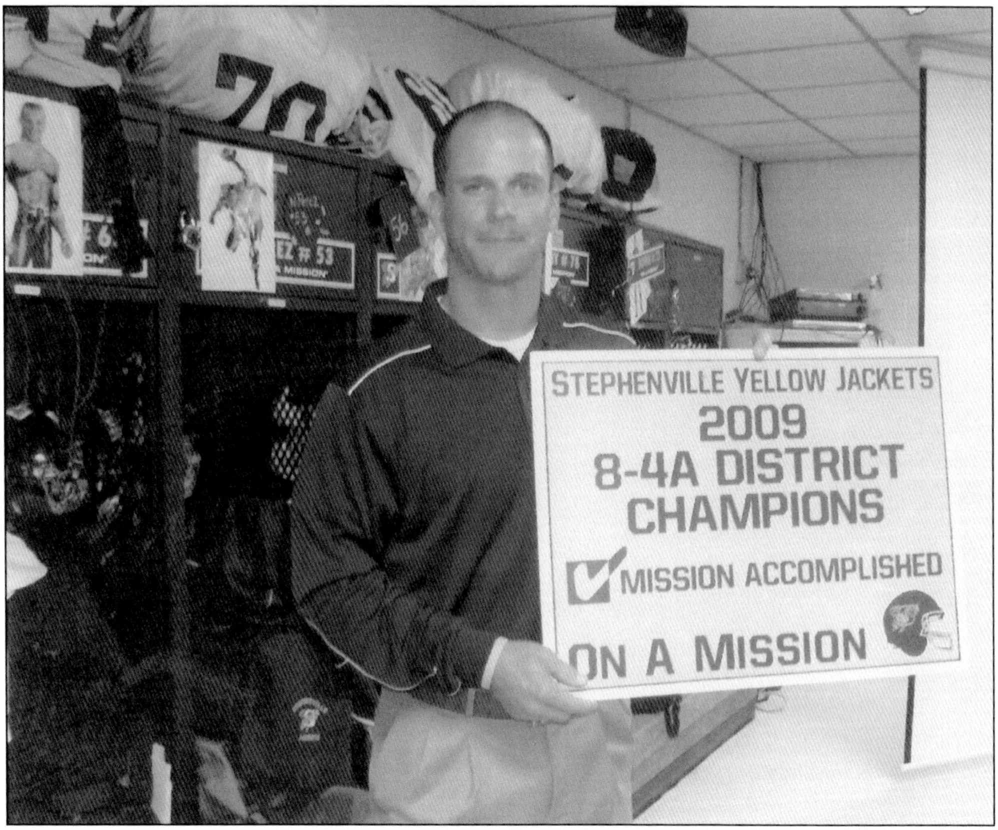

Five

Where Are They Now?

How many times do Texans follow the careers of their favorite high school athletes, only to find themselves asking a month, a year, or a decade later, "Where are they now?"

In Stephenville, that question is often the exception rather than the rule. No one has to ask. Thorough, heavily illustrated sports coverage provided by the local newspaper rarely allows its readers to forget its favorite sons. And locally, that is considered a very good thing. Living in one of the state's premier football towns, most Stephenville residents want to know how hometown heroes have fared beyond the high school gridiron.

Today, locals gleefully follow the storied career of current NFL quarterback Kevin Kolb. Like Jacket field generals before him, he jumped to the next level, enjoying a four-year, record-setting role as University of Houston's starting quarterback. His successes as a Cougar transformed him into an Eagle of the Philadelphia kind.

Kolb is not the only former Yellow Jacket to reach the NFL. He is the present, most recent bookend, opposite Hugh Wolfe, a 1930 schoolboy star who continued his football career at the local college, Tarleton, then at the University of Texas, and finally with the 1938 NFL champion New York Giants. In between Wolfe and Kolb is a host of others who have made their marks at the next level in college football. Some are players. Others are coaches. All embody the local refrain, "Once a Yellow Jacket, always a Yellow Jacket."

Stephenville's best remembered stars have extended their football careers at Texas A&M, Texas Christian, Southern Methodist, Baylor, Texas Tech, University of Texas, University of Houston, Abilene Christian, Tarleton State, Nebraska, Tennessee, Ole Miss, Iowa, New Mexico State, Southeast Missouri, West Point, West Texas State, Princeton, and elsewhere.

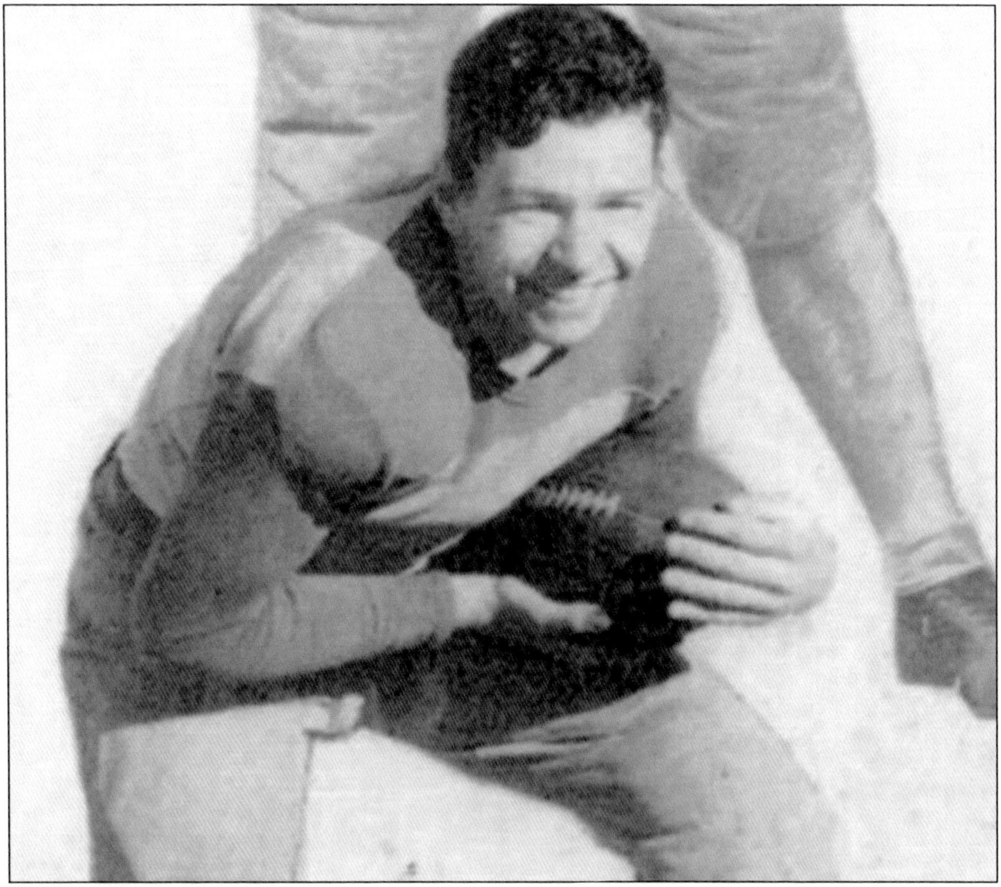

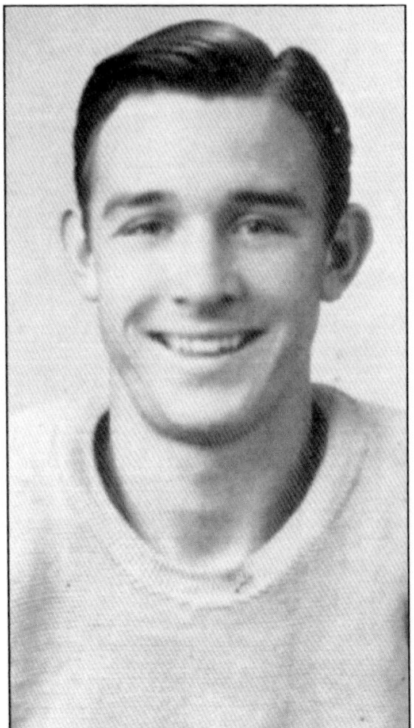

Hugh Wolfe (above) played fullback for the 1930 District Champion Yellow Jackets. He first continued his football career at home for John Tarleton Agricultural College. From there, Wolfe played at the University of Texas, where, after the 1937 season, he became the Longhorns first NFL draft pick. The following season, he was a member of the New York Giants NFL champion team. In 1977, Wolfe received induction into the Longhorn Hall of Honor. One of the greatest Yellow Jacket running backs following in Wolfe's wake was Derace Moser (left) who played for Mobley's celebrated 1936 and 1937 teams. This 170-pound halfback was renowned for long end runs and his remarkably accurate punts. (Above, Tarleton State University Dick Smith Library *Grassburr*.)

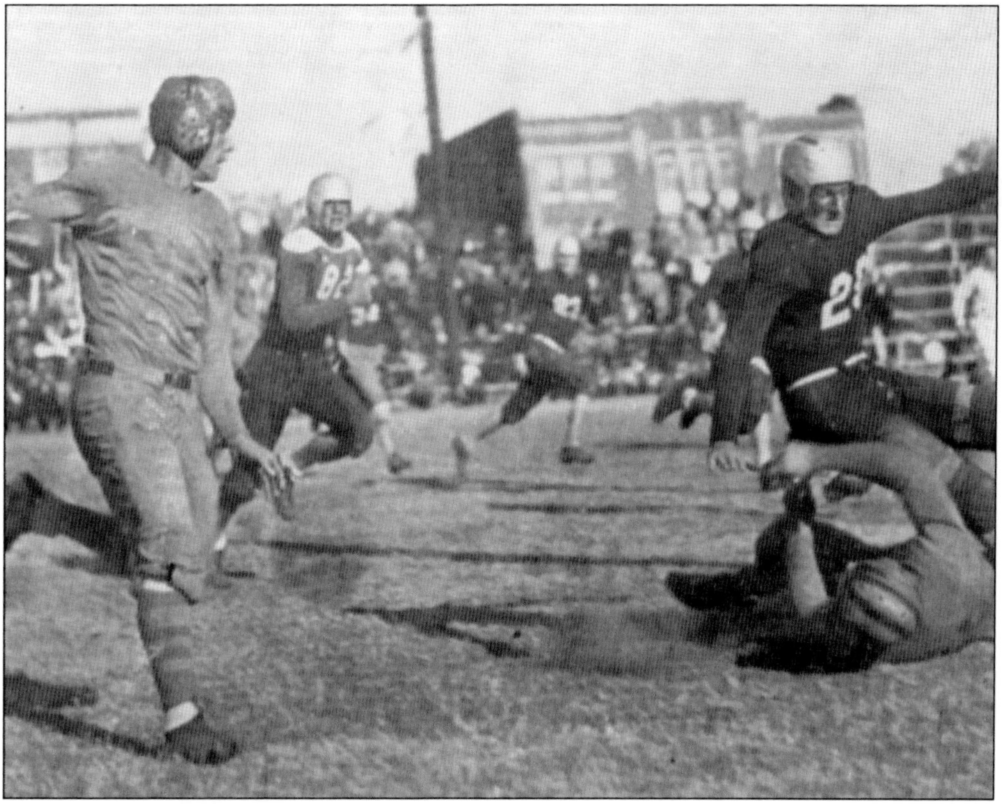

Above, Moser follows 190-pound fullback Norval Wood's lead block for a big gain. Described as the backbone of the SHS offense, this four-sport letterman was the team's leading scorer, all-district, and honorable mention all-state as well as student body president. After high school, Moser became an all-American and a 1990 Texas A&M University Athletic Hall of Fame inductee. Below, Moser runs the ball in a 1939 game against conference rival SMU. At A&M, he was a four-year letterman and played on the undefeated 1939 National Champion Aggie team. Those Aggies allowed only 76.3 yards per game. In 1941, Moser was Southwest Conference MVP. (Below, Thompson.)

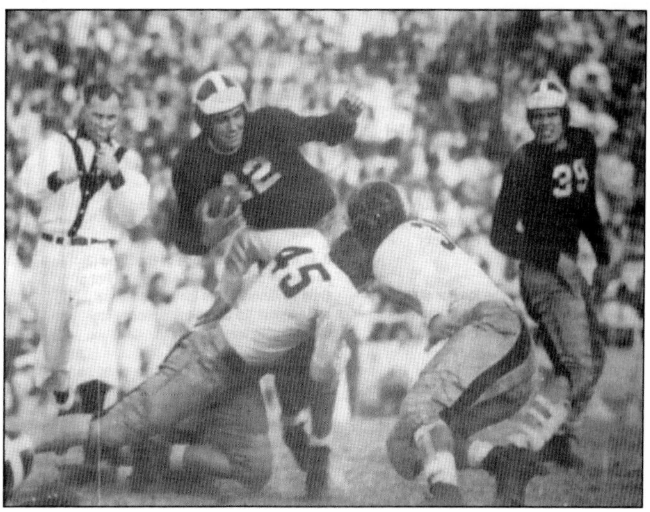

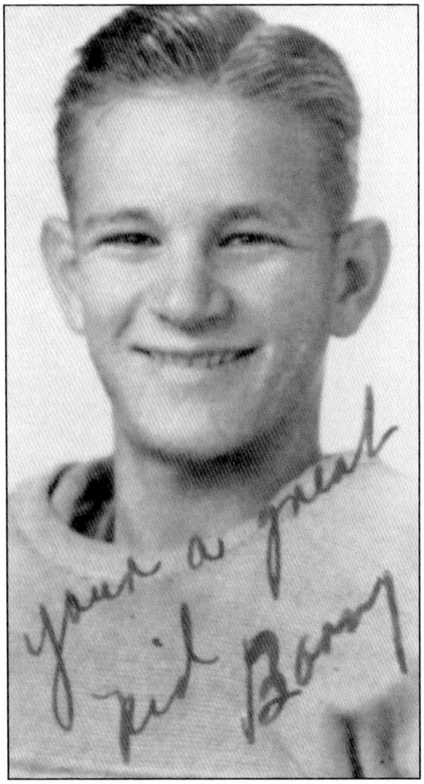

One of Moser's greatest gifts to A&M was high school teammate Barney Welch (left). Welch was the first Aggie to cross the goal line in Austin's Memorial Stadium. Five years before this historic 1942 punt return, Welch was a freshman varsity Yellow Jacket. In 1940, Welch runs, such as the one below, made Barney the leading Jacket ground-gainer and unanimous coaches selection as Outstanding 9-2A running back. Moser persuaded A&M coach Homer Norton to offer Welch a scholarship. World War II interrupted Welch's A&M career. It also cost him dear friend Derace Moser, who in November 1943 tragically died in a plane crash while flying from Waco to Florida on his way to deployment in Europe. After the war, Welch returned to A&M, where he resumed his football career, graduated in 1948, and eventually coached there under Gene Stallings.

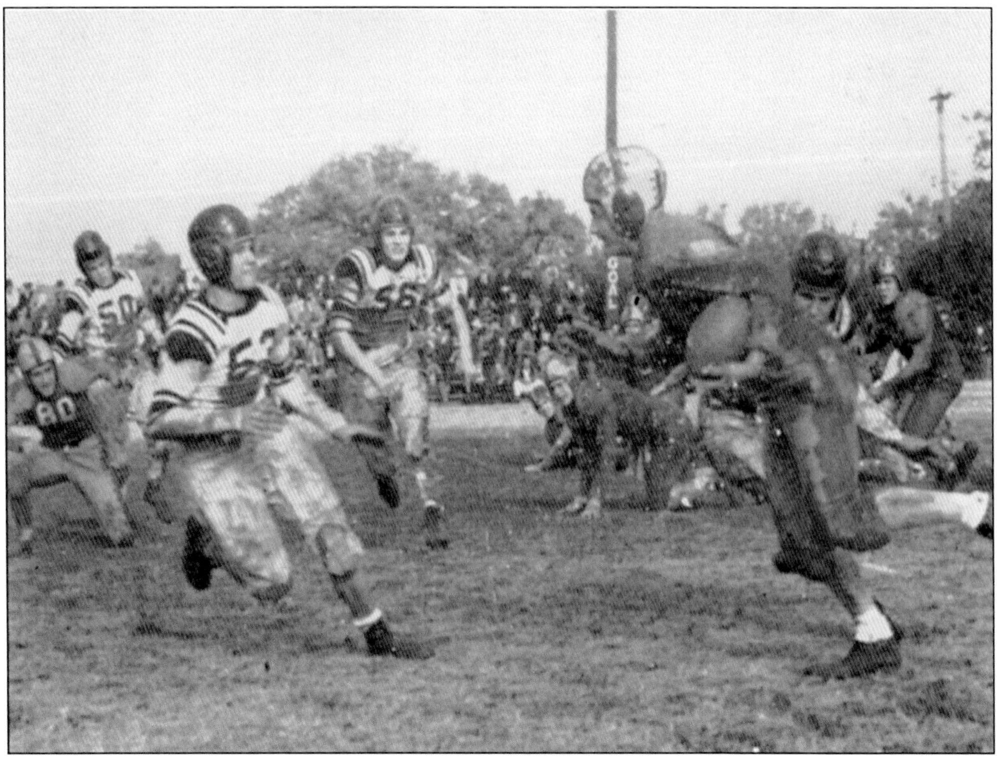

Welch and Moser were not the only 1937 Yellow Jackets to leave a mark after graduation. The 1938 SHS yearbooks notes that halfback-end 155-pound Cecil "Tail-light" Ballow's "nimble-foot running and bullet passing" made him "one of the best halfbacks in the [Oil Belt] conference." Ballow (right) went on to Tarleton, where as baseball coach his Plowboys were runners-up at the 1960 National Junior College Championship. In 2008, Cecil's son Pat (below, in 1962) received induction into the SHS Hall of Fame for his three years as an all-district Jacket football player. Pat Ballow also received honorable mention all-state.

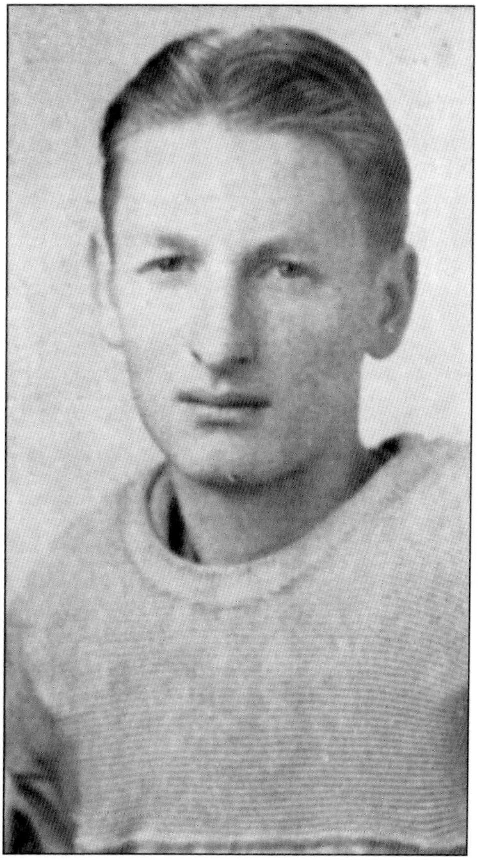

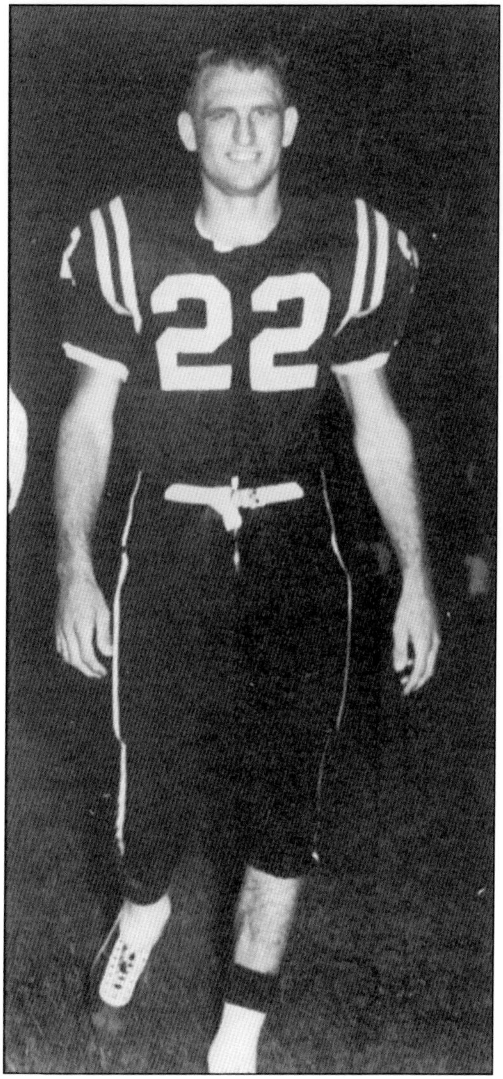

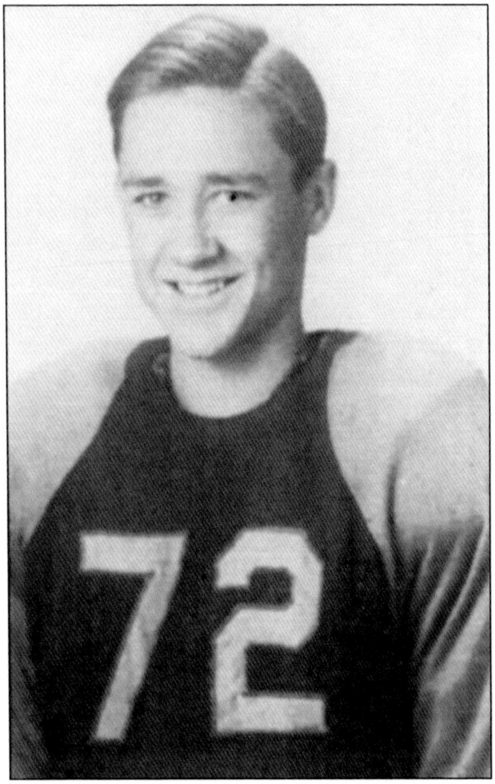

During the war years, one of Stephenville's greatest players was 175-pound fullback Ralph Poteet (left), a distant cousin of Lee, the first Jacket quarterback. Poteet continued his football career in Georgetown at Southwestern University. Immediately after the war, Southwestern was one of the best football schools in Texas. Poteet scored three touchdowns in Southwestern's 1945 El Paso Sun Bowl win. In appreciation for his productive 31-year career in Mesquite ISD (including 22 years as superintendent), the school district christened Mesquite Poteet High School in Dr. Poteet's honor. Below, hall of famer Harry "Bubby" Braeuer was a unanimous all-district quarterback for two seasons (1950–1951) and all-state for one. Braeuer played in the North-South High School All-Star Game and was part of the National High School All-American Team. He turned down a college football scholarship to go to UT Medical School.

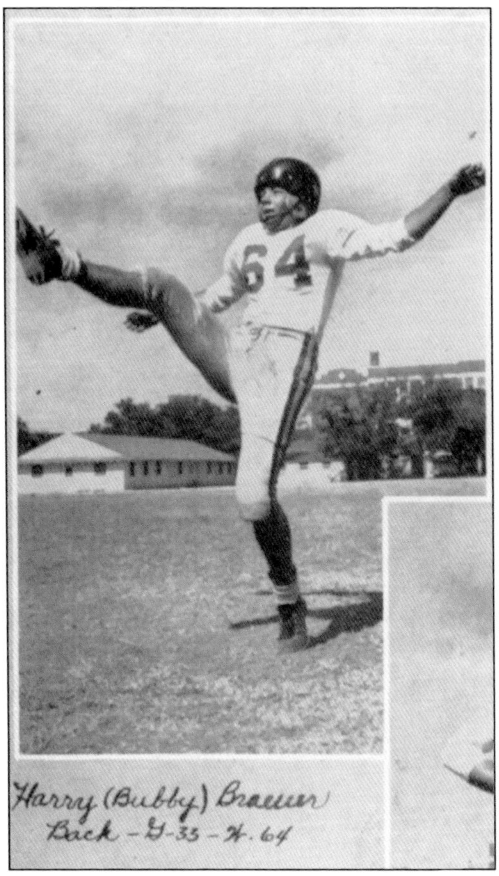

Speedy lineman Jay Ray McCullough (right) played on the 1952 Jacket team that went to the regional game and was 1953 team cocaptain. He went on to TCU, where he played in the 1955 and 1956 Cotton Bowls. McCullough's teammate Charles "Tubba" Roberson (below) played end, guard, tackle, and linebacker. During his 1953 senior season, he was team cocaptain, second team all-state, and honorable mention all-American. Roberson competed in the 1954 Green Belt Bowl and thereafter played at Tarleton.

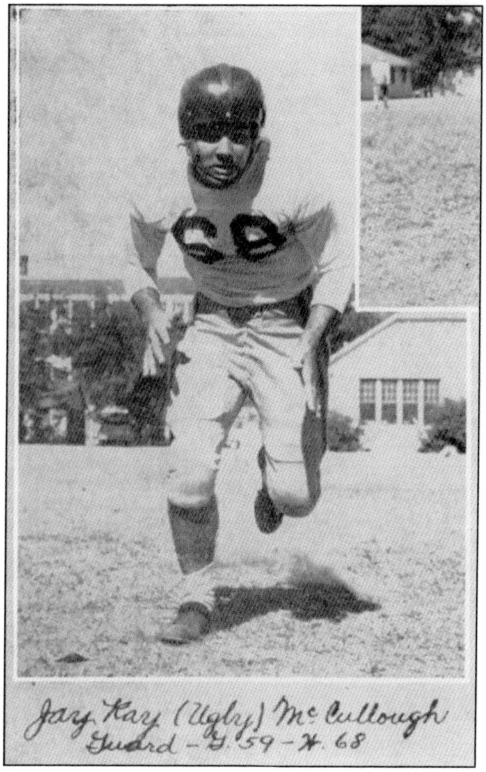

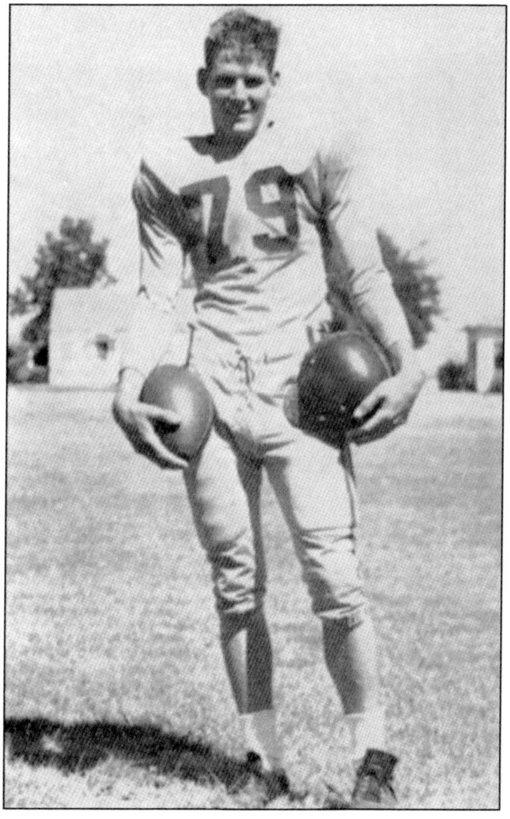

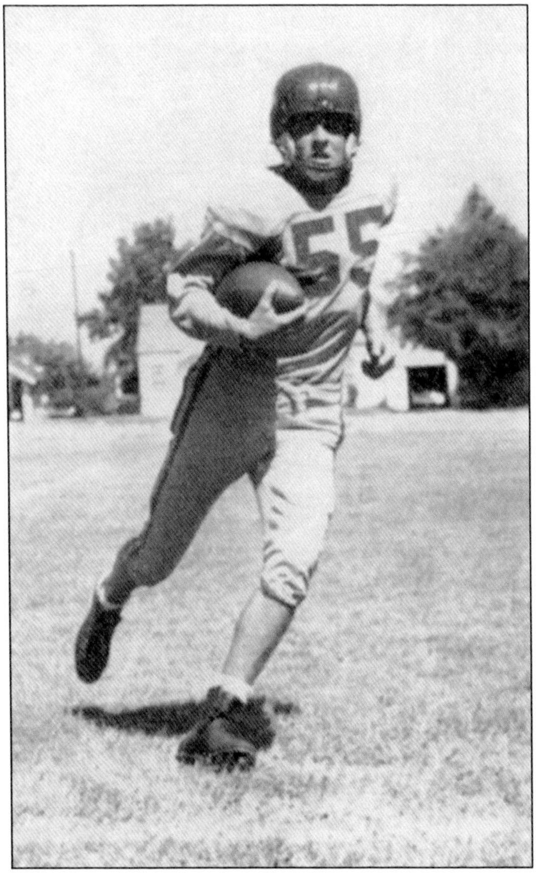

Jacket quarterback Jerry Flemmons (left) continued his football career at Tarleton as well. There, he played quarterback and after graduation became a highly popular newspaper columnist for the *Fort Worth Star-Telegram*. A later SHS quarterback, three-year letterman, and 1959 cocaptain, Bobby Glasgow (below), also attended Tarleton. In 1966, he was student body president and later was elected as a Texas state senator. Today, he is an attorney in the Stephenville firm of Glasgow Taylor Isham Glasgow. He is also the grandfather of four-year letterman Trey Taylor (page 68).

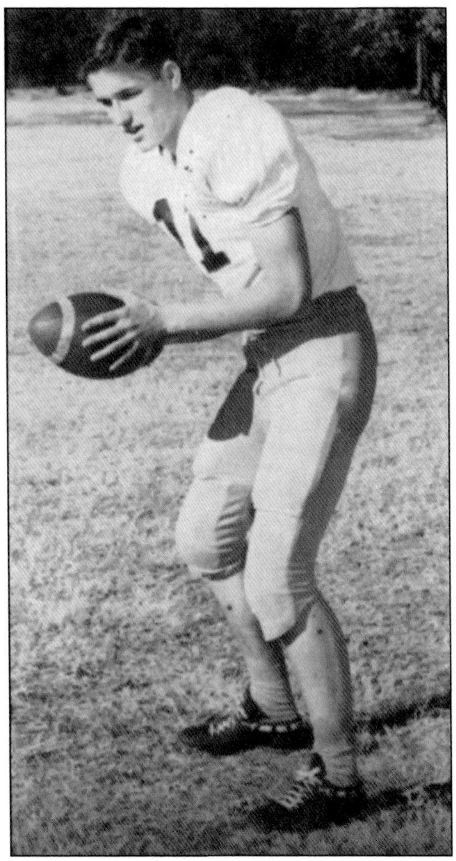

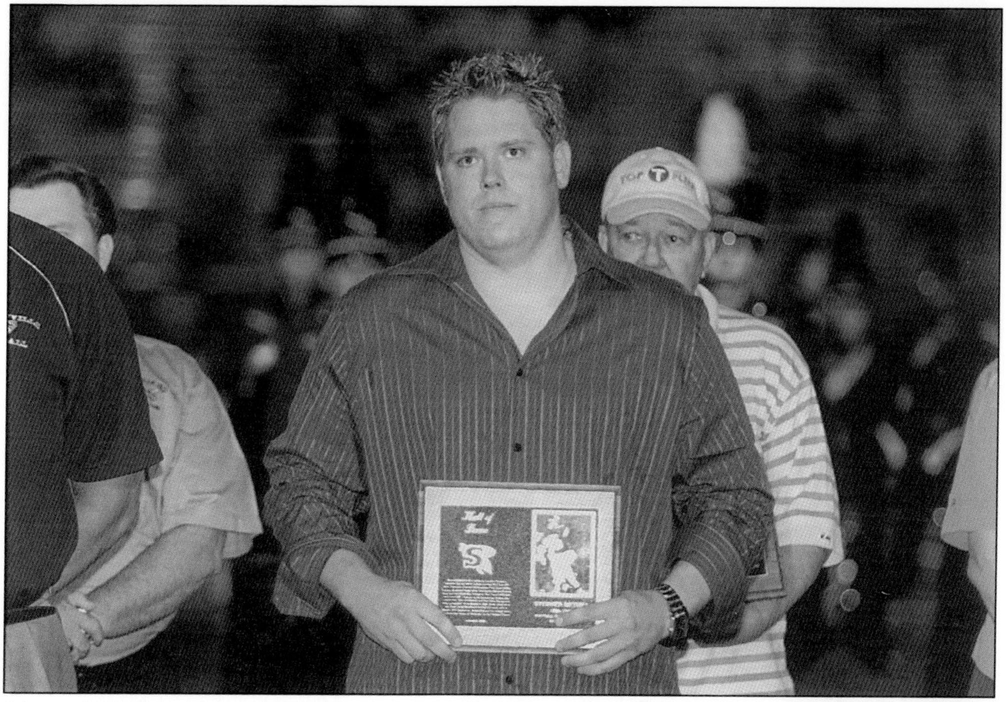

The early Briles years produced two outstanding future hall of famers—Stephen Bethea (above, at his hall of fame induction) and Kris Terrill (below left, holding the 1993 State Championship Trophy with teammate Branndon Stewart). At linebacker, Bethea received 1992 All-State honors as well as honorable mention all-American. Subsequently, Bethea was a three-year starting linebacker for Tarleton. Terrill's work as a Jacket offensive linemen earned all-state honors in 1992 and 1993. He later played football at West Point. (Both, Skipper.)

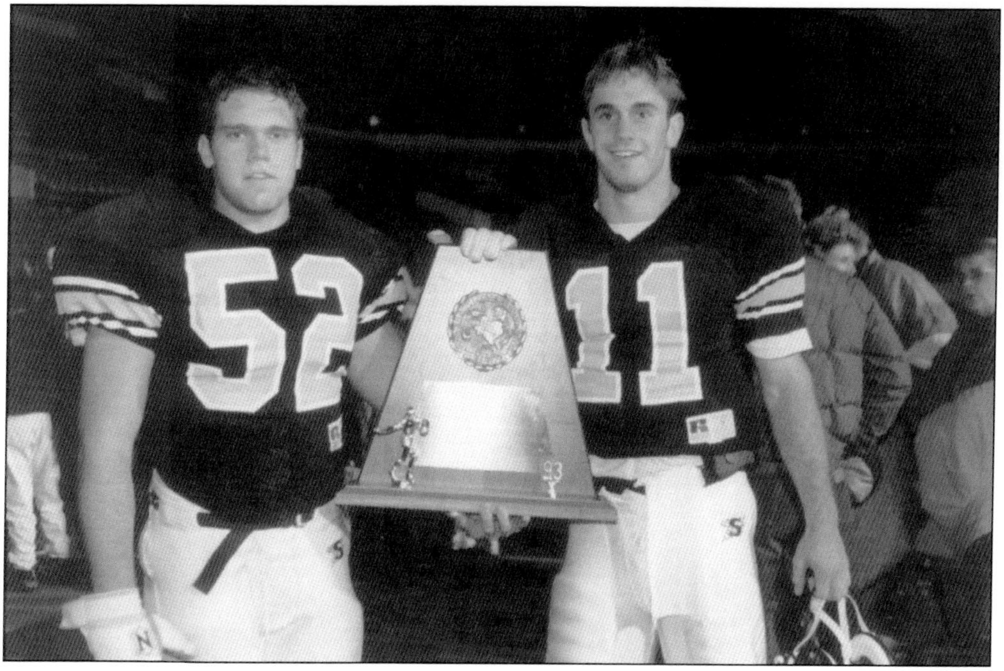

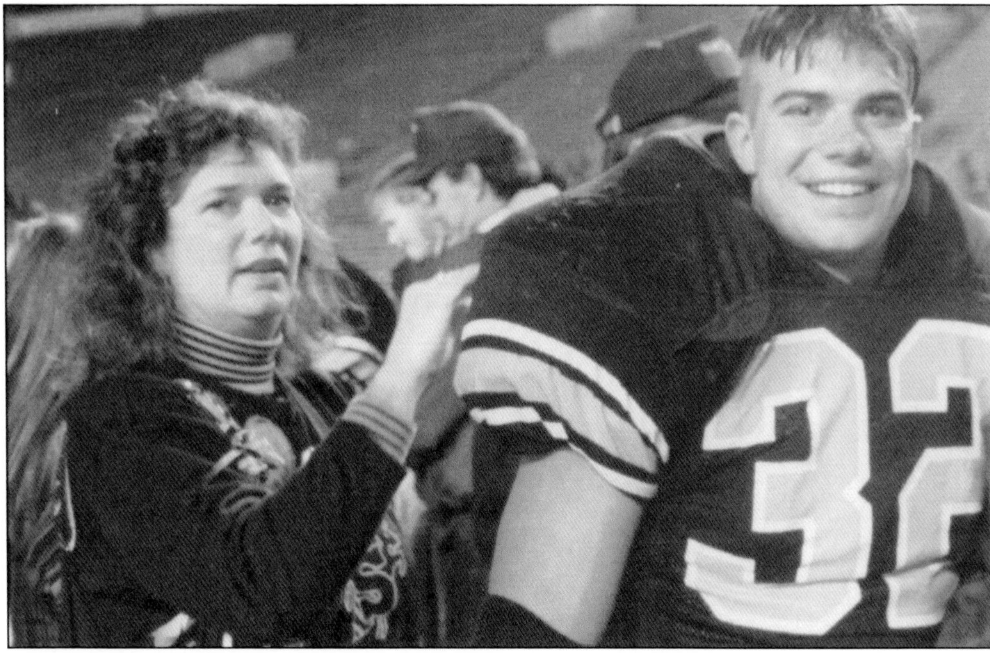

In the 1930s, fans called the defensive line the "Forward Wall." In 1998, inspired by all-state linebacker Jack Hodges, the Yellow Jacket defense collectively assumed a new name, War Dogs. Quoting Marcus Antonius in Shakespeare's *Julius Caesar*, Hodges admonished his fellow defenders to "Cry 'Havoc,' and let slip the dogs of war!" From that day forward, the name stuck. While many worthies have played at a high level on defense, one of the greatest was all-district and honorable mention all-state member of the 1993 championship team Shane Freels (above, with mother, Rita, in 1993). Freels's football career continued at Abilene Christian. Below, in the War Dogs tradition, a pack of 2008 defenders smothers Arlington Seguin runner Robert Owoyele. The players are, from left to right, Hayden Whitely, Nate Brady, Jared Slemmons, T.R. Varnado, Josh Emmons, and Dominick Jokel. (Above, Skipper; below, Huffman, *Stephenville Empire-Tribune*.)

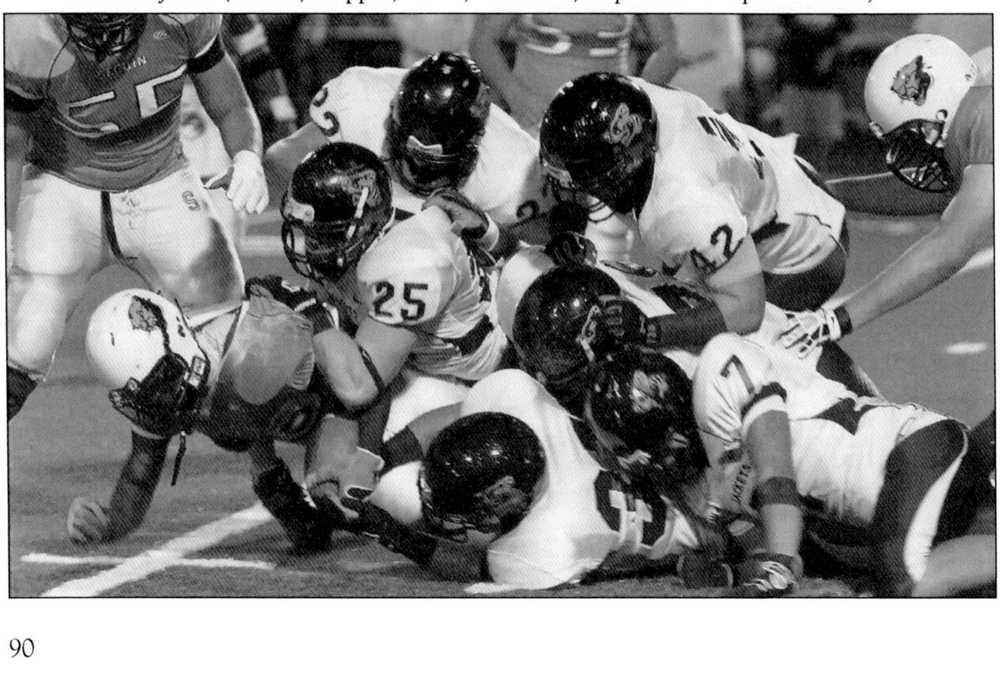

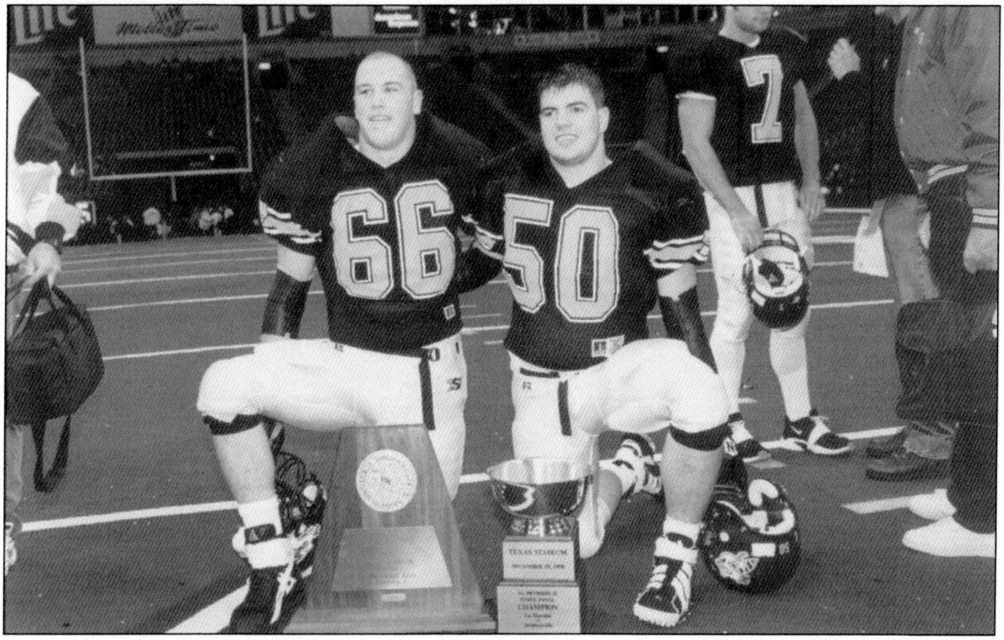

Another standout defensive lineman was three-year letterman Clayton Harmon, pictured above (left) with teammate Craig Parks and the 1998 State Trophy. After helping the Jackets win back-to-back state titles in 1998 and 1999, he continued his career at Texas Tech, where he earned Honorable Mention Big 12 and Texas Tech Freshman Player of the Year. Harmon also was state champion in the 4A 2001 shot put, with an SHS record of 62 feet, 0.75 inches. On the offensive line, few Jackets provided better protection than Shaylor Pryor. In the photograph below are, from left to right, coach Randy Clements; Shaylor's mother, Lisa Foster; and coach Briles. Pryor continued his football career at Iowa. (Both, Skipper.)

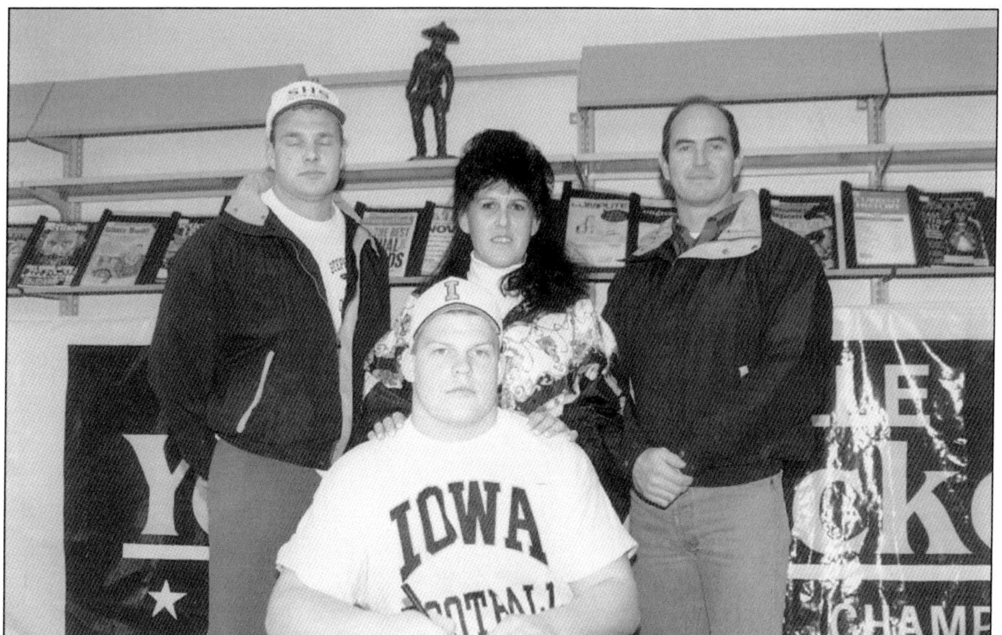

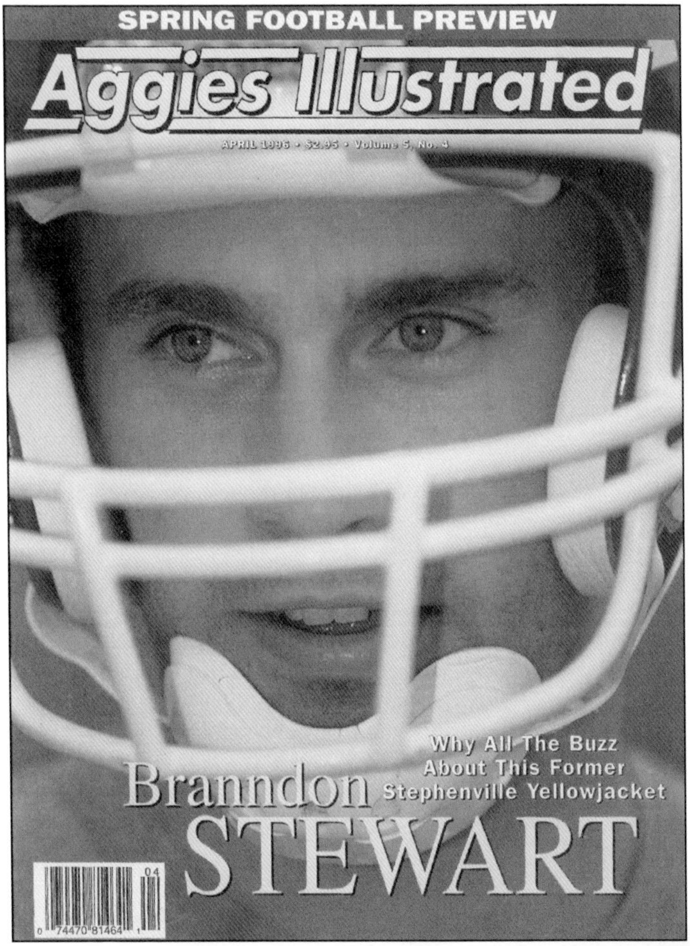

After graduation, Jacket quarterback Brannndon Stewart went to Tennessee, where he and Peyton Manning vied for the starting spot. Stewart later transferred to Texas A&M, where he led the Aggies to a double-overtime win against no. 2 Kansas State, the 1998 Big 12 title, and an invitation to the BCS Sugar Bowl. Left, Stewart graces the cover of the April 1996 *Aggies Illustrated*. Stewart's high school teammate Jason Bragg also played for A&M. Below, Bragg is flanked by his SHS English teachers Annette Pierce Sherrod (left) and Cristy Campbell-Furtick. They display Bragg's Big 12 Championship and Sugar Bowl rings. (Left, *Aggieland Illustrated*; below, author.)

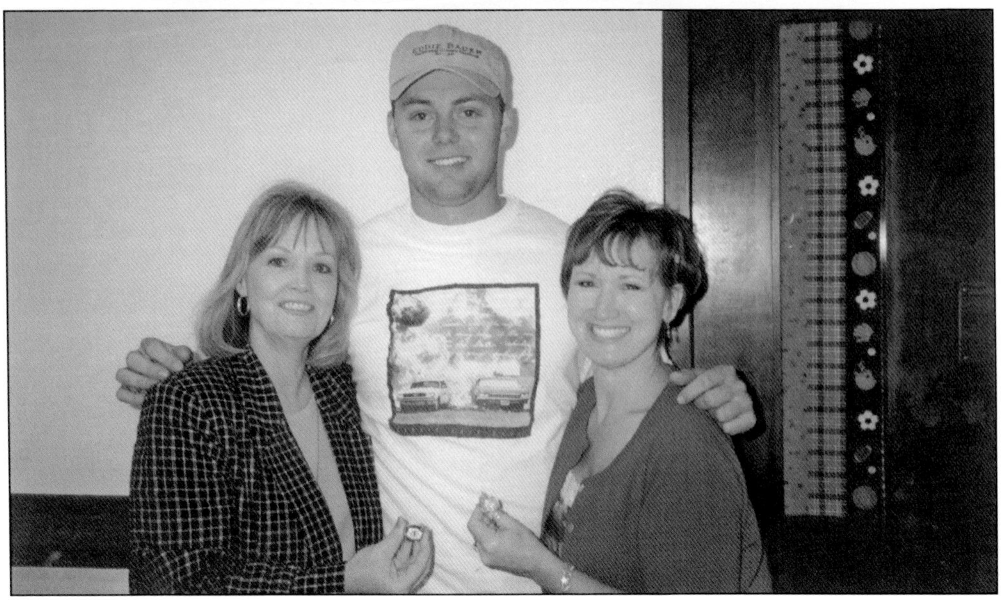

After high school, Cody Cardwell and Kelan Luker (right), the quarterback-receiver combination that gave opponents fits from 1996 through 1998, headed to Dallas. Both signed with SMU. Luker left SMU in 2002 to pursue a musical career with Submersed. In 2008, he left the band and returned to Stephenville where he played backup quarterback for Tarleton. As a Mustang, Cardwell was 2000 Western Athletic Conference Freshman of the year. In 2002, with 169 yards, he broke the immortal Doak Walker's single-game punt return record. Kendal Briles (below) also played college ball. After high school, this Texas Sports Writers Association's 1999 and 2000 4A Offensive Player of the Year played defensive back for the Texas Longhorns. After one season in Austin, he followed his father to University of Houston, where he played wide receiver and backup quarterback. (Right, *Stephenville Empire-Tribune*; below, Skipper.)

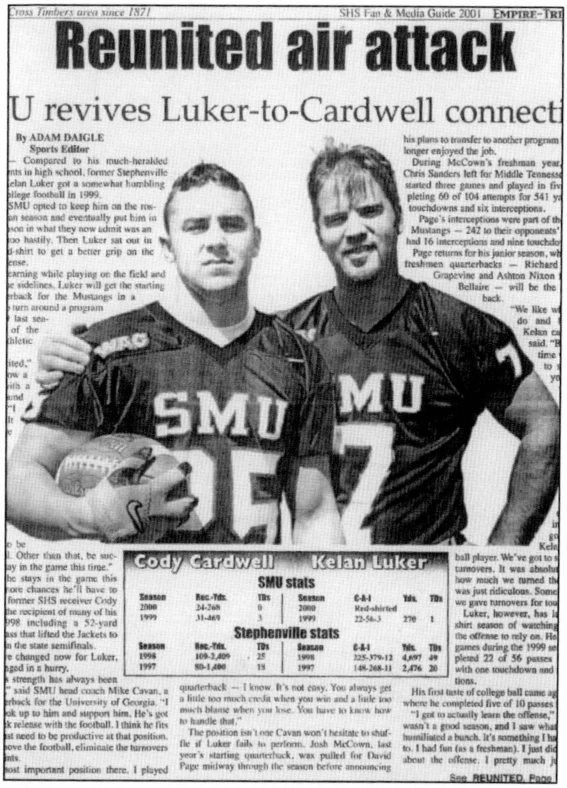

ross Timbers area since 1871 SHS Fan & Media Guide 2001 EMPIRE-TRI

Reunited air attack

U revives Luker-to-Cardwell connecti

By ADAM DAIGLE
Sports Editor

– Compared to his much-heralded
nts in high school, former Stephenville
elan Luker got a somewhat humbling
llege football in 1999.
SMU opted to keep him on the ros-
n season and eventually put him in
son in what they now admit was an
oo hastily. Then Luker sat out in
-shirt to get a better grip on the
ense.
earning while playing on the field and
e sidelines, Luker will get the starting
rback for the Mustangs in a
turn around a program
last sea-
of the
hletic

ited,"
ow a
ith a
und
"I

o be
l. Other than that, be suc-
ay in the game this time."
he stays in the game this
ore chances he'll have to
former SHS receiver Cody
he recipient of many of his
998 including a 52-yard
ss that lifted the Jackets to
n the state semifinals.
e changed now for Luker,
ged in a hurry.
s strength has always been
" said SMU head coach Mike Cavan, a
rback for the University of Georgia. "I
ok up to him and support him. He's got
k release with the football. I think he fits
st need to be productive at that position.
ove the football, eliminate the turnovers
nts.
ost important position there. I played quarterback — I know. It's not easy. You always get a little too much credit when you win and a little too much blame when you lose. You have to know how to handle that."

The position isn't one Cavan won't hesitate to shuffle if Luker fails to perform. Josh McCown, last year's starting quarterback, was pulled for David Page midway through the season before announcing his plans to transfer to another program
longer enjoyed the job.

During McCown's freshman year,
Chris Sanders left for Middle Tenness
started three games and played in fiv
pleting 60 of 104 attempts for 541 ya
touchdowns and six interceptions.

Page's interceptions were part of th
Mustangs — 242 to their opponents'
had 16 interceptions and nine touchdo

Page returns for his junior season, wh
freshmen quarterbacks — Richard
Grapevine and Ashton Nixon
Bellaire — will be the
back.

"We like w
do and
Kelan ca
said. "B
time
to
yo

Kela
ball player. We've got to s
turnovers. It was absolu
how much we turned th
was just ridiculous. Some
we gave turnovers for tou

Luker, however, has l
shirt season of watching
the offense to rely on. He
games during the 1999 se
pleted 22 of 56 passes
with one touchdown and
tions.

His first taste of college ball came ag
where he completed five of 10 passes

"I got to actually learn the offense,"
wasn't a good season, and I saw what
humiliated a bunch. It's something I ha
to. I had fun (as a freshman). I just did
about the offense. I pretty much ju

Cody Cardwell — Kelan Luker

SMU stats

Season	Rec.-Yds.	TDs	Season	C-A-I	Yds.	TDs
2000	24-268	0	2000	Red-shirted		
1999	31-469	3	1999	22-56-3	270	1

Stephenville stats

Season	Rec.-Yds.	TDs	Season	C-A-I	Yds.	TDs
1998	109-2,409	25	1998	225-379-12	4,697	49
1997	80-1,400	18	1997	148-268-11	2,476	20

See REUNITED, Page

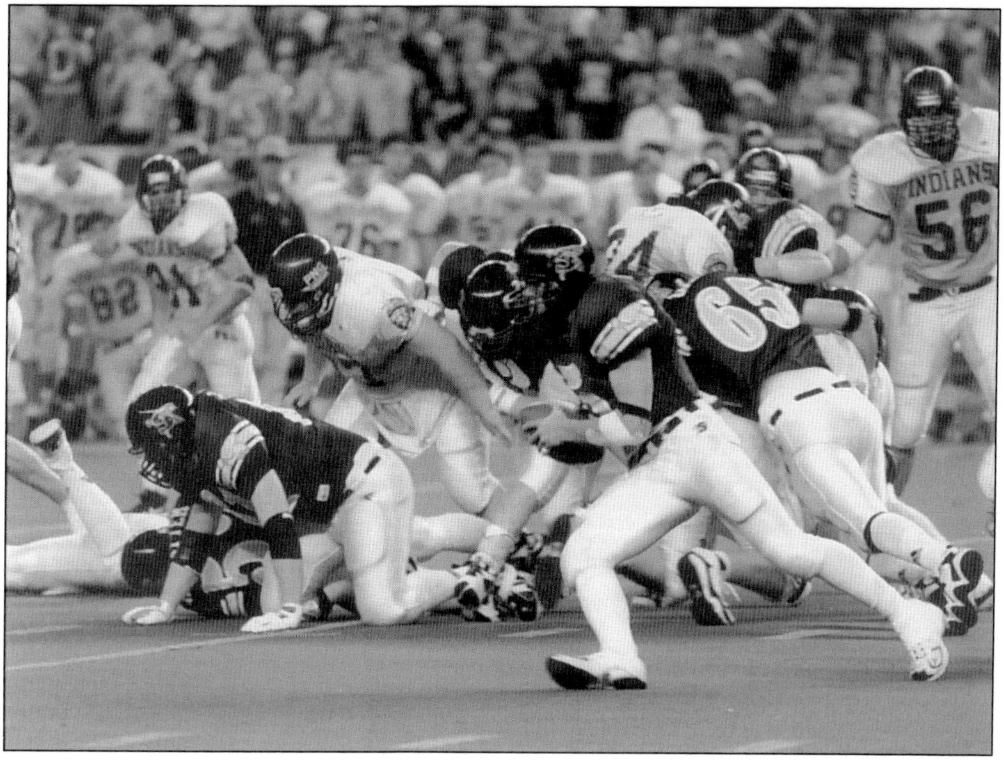

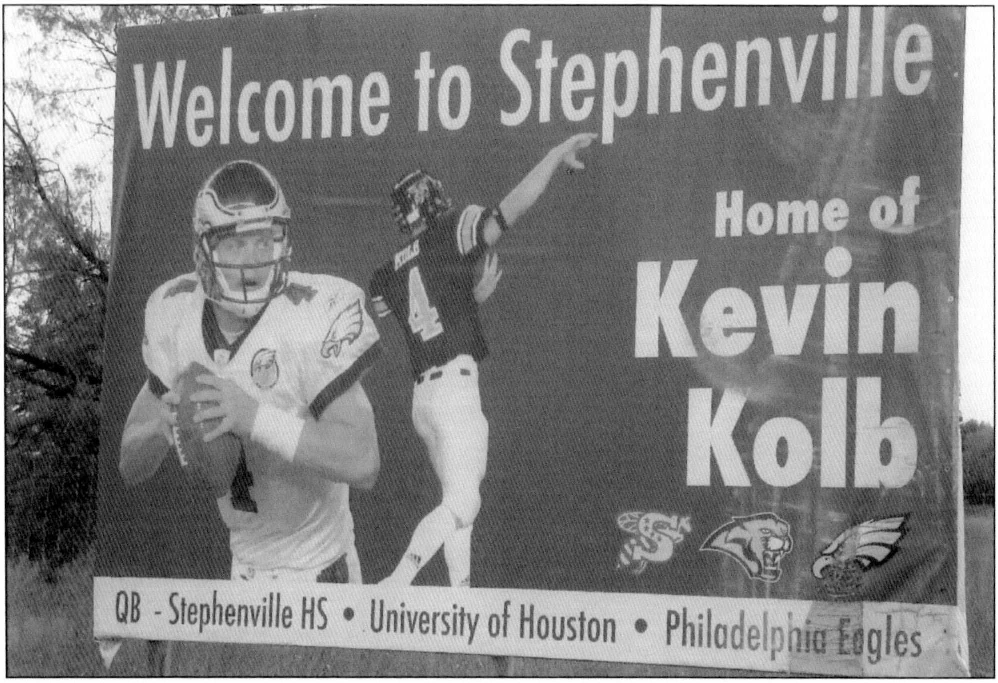

As a four-year starter for University of Houston, Kevin Kolb put his name in the record books. His 12,964 passing yards placed him fifth on the NCAA Division I all-time list. Kolb's 85 touchdowns ranked him 22nd. On Highway 377 leading into Stephenville, the sign above celebrates Kolb's present career with the Philadelphia Eagles. In the September 4, 2010, *Philadelphia Inquirer,* staff writer Jeff McLane understandably mused, "Imagine if Tony Romo were from the Philadelphia area and a similar billboard were erected in honor of the Cowboys quarterback on I-95." Jevan Snead (below) played a year at Texas before leaving the Big 12 and transferring to the SEC's Ole Miss. During Snead's tenure as starting quarterback, the Rebels won back-to-back Cotton Bowl victories (2008 and 2009). (Above, author; below, *Fort Worth Star-Telegram.*)

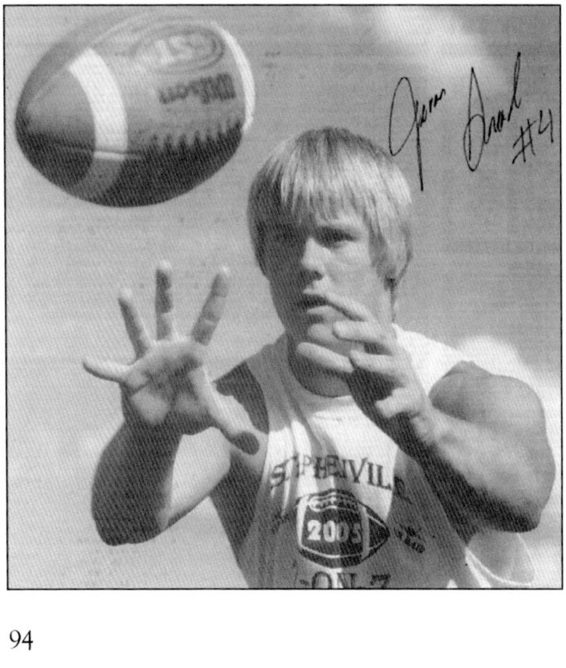

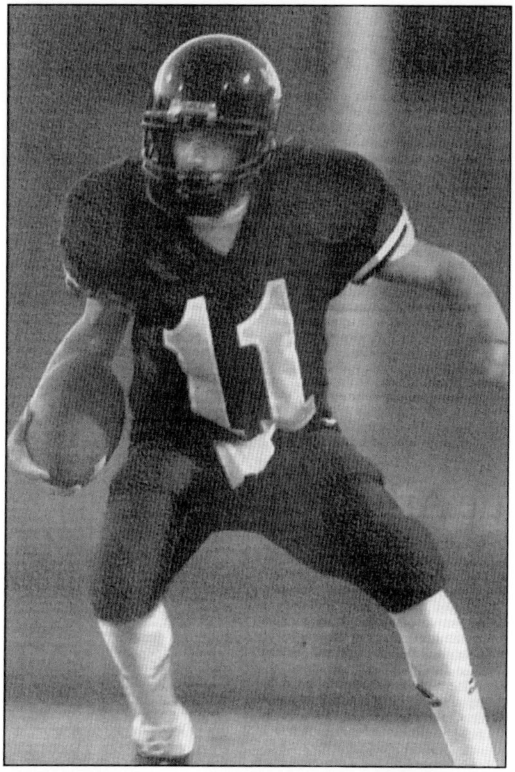

Right, Jacket quarterback and wide receiver Tie Lasater played at Tarleton in 2003 and later at Abilene Christian during the 2004 and 2005 seasons. Below, hall of famer Jeffrey Thompson (left) played cornerback and free safety for New Mexico State while teammate and fellow hall of famer Jody Bill Brown (right, blocking) continued his football career at Abilene Christian University. (Right, *Fort Worth Star-Telegram*; below, Wendy Jo Brown, *Stephenville Empire-Tribune*.)

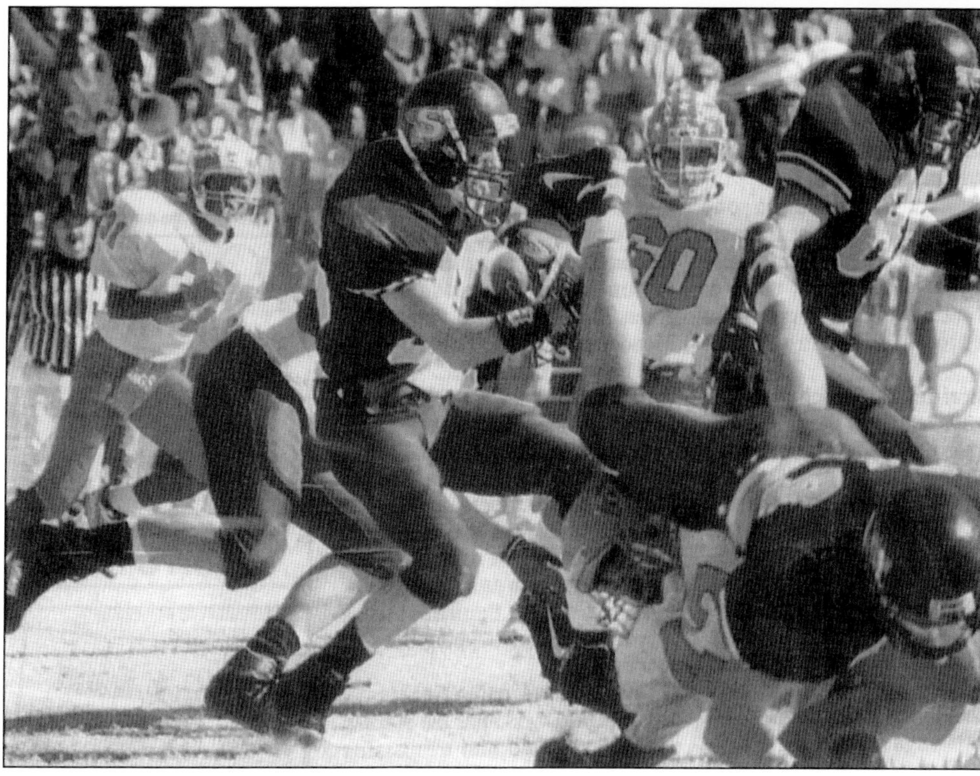

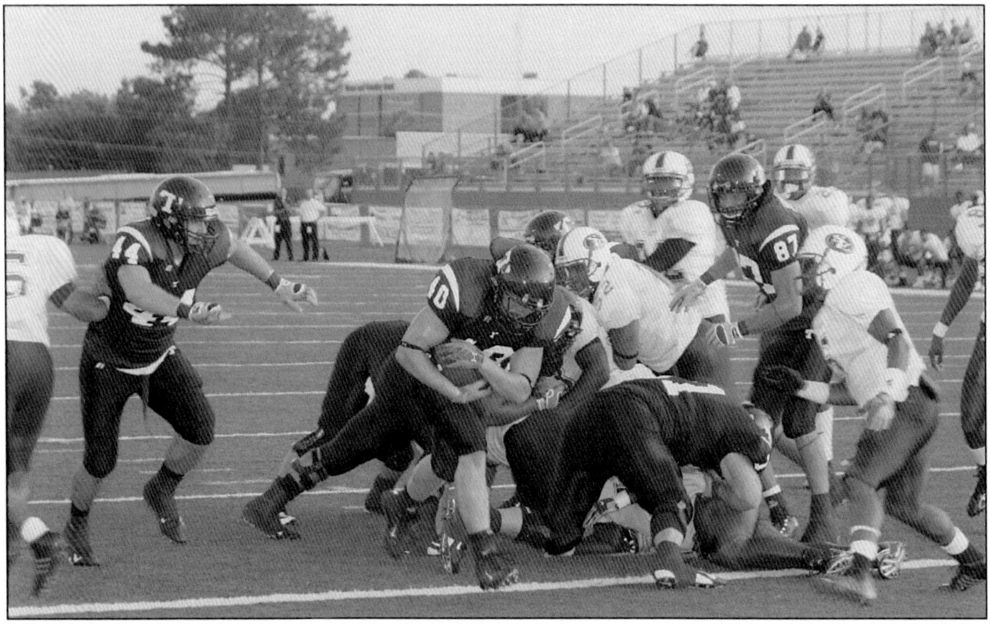

Among many former Jackets who played for Tarleton State, George Murray, seen above scoring a touchdown, became one of the most effective blocking backs in the Lone Star Conference. In 2008, Murray won the John Fielding Higgs Award for Most Valuable Player on the Tarleton football team. Three-time all-state defensive back Cody Davis played on the 2005 semifinal team. Today, he plays for Texas Tech, where he started as a redshirt freshman safety. He was a 2009 first team freshman all-American, Big 12 Honorable Mention Freshman of the Year, and second in total tackles for the Red Raiders in both 2009 and 2010 (with 81 and 87, respectively). Below, Davis appears in his Texas Tech jersey flanked by his mother, Cindy, and his father, David. (Above, Tarleton Athletics; below, Cindy Davis.)

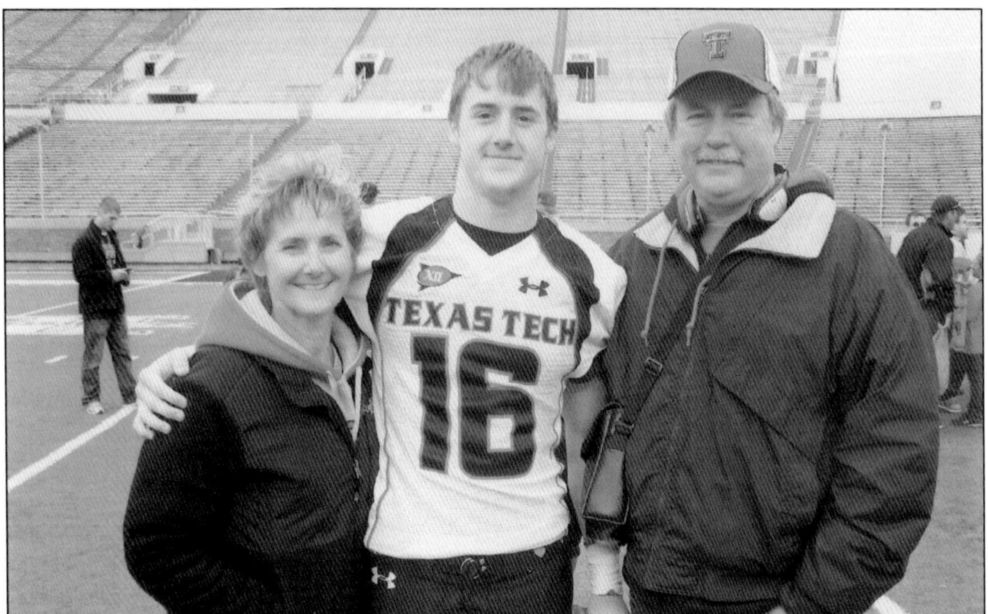

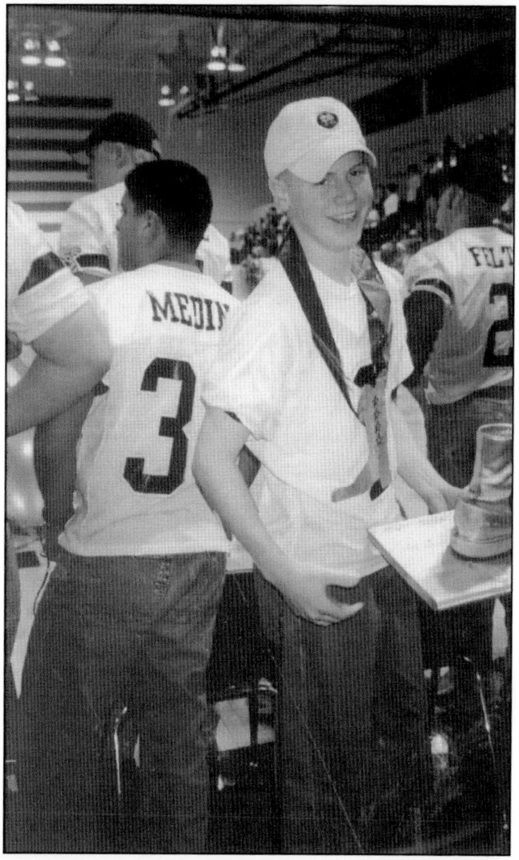

Right, Eben Nelson, whose end-of-the-game semifinal field goal against the Ennis Lions carried the Jackets to state in 1999, continued play at Abilene Christian. There, he handled kicking duties from his 2001 freshman year. In conjunction with the 2006 ACU Centennial Celebration, he was named a member of ACU's Team of the Century. The string of Jacket football players in college continues today. Below, Jacket offensive lineman Kody Travis signs a letter of intent to play with Tarleton State University in 2011. In this photograph, from left to right, are (seated) his father, Kerry, Kody, and his grandfather Melvin Travis; (standing) Joseph Gillespie, Kody's grandmother Sherri Travis, and O-line coach Curtis Lowery. (Right, author; below, Brad Keith, *Stephenville Empire-Tribune*.)

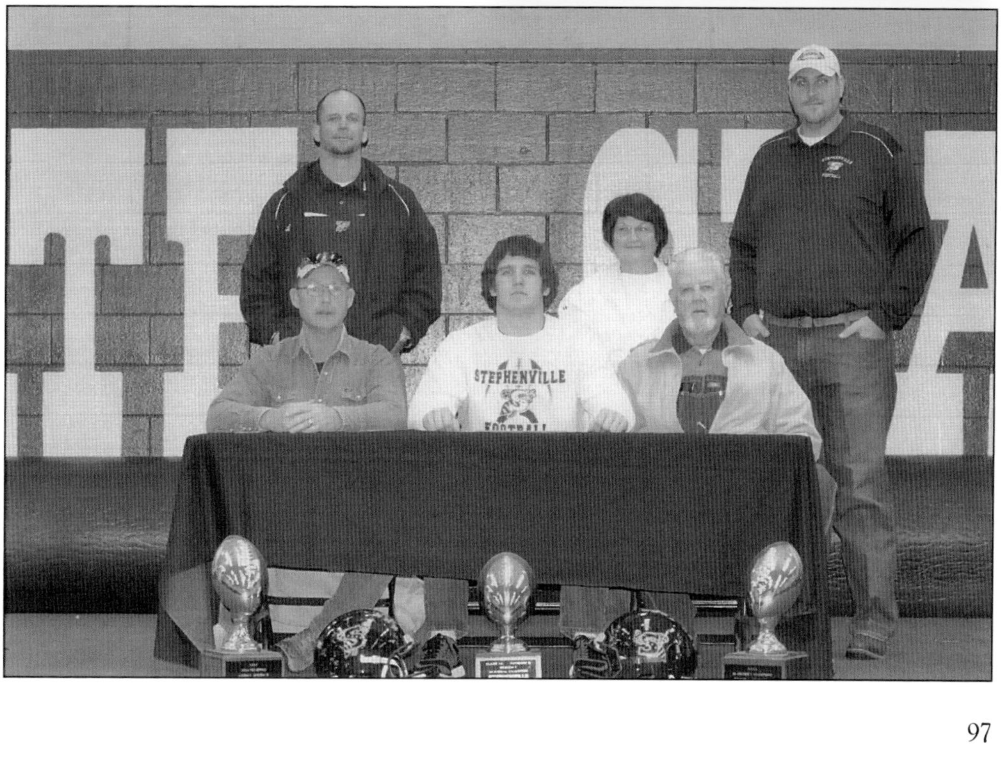

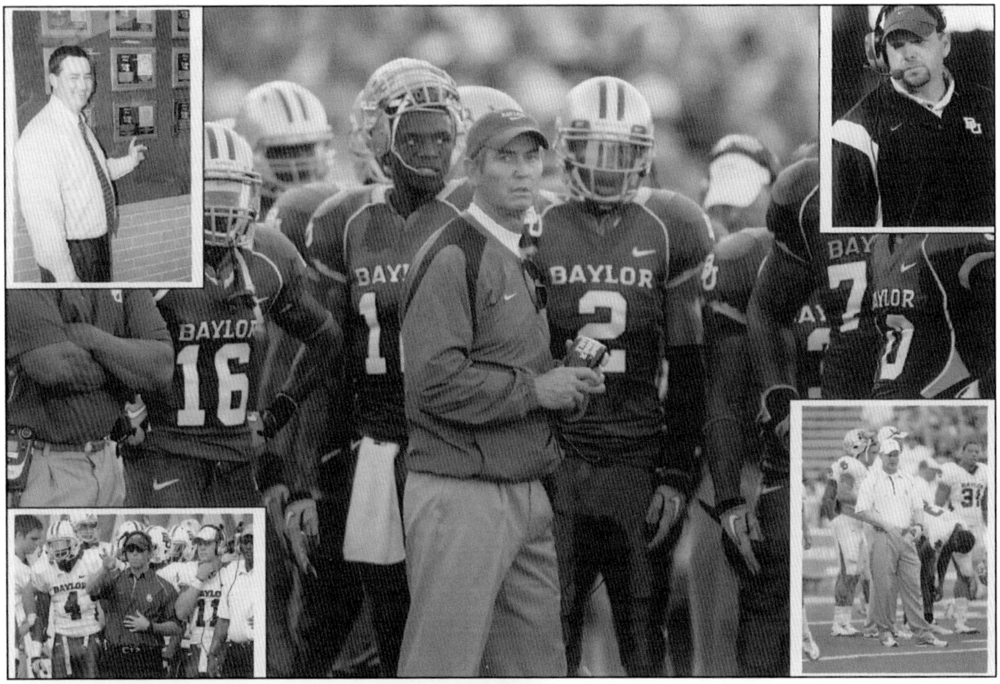

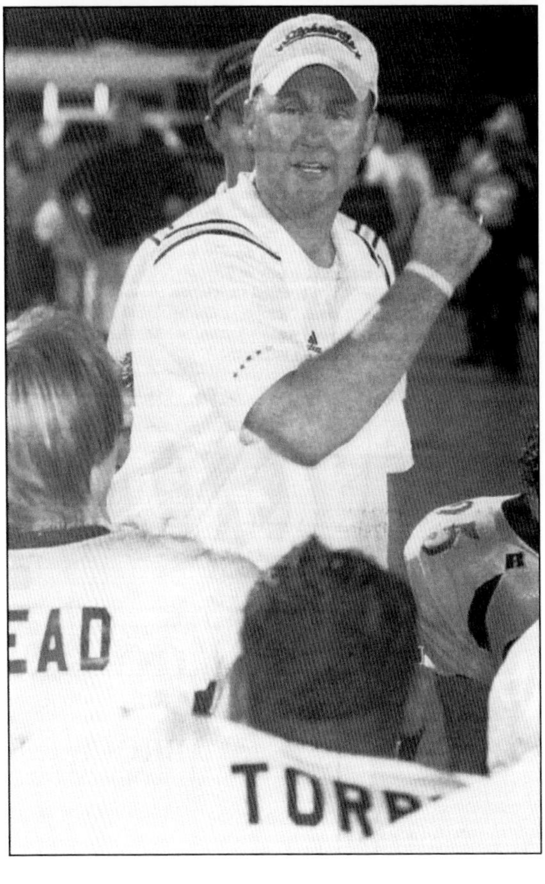

Art Briles left SHS for Texas Tech in 2000. As Houston head coach (2003–2007), he hired former SHS coaches Colin Shillinglaw, Randy Clements, and Philip Montgomery. He continues to surround himself with Stephenville exes, including, clockwise from upper left, Shillinglaw (director of football operations), Clements (co-offensive coordinator), Montgomery (co-offensive coordinator), and Kendal Briles (assistant coach). They led the Baylor Bears to the 2010 Texas Bowl. Left, Chad Morris (49-10) came to SHS in 2003. In 2008, he went to Lake Travis, winning back-to-back state titles. In 2010, as the Tulsa Hurricane's offensive coordinator, Morris contributed to victory over Notre Dame (28-27) and a 62-35 win over the Hawaii Warriors at the Hawaii Bowl; he directed the sixth-ranked Football Bowl Subdivision Offense in the nation. After 2010, Morris moved to Clemson University as offensive coordinator. (Above, Baylor Football and Thompson; left, Bud Jones, *Stephenville Empire-Tribune*.)

Six

Our 12th Man

J.C. Dykes came to Stephenville as 1921–1922 principal and football coach. The community celebrated his credentials from Texas A&M, some 180 miles southeast of Stephenville. At the end of that particular football season, a game played in College Station gave birth to one of the grandest Lone Star football traditions. During a January 2, 1922, contest between A&M and no. 1–ranked Centre College, E. King Gill left the press box, donned football gear, and stood ready on the sideline to play if limited Aggie reserves ran short.

Henceforth, the tradition of the 12th man—being ready to serve the team if called on to help—has inspired what the *Aggie Traditions* website calls a "spirit of readiness for service, desire to support, and enthusiasm" that makes College Station's Kyle Field one of the toughest home-field venues in America.

The Yellow Jackets have a 12th man of their own. That man's impact is felt both at home and away. It dates from the Briles years, when Stephenville fans began "shaking their cans." Specifically, can fans shake metal containers ranging in size from handheld vessels to multiple butane tanks welded together. Most are filled with ball bearings provided gratis (along with ear plugs) by Stephenville's FMC Technologies. The racket created rivals Gabriel's final trumpet. In recent years, opposing high schools have tried in vain to ban cans from their stadiums. Happily, this unique Stephenville tradition survives.

Meanwhile, the SHS 12th man includes a host of other loyal, devoted supporters, including team managers, athletic trainers and their student staff, KSTV Radio "Voice of Yellow Jacket Football" Boots Elliott, cheerleaders, the Bee mascot, members of the marching band, the award-winning SHS Stingerette dance team, and one of the most enthusiastic booster clubs in all of Texas. If they, like E. King Gill, never make a play on the gridiron, their contribution is no less a part of what makes Yellow Jacket football a cut above.

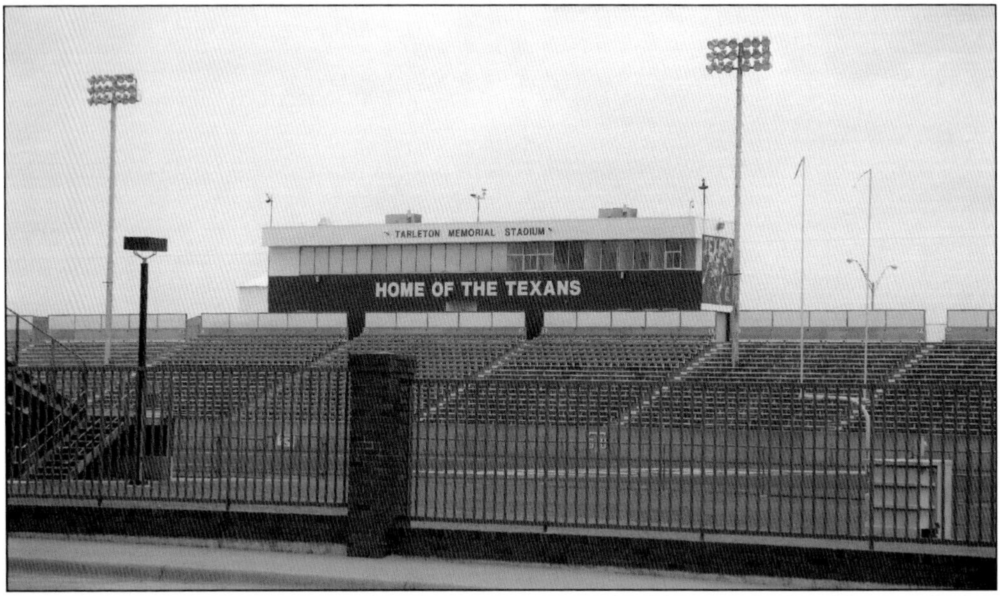

Stephenville's earliest games were played on an improvised field at popular local landmark City Park. Occasionally, the high school played on Tarleton's Hays Field (long since gone but then located southeast of Memorial Stadium on today's TSU campus). Hays Field was the site of the highly anticipated 1923 late-season matchup between two undefeateds, SHS and Abilene High (who went on to beat Waco 3-0 for the 1923 state title). Tarleton Memorial Stadium (above) is the venue for today's Jacket home games. Team managers play an important role in the locker room and on the sideline for any program. Below, guardians of the 1940 equipment were Eugene "Fakey" Ferguson (left) and Bud "Motto" Casstevens. Ferguson received recognition as all-district manager. (Above, Cashell.)

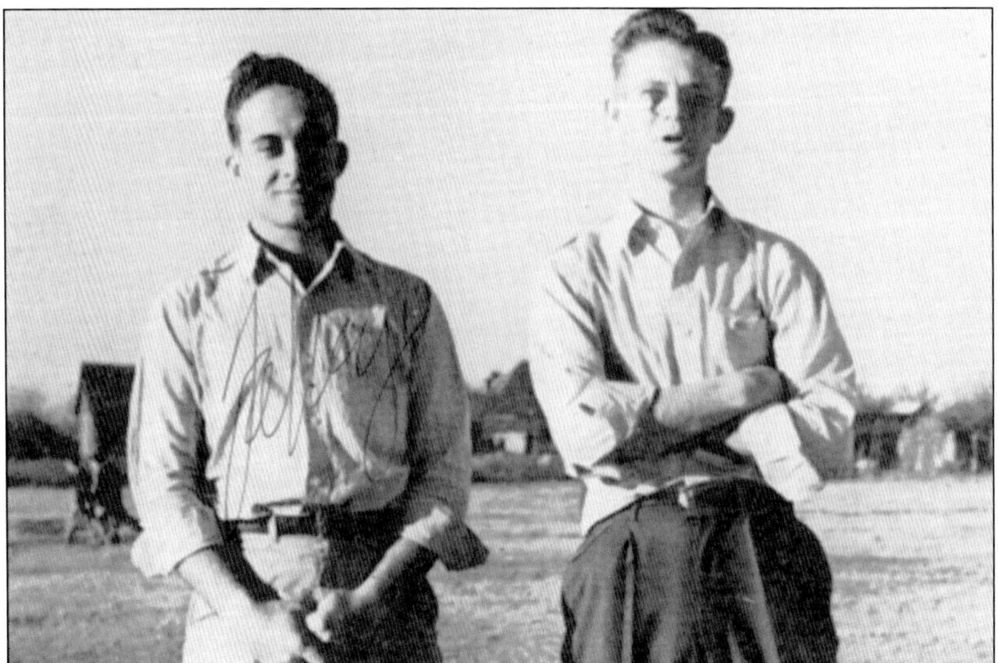

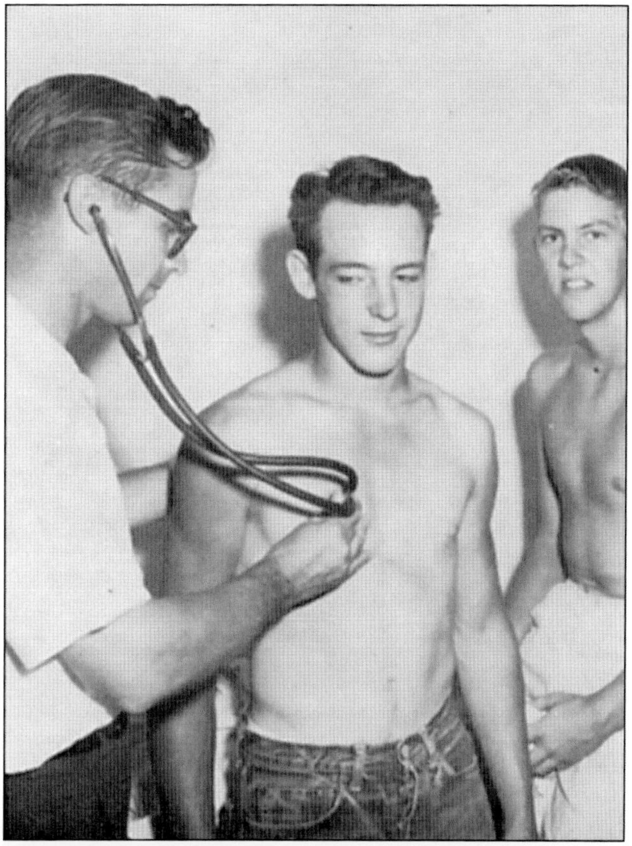

Local physicians have often helped keep players healthy. Right, Dr. Bruce Terrill gives physical exams to members of a 1950s team. More recently, head athletic trainer and assistant athletic director Mike Carroll and his corps of student trainers tend to the many needs of injured players, both in practice and during games. Below, Carroll (right) and Stephenville doctor William Evans escort an injured Alex Chavez off the field. (Below, Skipper.)

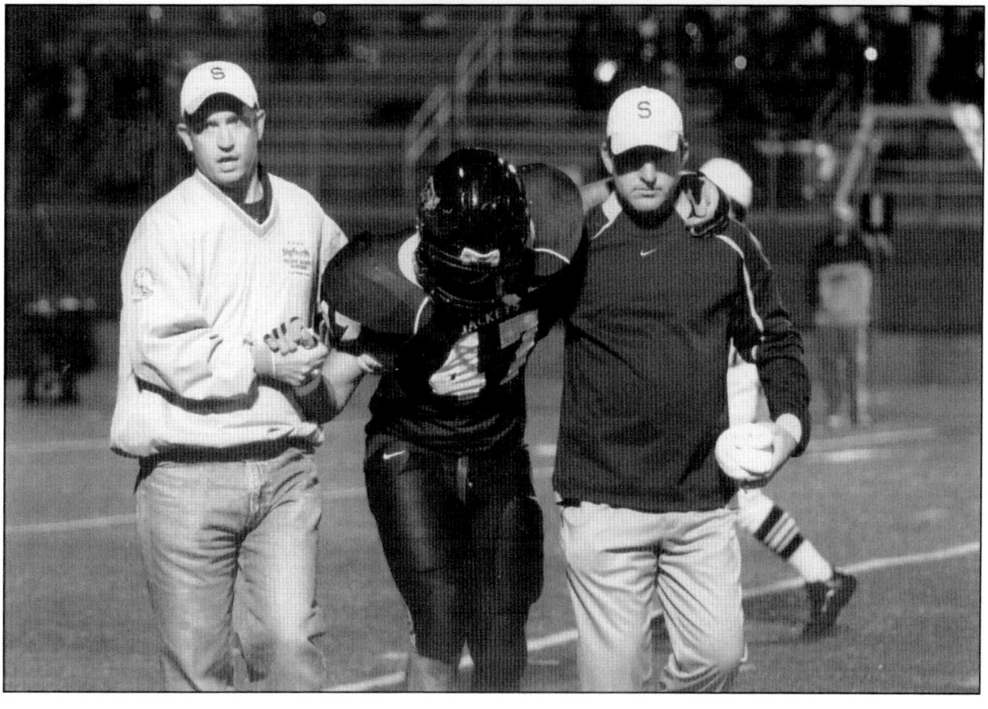

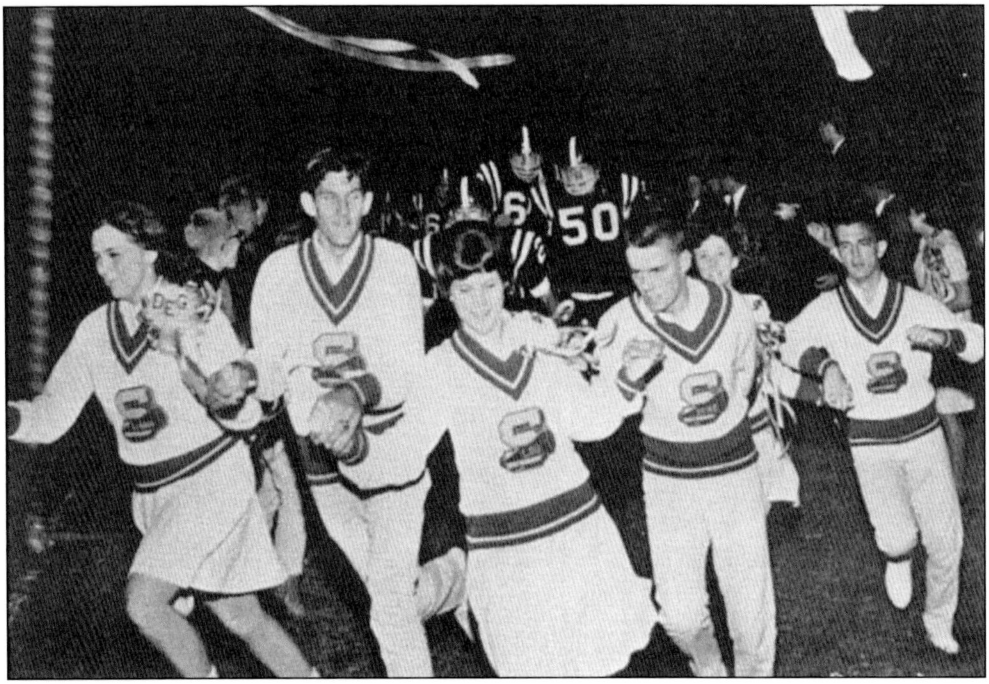

The yell leaders of yore, like the cheerleaders today, performed the critical role of keeping the crowd in the game. Above, from left to right, cheerleaders Di-Ann Gunn, David Self, Lou Greenway, Mike Starnes, Sissie Williams, and Tony Price lead the 1965 team onto the field. Also important is the Yellow Jacket Band playing the fight song, alma mater, and a legion of other tunes that celebrate scores and keep fighting spirit high. Organized in 1936, the band does more than provide musical support during the game. From then to the present day, crowds have reveled in halftime entertainment provided by the marching band. Below, the 1940 Jacket band, led by the drum major and five majorettes, displays its skill moving up and down the field.

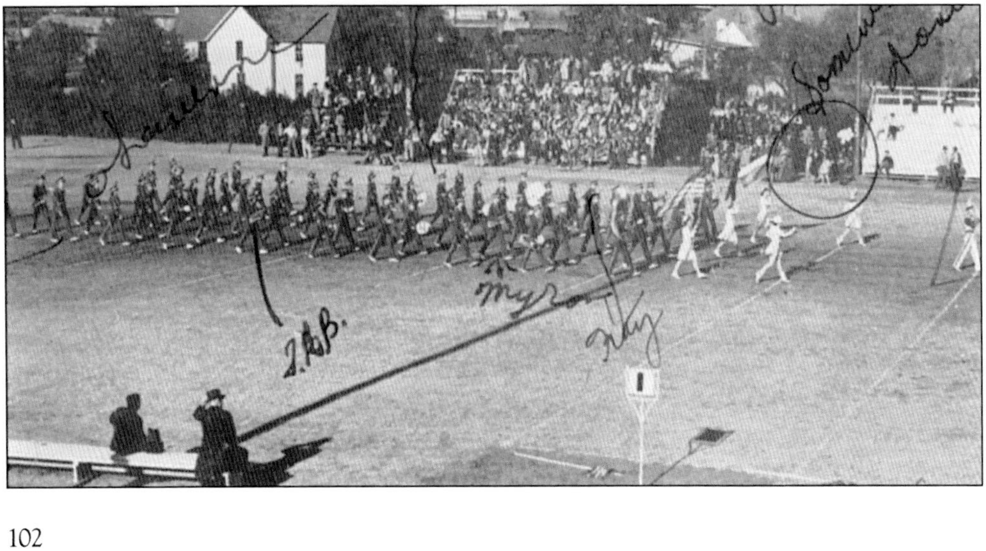

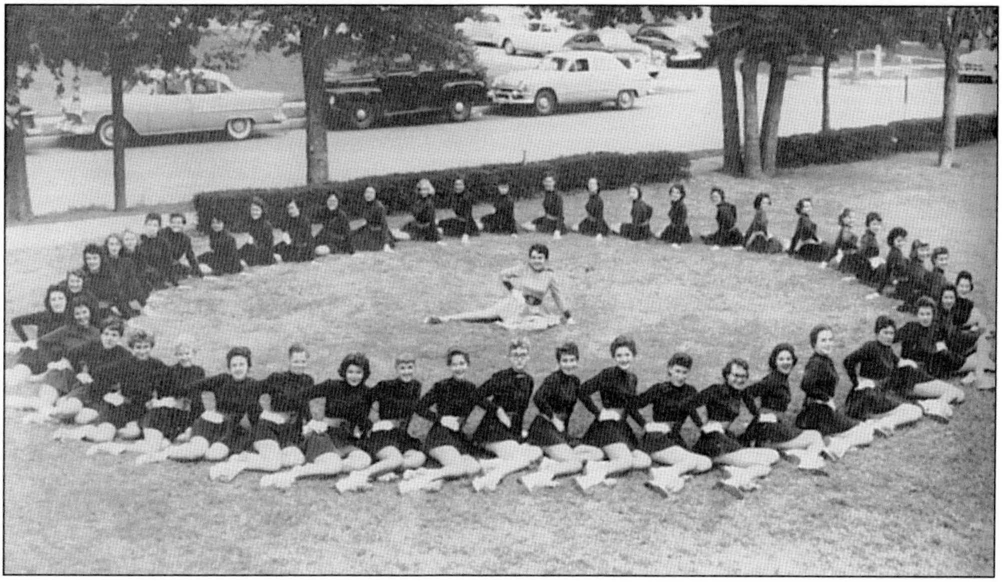

The Stingerettes, an award-winning precision performance dance team created in 1953, add a special dimension to Friday morning pep rallies and halftime entertainment. Above, the 1956 "Stings" pose for a picture on the high school grounds. In the 1930s, pep meetings generally convened the night before the game. An October 24, 1930, *Empire* report indicates that a crowd of 75 to 80 participated. Below, the author (left) and his father, Marshall Sherrod, who played in the first Stephenville-Brownwood contest in 1937, encourage the student body and players to whip the Lions in that night's rivalry matchup. (Below, Cashell.)

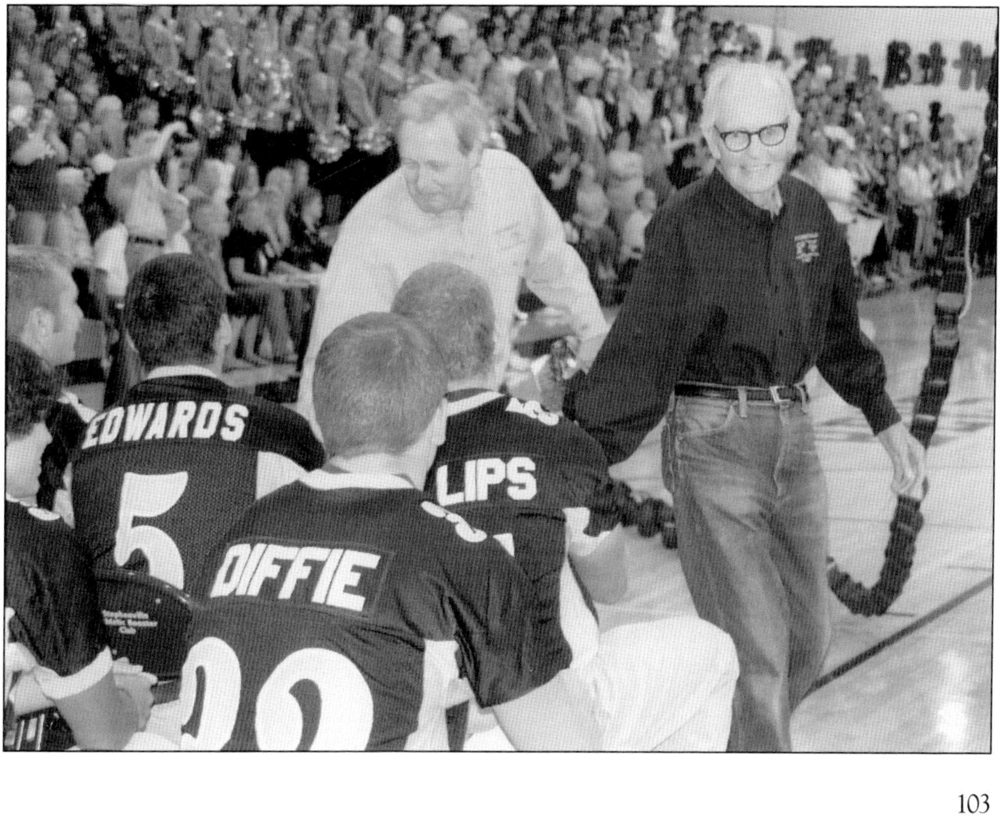

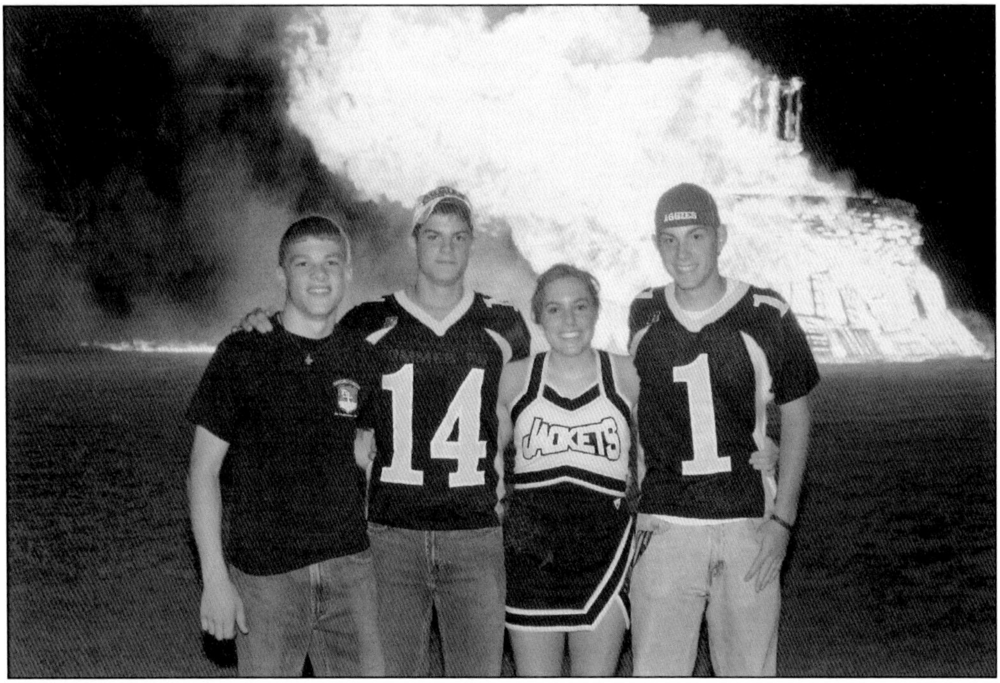

In recent years, Thursday nights preceding Brownwood games have been occasioned by a heavily attended bonfire in City Park. Above, the Thompson quadruplets—Daniel, Patrick (second team all-district kicker), Kayla (cheerleader), and Reagan—who graduated from Texas A&M in 2010, pose in front of 2005's fiery conflagration. The bonfire tradition long predates the Stephenville-Brownwood rivalry. Below, a 1941 pregame bonfire precedes the contest with nearby Ranger. (Above, Cashell.)

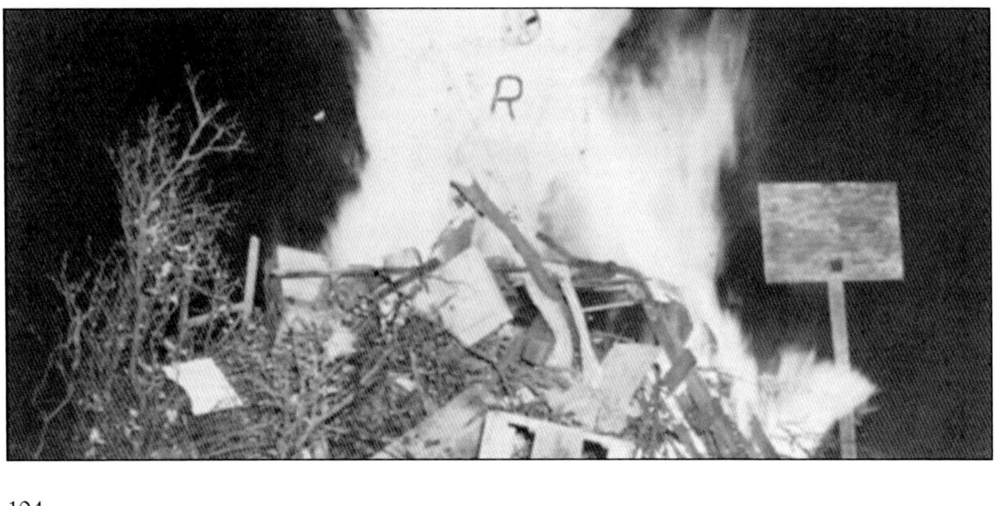

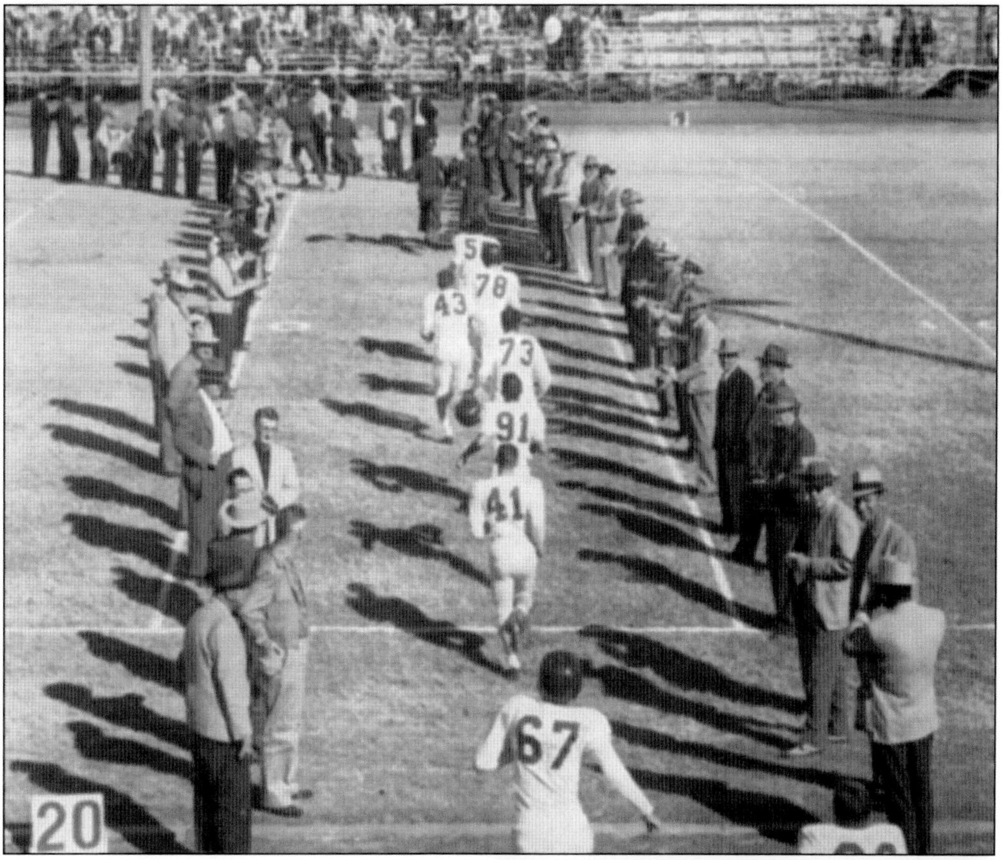

Above, the 1956 Booster Club and other fans form a human tunnel guiding the team onto the field. Boosters played a central role from the start. In early September 1923, to prepare for the Yellow Jackets opening game coincident with the Erath County Fair, principal and coach J.C. Dykes, aided by Tarleton football star "Tattie" Tate, took 35 prospective team members to Moore's Tank, three miles south of Comanche County's Proctor. There, the September 7, 1923, *Empire* documents, they participated in a 10-day pre-school training session (a standard practice in the 1920s). The September 5 *Empire* reports that in one of the earliest examples of boosterism, Stephenville businessmen financed the entire enterprise. As the 12th man tradition evolved, cheerleaders devoted untold hours creating decorated stand-up signs through which the players ran as they took the field. A 1956 version of the practice is pictured right.

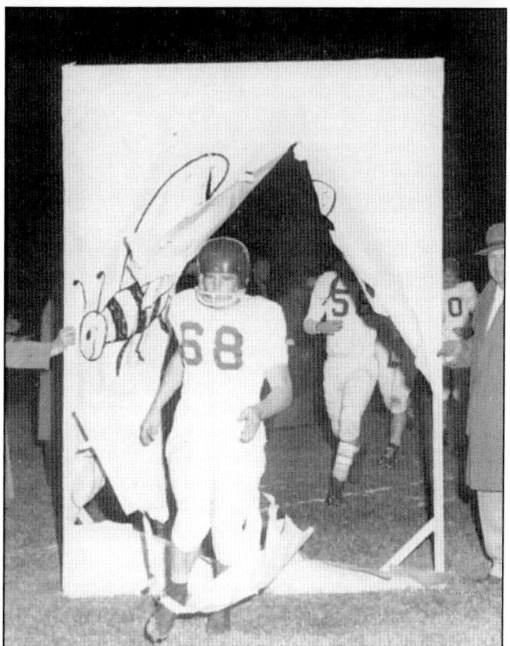

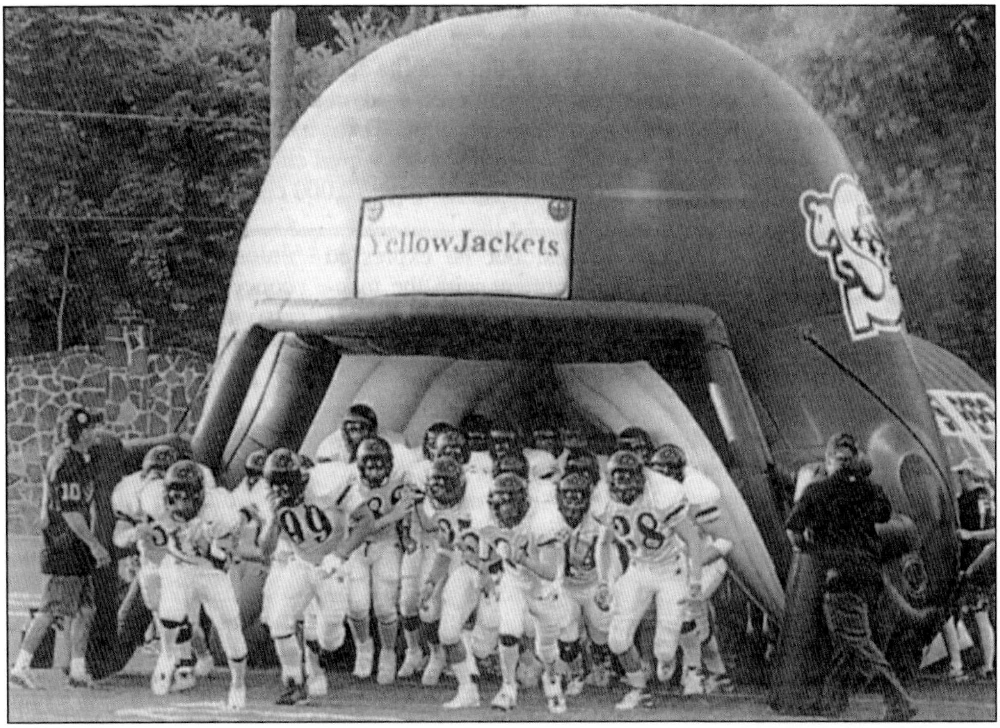

By the Briles era, more than the signs became significantly more sophisticated. Above, prior to taking the field, players raucously convened in the enormous inflatable Yellow Jacket helmet. As smoke produced by dry ice envelops the helmet, players and coaches run pell-mell out of the helmet and through supportive banners—different ones each week—that dwarf the 1950s models. Below, after running down a corridor composed of Stingerettes, the modern Jackets burst through a banner in Floyd Casey Stadium at the 2010 quarterfinal contest against Aledo. (Above, Jones, *Stephenville Empire-Tribune*; below, Skipper.)

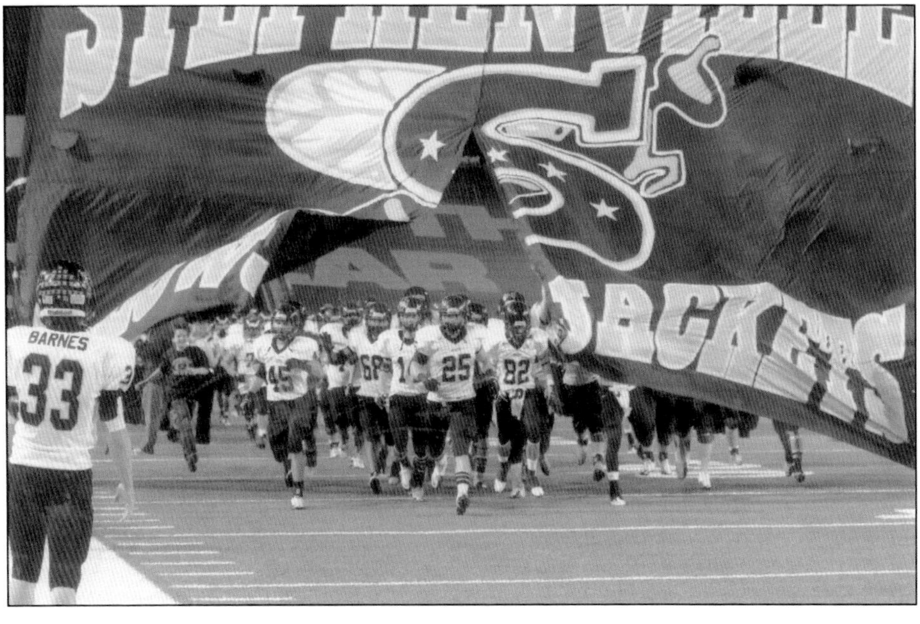

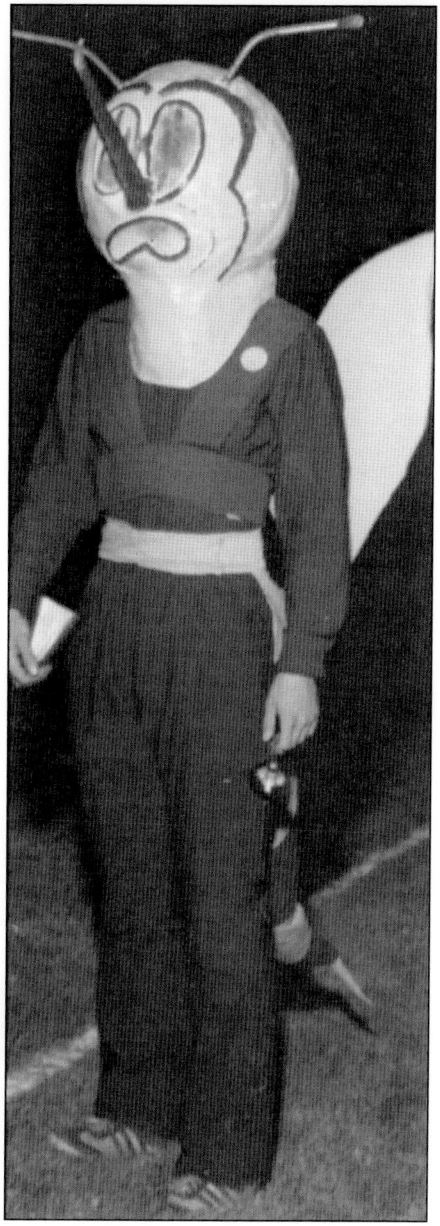

According to the 1921 yearbook, the SHS mascot was Wayne "Chicken" McCluskey, "who did much to keep the spirit in the boys through the season." Over time, a costumed Bee replaced Chicken as mascot and by 1977 took the form pictured at right. Below, a new and improved 2005 Bee strolls the bleachers, entertaining children and encouraging fan support.

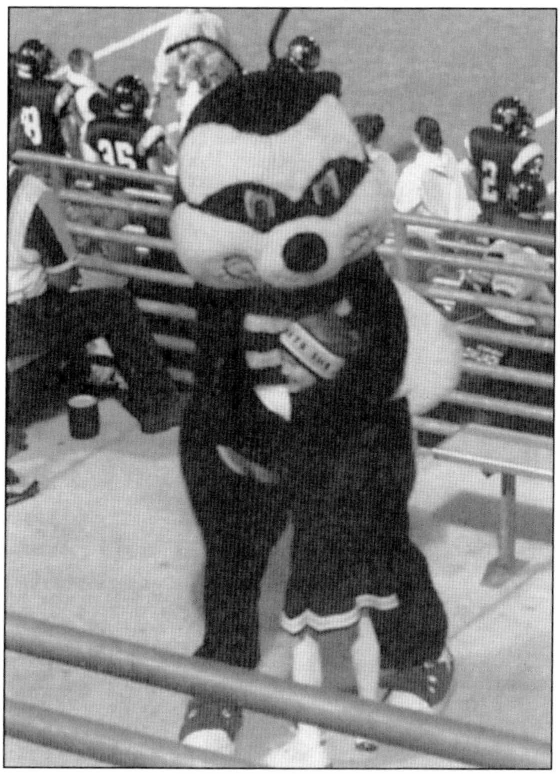

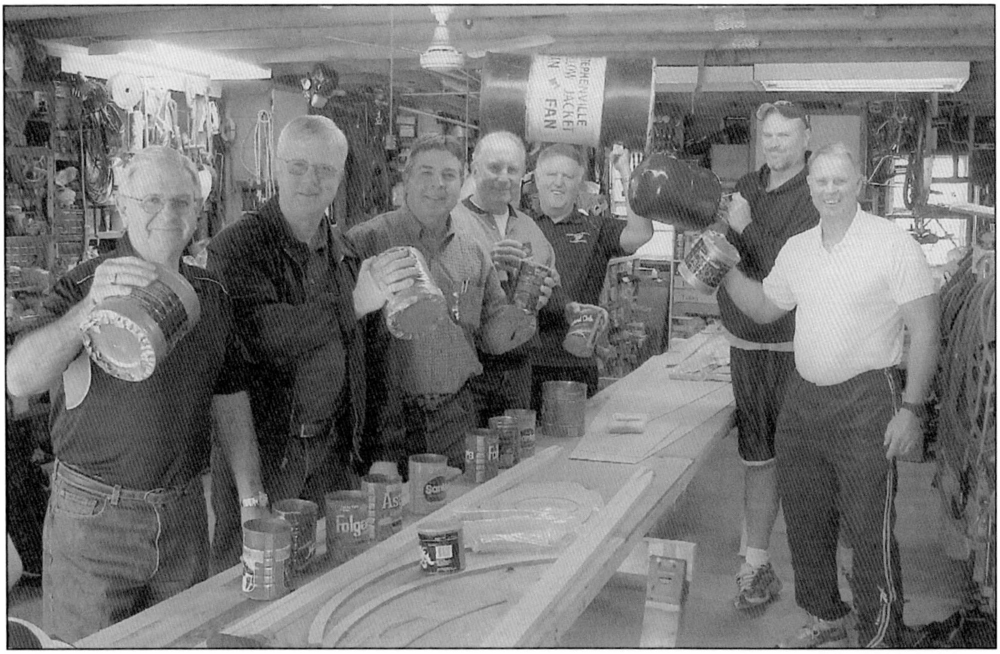

"I have spectators—I need fans," said Art Briles in 1988 to Stephenville TSU professor Steve Steed. The lightbulb moment came when Steed's preteen son, T.J., began vigorously shaking a partially filled Planters Mixed Nuts can, yelling "Beat Brownwood!" Thus, a mighty movement began in Steed's garage, where the earliest cans were "mass produced" (above). Included in this 2010 image of some who gave birth to the can fan are, from left to right, Larry Branch, Steve Peacock, Monty Bedwell, John Moore, Daniel Devivo, T.J. Steed, and Steve Steed. Until FMC Technologies began regularly donating ball bearings, almost every imaginable metal item was used to fill the cans, including nails, nuts, washers, and bolts. If can fans initially met vigorous resistance, they were infinitely creative in getting cans into stadiums. Below, they shake them at a Memorial Stadium home game. (Above, author; below, Cashell.)

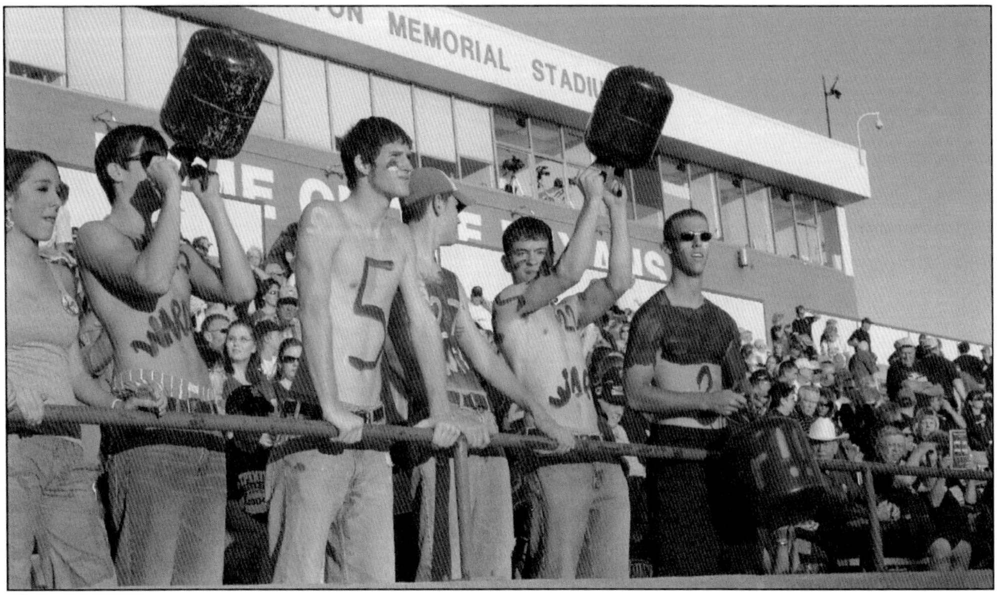

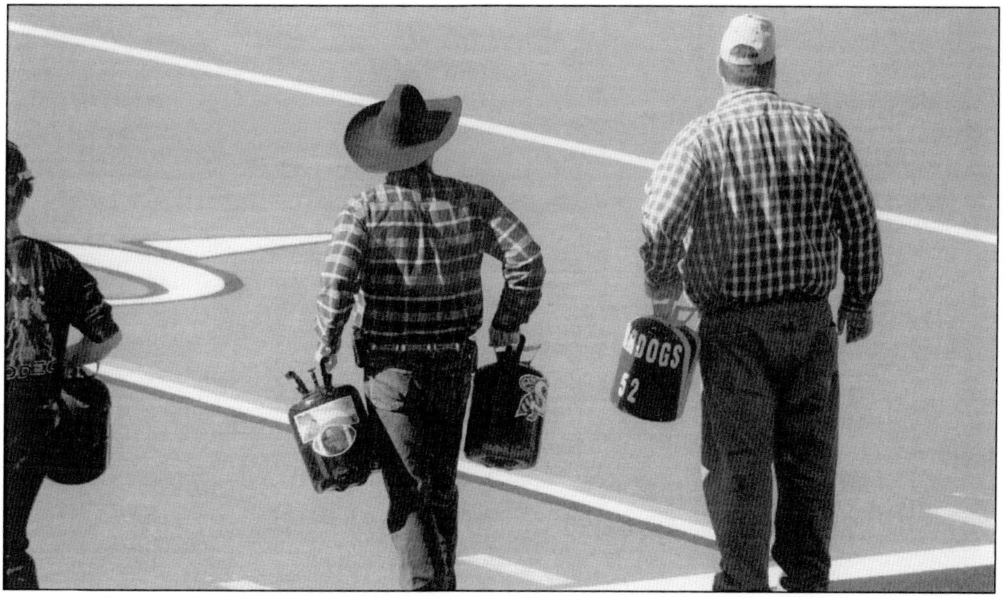

In time, the can fans prevailed both at home and away, establishing a tradition known today throughout Texas. At the 1998 state 4A D-2 final, one Fox Sports Southwest analyst estimated 10,000 cans of various shapes and sizes populated Texas Stadium. Typically, Booster Club members and football dads shake their cans on the sideline during the pregame warm-up. Above, from left to right, Jaylon Snead (the quarterback's father) and Dennis Hughes (all-district defensive end, Dustin Hughes's dad) follow this tradition prior to the Jacket quarterfinal double-overtime win over Plainview at Texas Tech's Jones AT&T Stadium on November 26, 2005. Below, the following week, in the 2005 semifinal at Denton's University of North Texas Fouts Field, can fans liberally season stadium seating. In the end, Coach Briles got not only fans but also perhaps the most special tradition in Texas high school football. (Above, Debbie Cashell; below, Emily Hoke.)

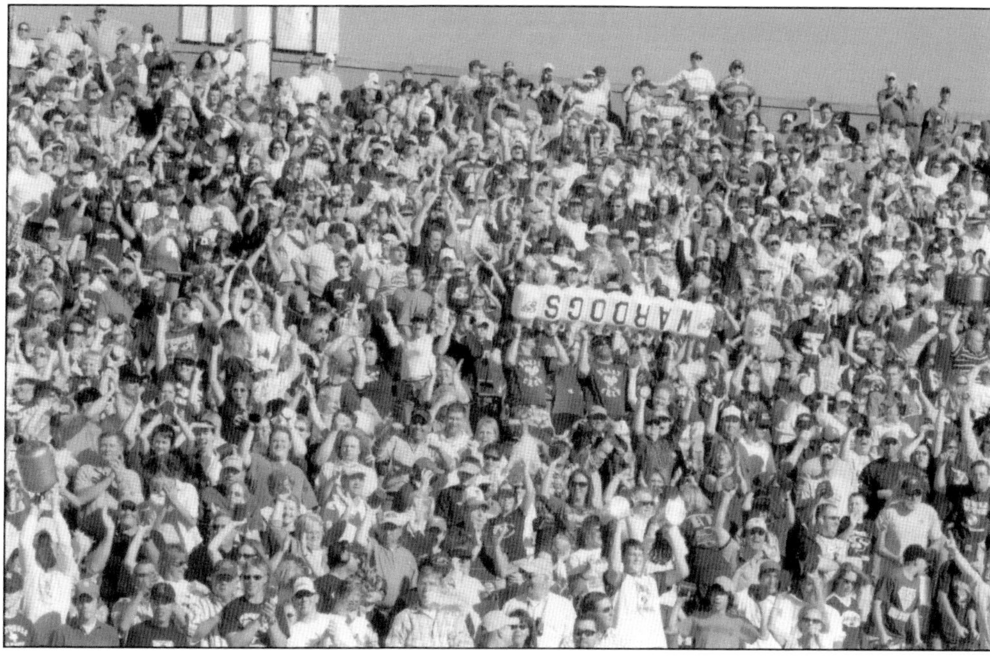

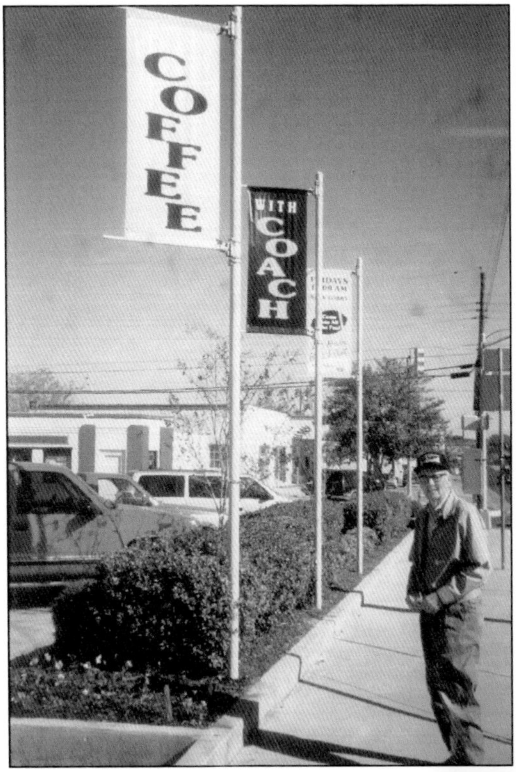

The Briles era brought another popular innovation—a weekly 30-minute Friday morning radio interview called *Coffee with Coach*. Radio's Voice of the Yellow Jackets, 93.1 KSTV's Boots Elliott continues the tradition every football season. Left, elevated banners alongside Bank of America advertise the program in 1998. Below, Elliott models his new double back-to-back state championship cap after the Jackets won their fourth state title. (Left, author; below Stephany Elliott.)

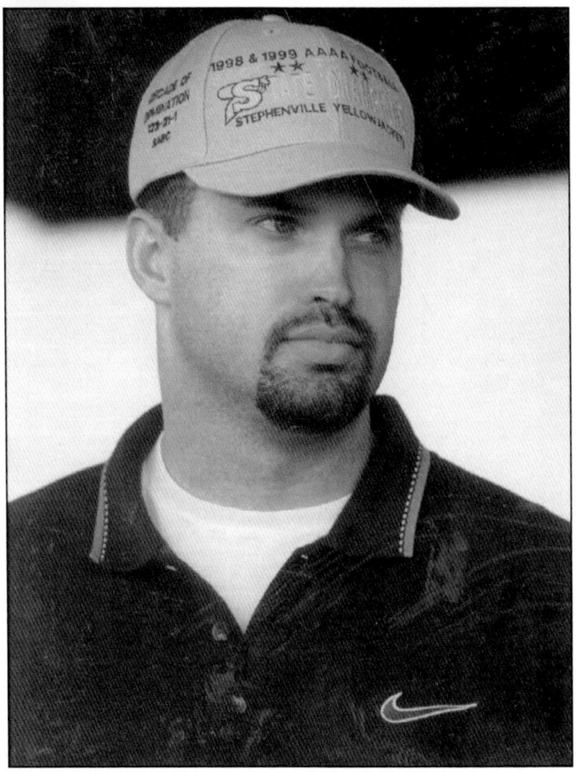

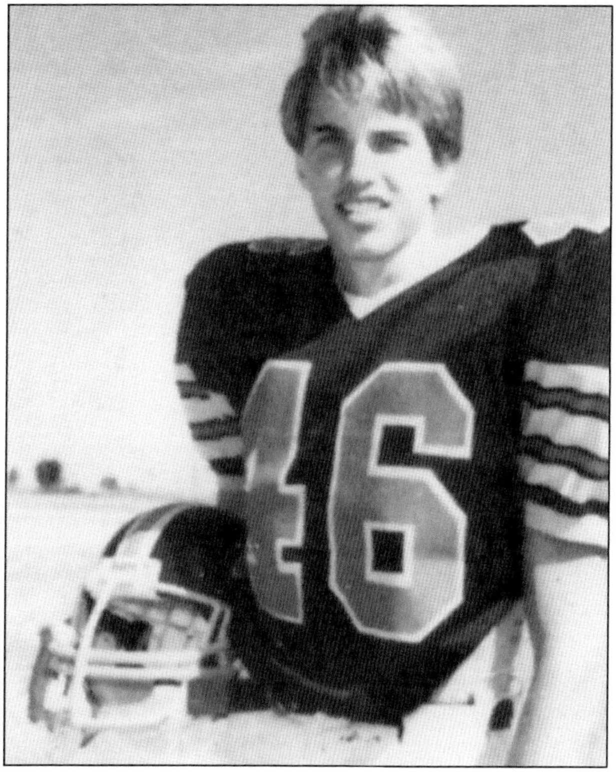

Elliott comes to the radio program with considerable personal experience. He was a first team All–Cross Timbers Jacket tight end on the 1984 and 1985 teams (right). As it was for so many others, Elliott's schoolboy football career was part of a larger family tradition. His father, Robert Elliott (below), was a three-year letterman at end on the Jacket team from 1959 through 1961.

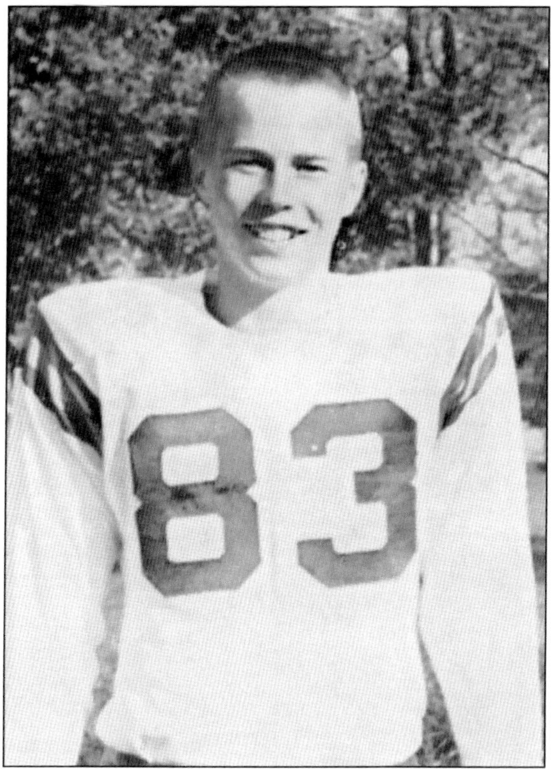

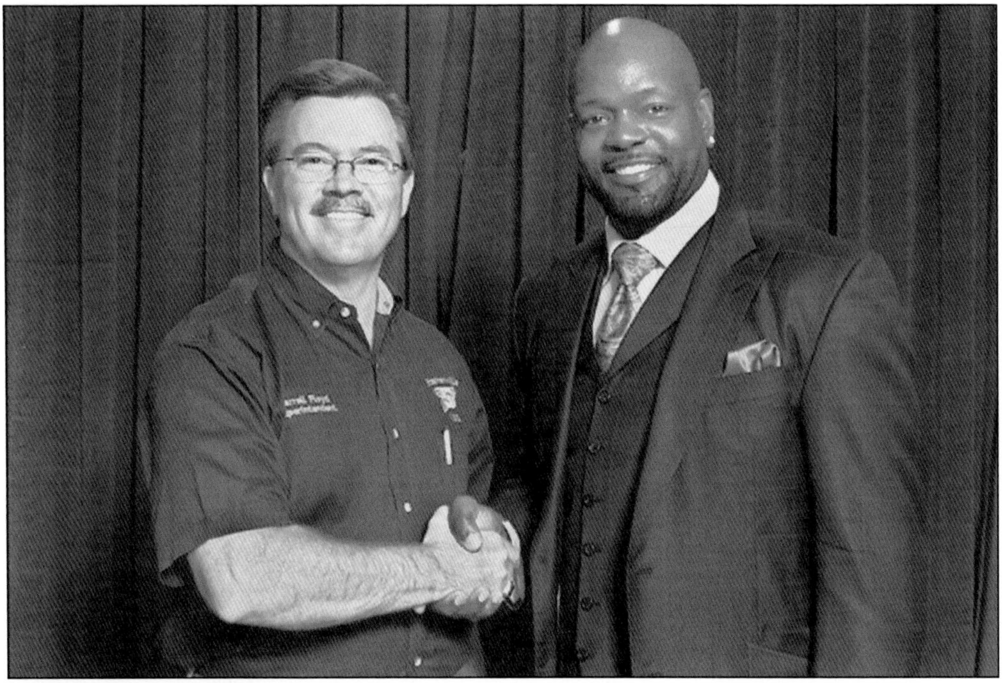

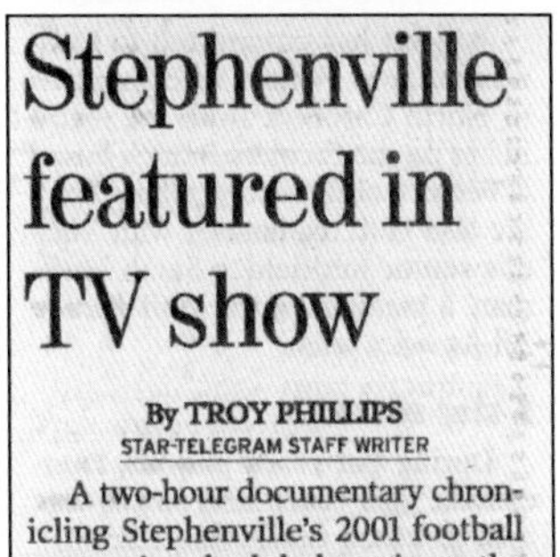

Stephenville featured in TV show

By TROY PHILLIPS
STAR-TELEGRAM STAFF WRITER

A two-hour documentary chronicling Stephenville's 2001 football season is scheduled to air on the A&E cable network at 8 p.m. Feb. 1.

Part of A&E's *Investigative Reports* series, the documentary is titled *Wide Open: Inside the World of High School Football.* Starting in August, cameras followed Yellow Jackets players, coaches and fans through the team's 35-21 loss to Dunbar in the Class 4A Division II bi-district playoffs.

The documentary also focuses on a team in South Central Los Angeles, Jefferson High School, in attempts to contrast football in rural and urban environments.

"The first week, you notice there's a camera around you," Stephenville coach Mike Copeland said. "After that, you're used to it. What you see is a true picture of the way things are."

A&E sent Copeland a four-minute preview of the documentary. Asked if he was concerned

From the earliest days, supportive administrators have consistently contributed to Stephenville's football success. An enthusiastic football fan, today's SISD superintendent Darrell Floyd appears above in 2010 with Dallas Cowboys great Emmitt Smith. If the Jackets are not quite "America's Team," found 75 miles east-northeast up I-20, they enjoyed national celebrity in 2002, when 44 Blue Productions out of California featured SHS in a nationally televised two-hour documentary that was part of A&E's *Investigative Reports* series. Troy Phillips's *Fort Worth Star-Telegram* article (left) announces the program's February 1 airing. (Above, Dr. Darrell Floyd; left, *Fort Worth Star-Telegram.*)

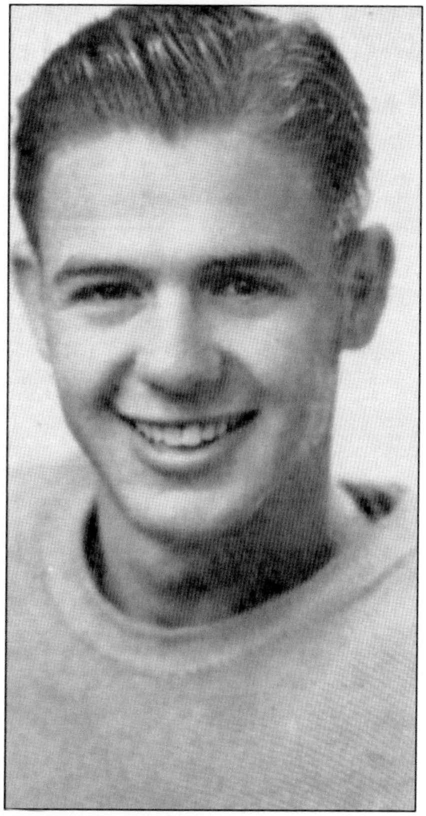

Today, there exists a Yellow Jacket brotherhood, a fraternity of players transcending space and time. Jackets old and new share a bond that holds young and old together. Below, coach Joseph Gillespie and members of the 2010 team present the autographed round three Canyon Randall game ball to 90-year-old Marshall Sherrod, who was convalescing in the Stephenville Community Nursing and Rehabilitation Center. Sherrod was born 22 days before the first SHS game under UIL auspices. Included in this photograph are, from left to right, (first row) Padyn Giebler, D.J. Vanden Berge, Gabe Barrios, Witt Westbrook, Keaton Trinkle, Connor Washington, and Tyler Floyd; (second row) Coach Gillespie, Travis Crittenden, Stephen Harrell, Hunter Bernays, Jared Slemmons, Holton Westbrook, and Aiavion Edwards. Right, a much younger Sherrod appears in his 1937 Yellow Jacket uniform. (Below, author.)

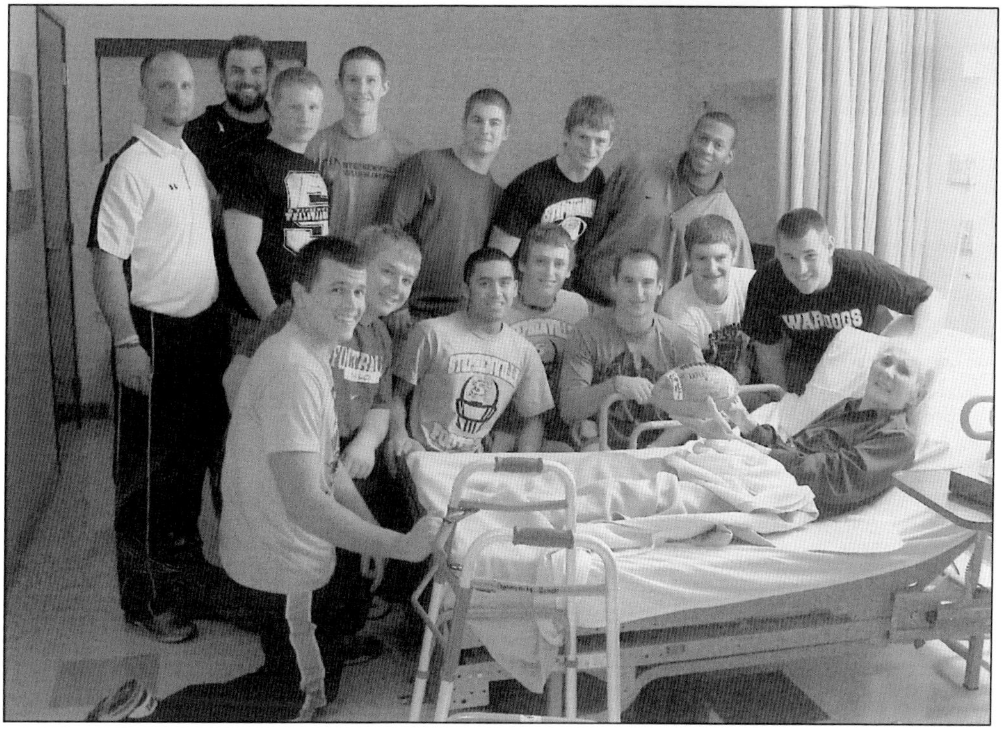

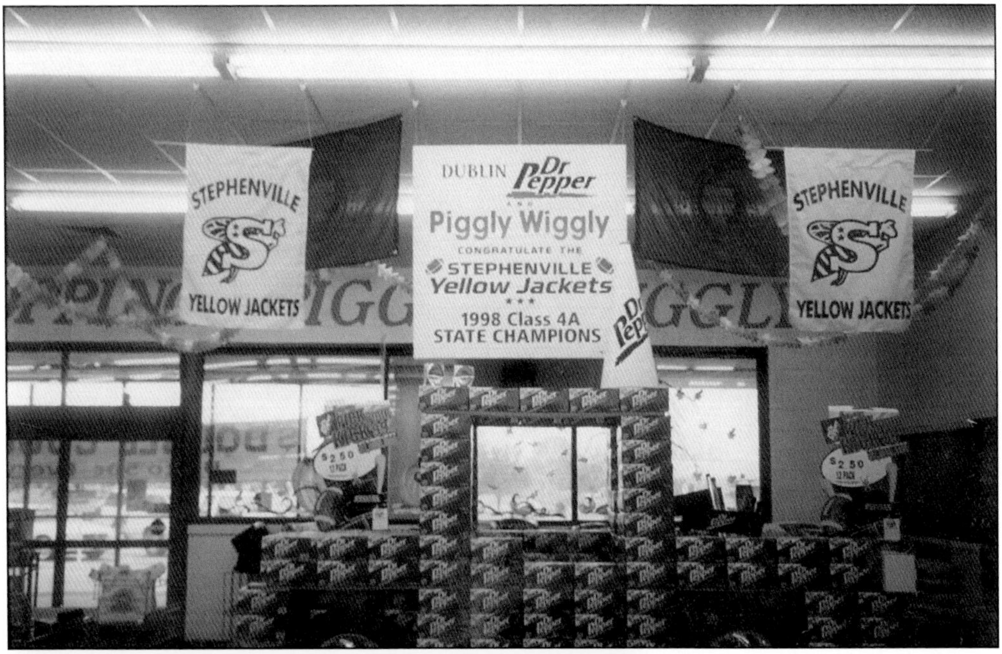

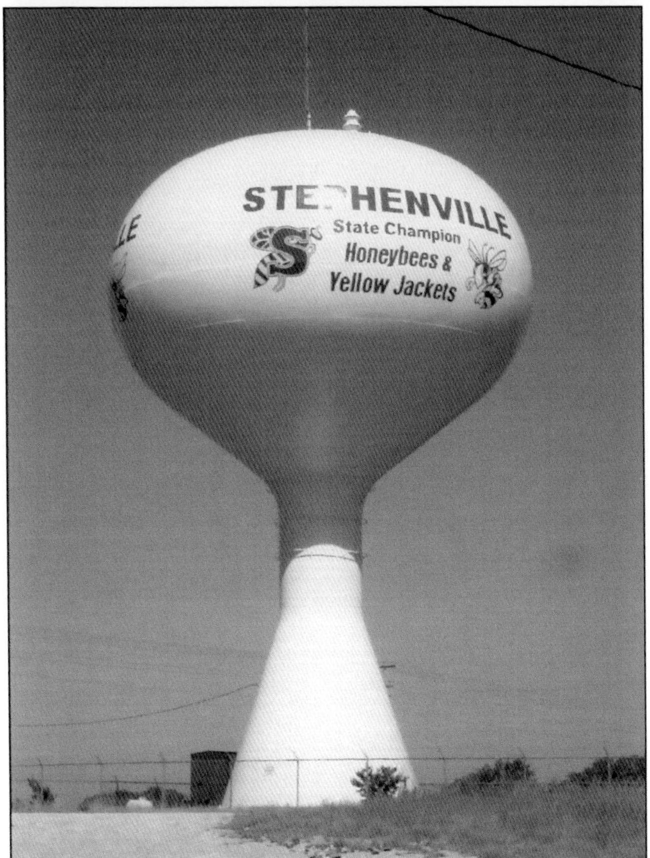

Whether or not a Stephenville resident has played on the team, communitywide support is comprehensive, even for a football-crazy state like Texas. A 1999 Piggly Wiggly display (above) is typical of encouragement extended by local businesses from one end of town to the other, especially during a playoff run. The city itself trumpets support on the water tower surmounting the local landscape (left). The structure proudly bears the high school logos. (Both, author.)

Seven

For the Record

For high school football players, recognition comes in many shapes and forms—a letter jacket, a trophy awarded at the conclusion of a playoff win, the conferring of all-district or all-state status at season's end. Since 1920, recognition of every stripe and hue has come to Jacket players in each and every position. Many Jackets have received acknowledgement as all-district offensive or defensive Player of the Year. Six have received Player of the Year honors at the 4A all-state level.

Since the Lions Club's 1991 creation of a Stephenville High School Athletic Hall of Fame, 58 Yellow Jacket football players and 8 SHS football coaches—66 percent of the hall's inductees—are remembered by their plaques, which are housed in the display cases flanking the high school's central entryway.

Perhaps the greatest Jacket records have come at the state and national levels. During the unforgettably successful 1998 State Championship season, quarterback Kelan Luker and receiver Cody Cardwell rewrote the schoolboy record books. Some of their standards endured for almost a decade. Cardwell still holds individual SHS records in eight categories and Luker in six.

But in football, there is no *I* in team. The most remarkable 1998 Jacket achievement is the 8,664 yards in total-season offense that established new state and national standards. The mark surpassed Sugar Land High School's total of 8,375, a Texas record that had endured since 1953. The Jackets also eclipsed the 74-year-old national mark of 8,588 set by Pine Bluff, Arkansas, in 1925. Together, Luker, Cardwell, Chris Evatt, K.C. Steed, Toby O'Neal, T.J. Douglas, A.B. Combs, Zac Hunter, Jimmy Ferrazas, Matt Tinklenberg, Kendal Briles, J.W. Boren, Robert Lilly, Aaron Collier, Matt Van Hattem, Derek Haney, Jay Doty, Sterling Doty, and Felix Alvarado established a high school mark almost impossible to rewrite, inside Texas or out. The small selection of pictures below are representative of the many Yellow Jacket records and achievements that testify to one of the finest football programs ever produced in the Lone Star State.

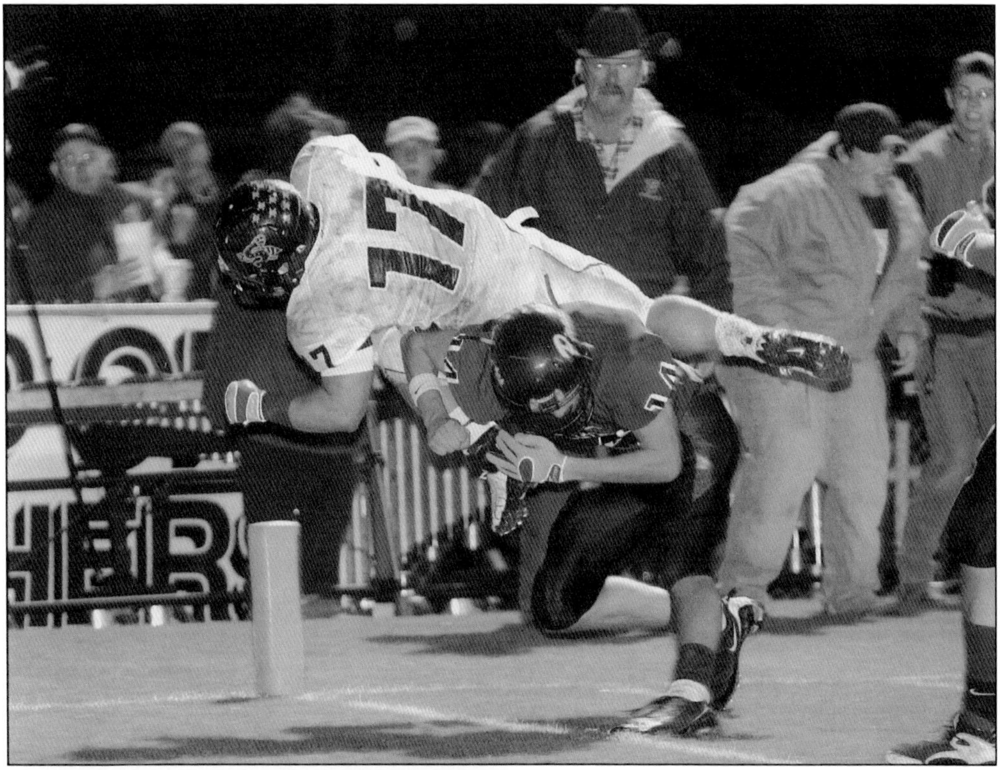

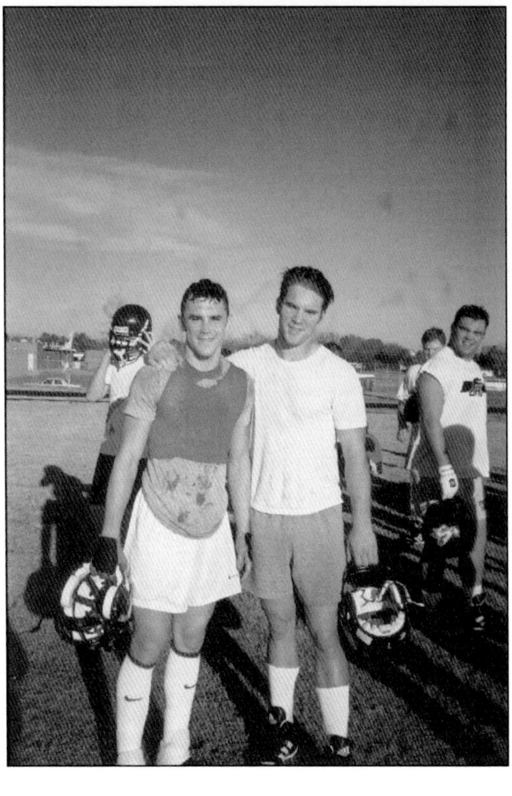

Historically, great Jacket accomplishments have been the product of the 2007 team motto, One More Yard. Expressing the spirit of going above and beyond, this mantra is captured in the image above by Jacket linebacker Tyler Floyd stretching to break the plane after a 2009 interception against Granbury. At left, all-staters Cody Cardwell (left), Kelan Luker (center), and offensive lineman Robert Lilly (right) prepare for the 1998 4A D-2 Championship Game that pushed the Jackets' season yardage total beyond the national record. The 1993 and 1994 teams also set national single-season marks for most offensive plays—1,037 and 944. In 1998, Cardwell's 2,427 receiving yards rewrote the national single-season standard. His 4,241 career yards was a Texas best. Meanwhile, Cardwell's quarterback, Luker, set state marks for single-season and career passing yardage—4,697 and 8,297, respectively. (Above, Jones; left, author.)

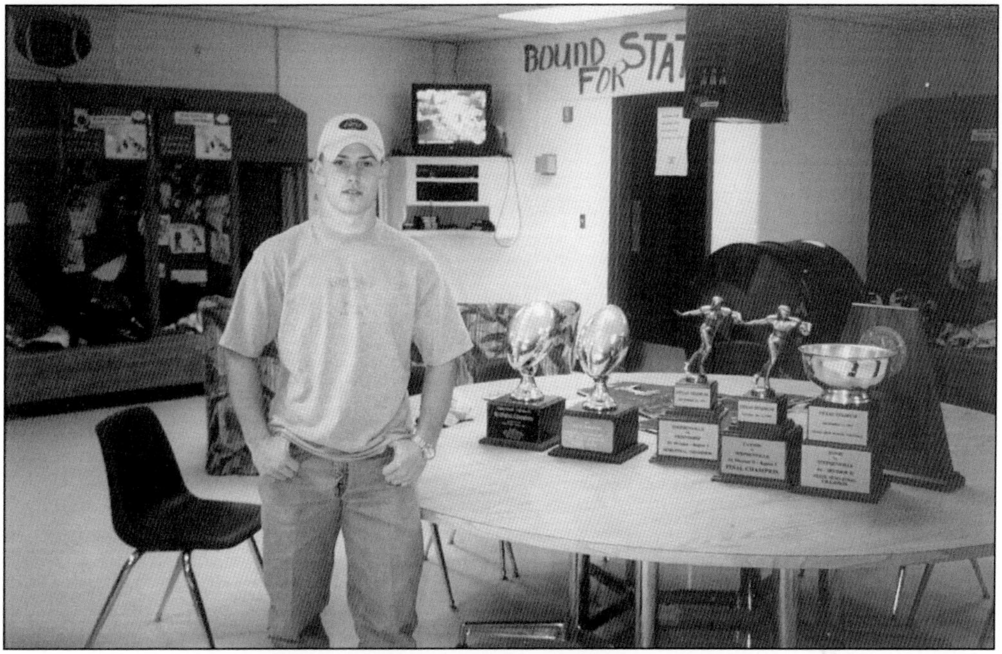

The run-and-gun passing attack that distinguished the Briles era and beyond can easily overshadow the strides made by Stephenville running backs since 1988. Between 1998 and 2010, four running backs posted enviable numbers for any Texas program. Above, Zac "Rabbit" Hunter stands beside the six playoff trophies SHS earned in 1999. With 1,833 yards, Hunter is second on the Jacket all-time single season rushing list. His 4,376 career total makes him the leading ground-gainer ever. Below, Brad Mills races for a touchdown against Aledo in 2008. His career total (2005–2007) places him second, with 3,452. With a 1,830 yard single-season total, Mills narrowly missed overtaking Hunter for second place. (Above, author; below, Huffman, *Stephenville Empire-Tribune*.)

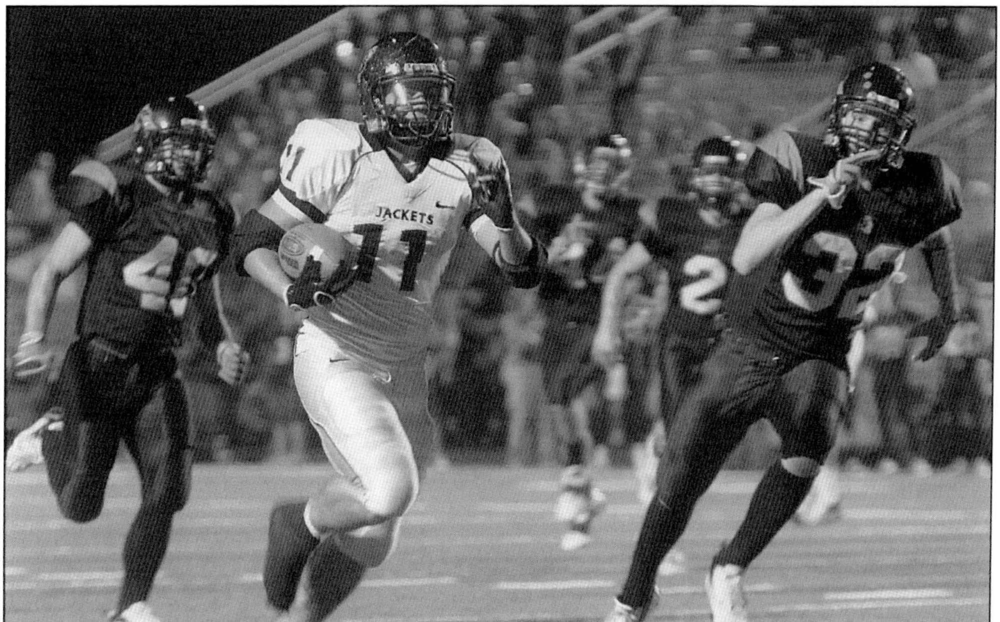

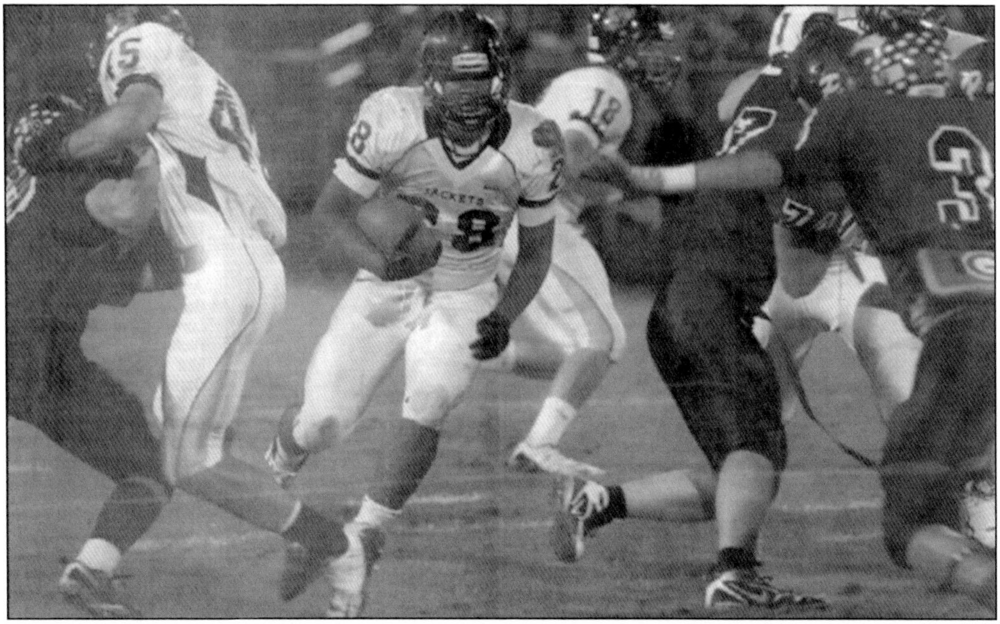

In 2009, with 1,853 rushing yards, James Myles (above) surpassed Hunter's 1999 single-season mark. The 2010 season witnessed a breakout year for junior running back Aiavion Edwards. Below, he races for a big gain against the Crowley Eagles in the bi-district playoff round. With 1,744 yards for the year, Edwards promises to complete his Yellow Jacket career in 2011 as one of the most productive runners in SHS history. (Both, Huffman, *Stephenville Empire-Tribune*.)

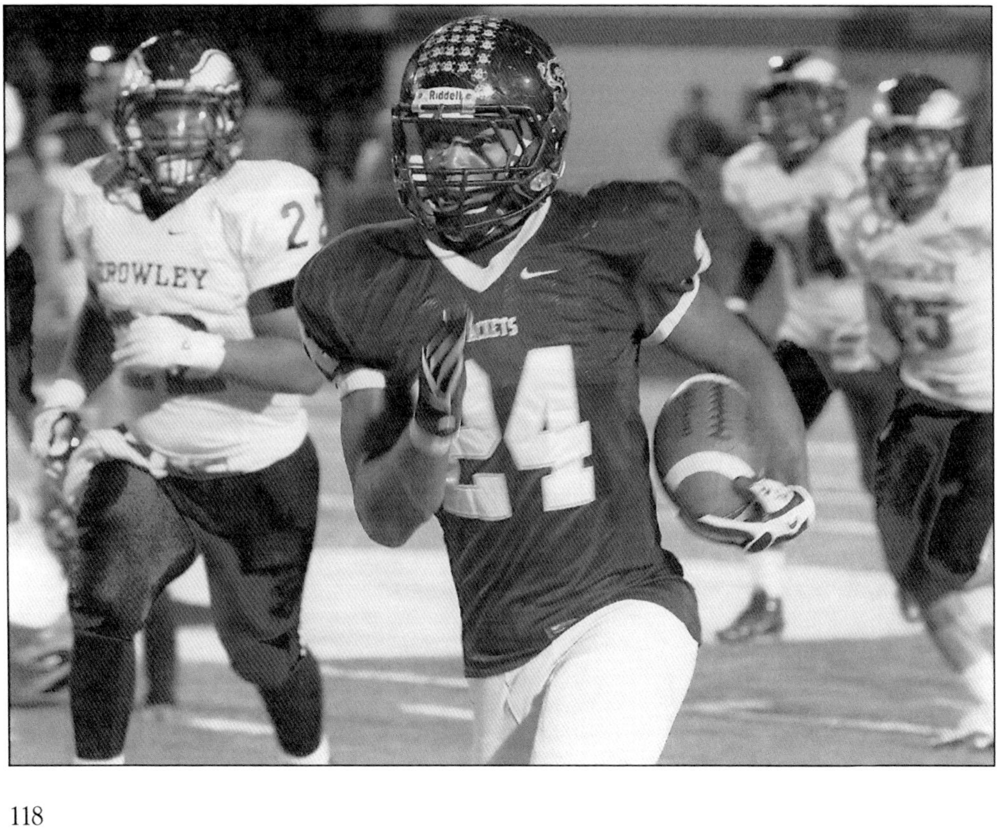

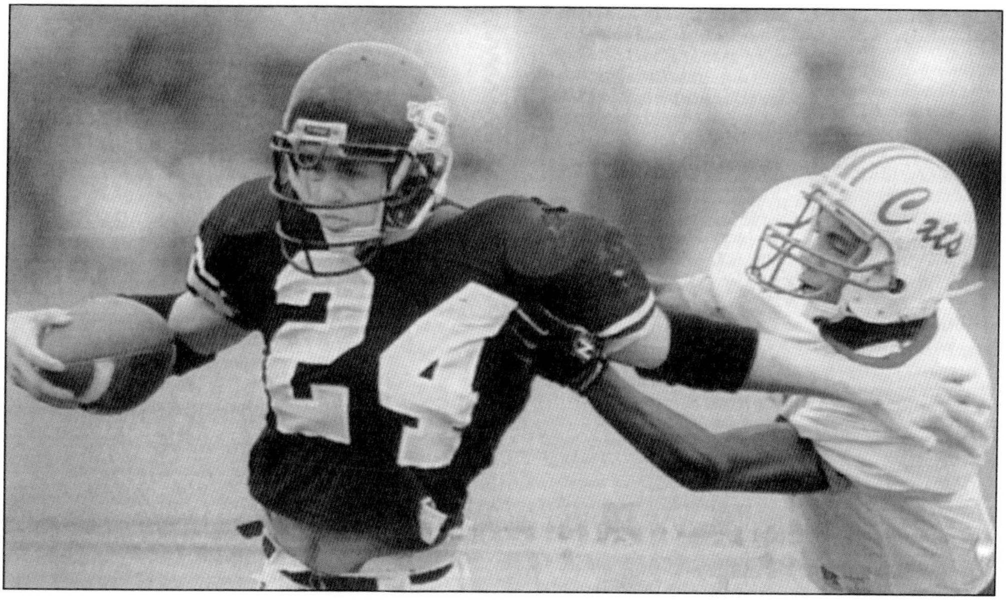

Jason Bragg and Kendal Briles are two of the three Yellow Jackets who have received 4A Offensive Player of the Year awards. Although Bragg (above) played both ways, his offensive exploits garnered Player of the Year awards for him in 1994. Five years later, Briles (below) received the same distinction for outstanding performance in the quarterback role. (Above, *Fort Worth Star-Telegram*; below, Skipper.).

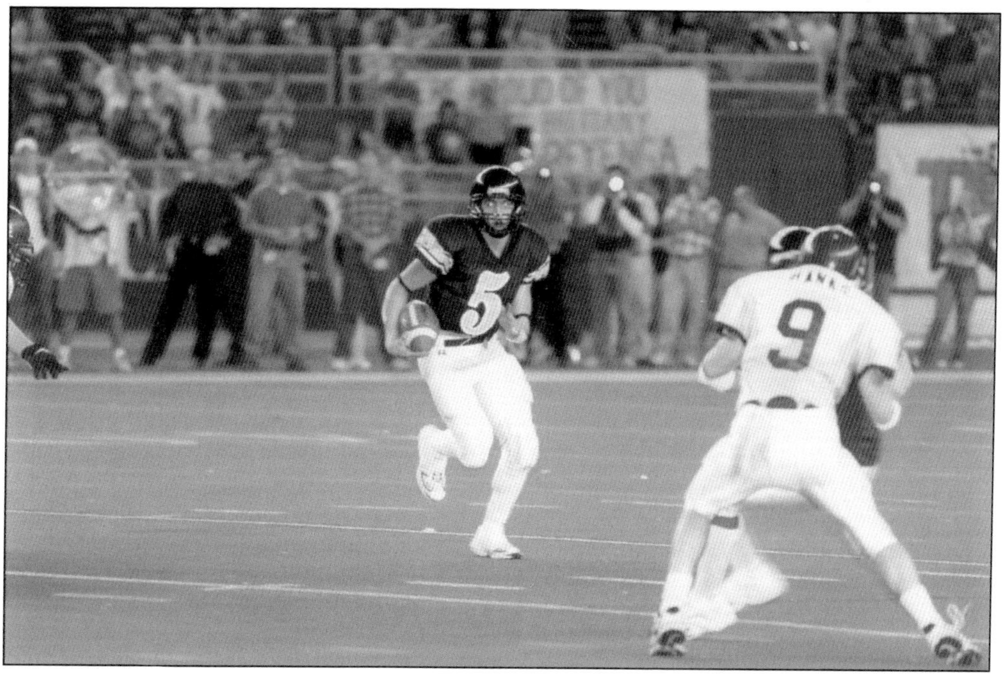

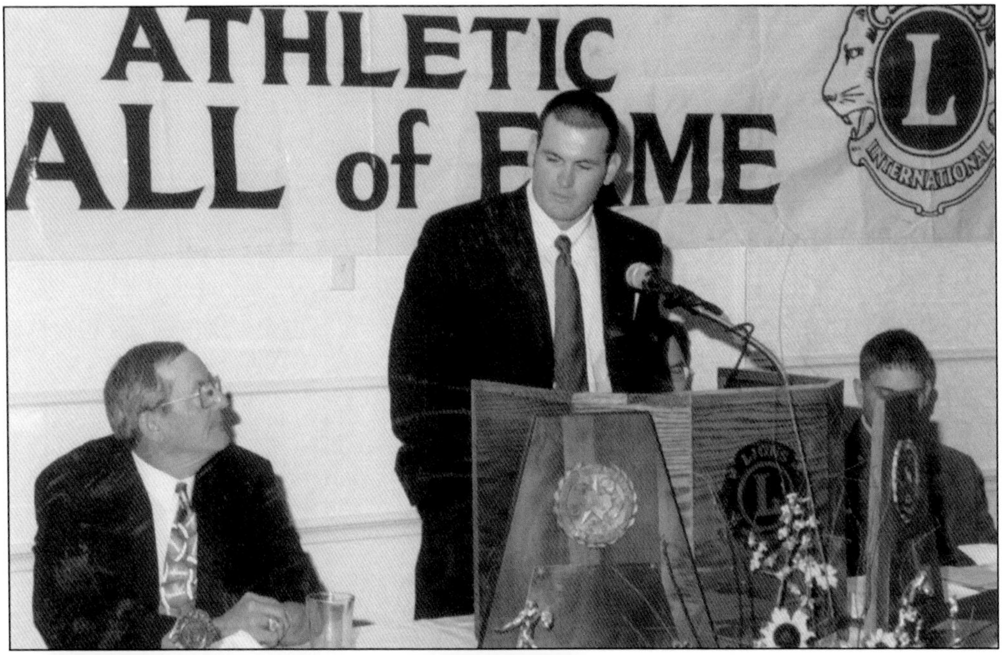

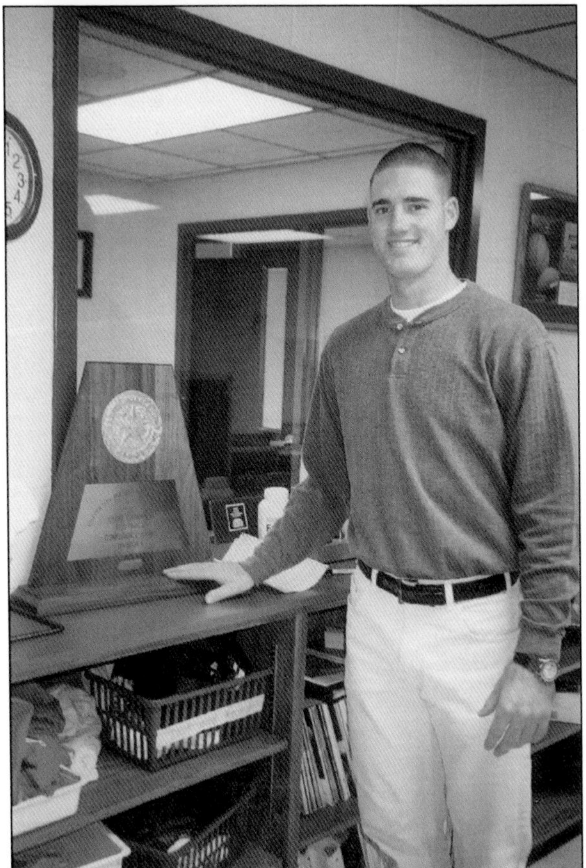

On the other side of the ball, Mitch Copeland earned 1994 4A Defensive Player of the Year. In addition to all-state honors in both 1993 and 1994, Copeland was a three-year letterman who started 46 consecutive games. Above, his father (left) and he appear at Mitch's induction into the SHS Athletic Hall of Fame. In 1999, Cal Jillson brought a second 4A Defensive Player of the Year award back to Stephenville. Pictured at left alongside the 1999 State Championship Trophy, Jillson was a member of both the 1998 and 1999 title teams. He continued his football career playing defensive end for the Southeast Missouri Redhawks. (Above, Skipper; left, author.)

In 2002, three-year letterman John Harrell brought a third Defensive Player of the Year award to SHS. After a successful high school career, Harrell played football at University of Houston but later transferred to Tarleton State. There, in 2006, he was first team Lone Star All-Conference and second team All-American center. Another Jacket hall of fame War Dog deserving special mention is tough-as-nails Jack Hodges. At middle linebacker, he was 1998 first team all-district and all-state. Playing in that year's title match, Hodges had a career game in spite of performing from beginning to end with a heavily braced broken ankle. Below, he appears (left) in 1998 with fellow linebackers Keith McCormick (center) and Justin Monk. In the Heart-of-Texas All-Star Classic, Hodges earned Defensive MVP honors. (Right, *Stephenville Empire-Tribune*; below, Skipper.)

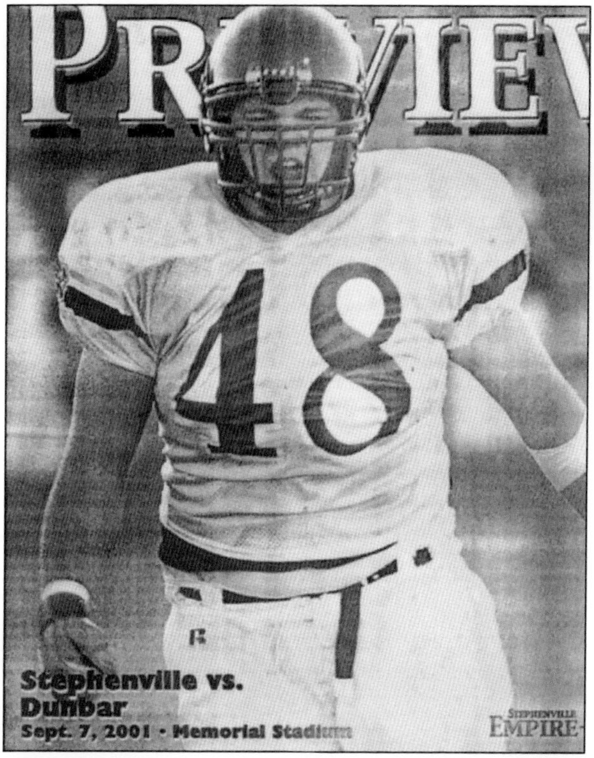

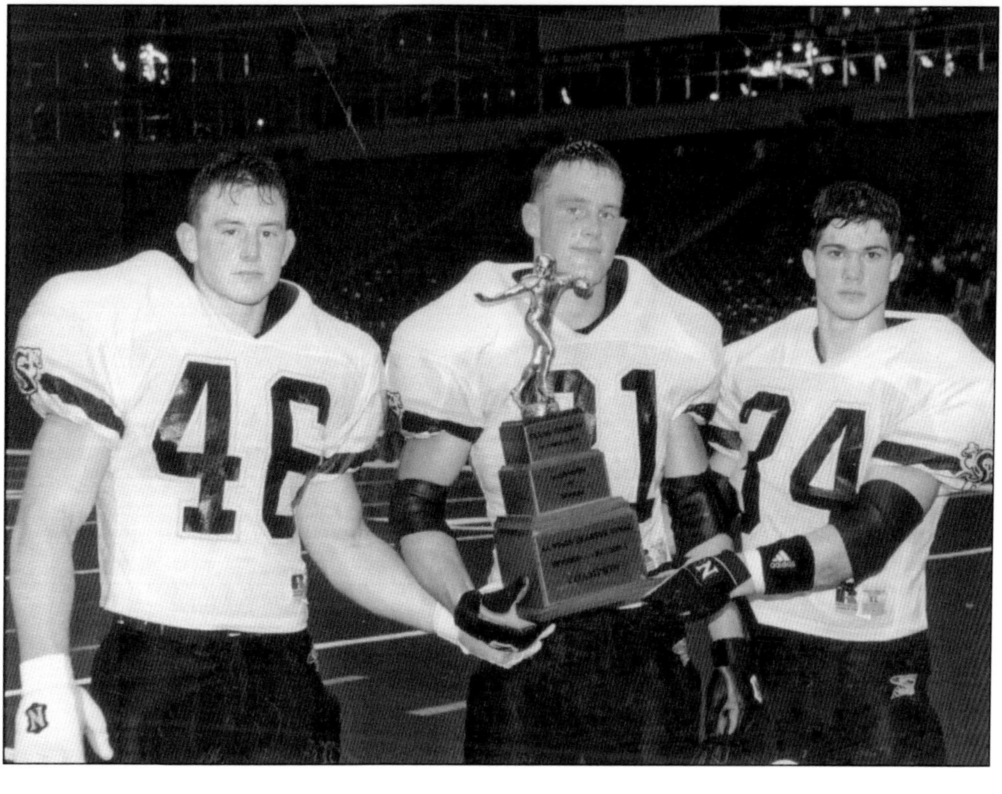

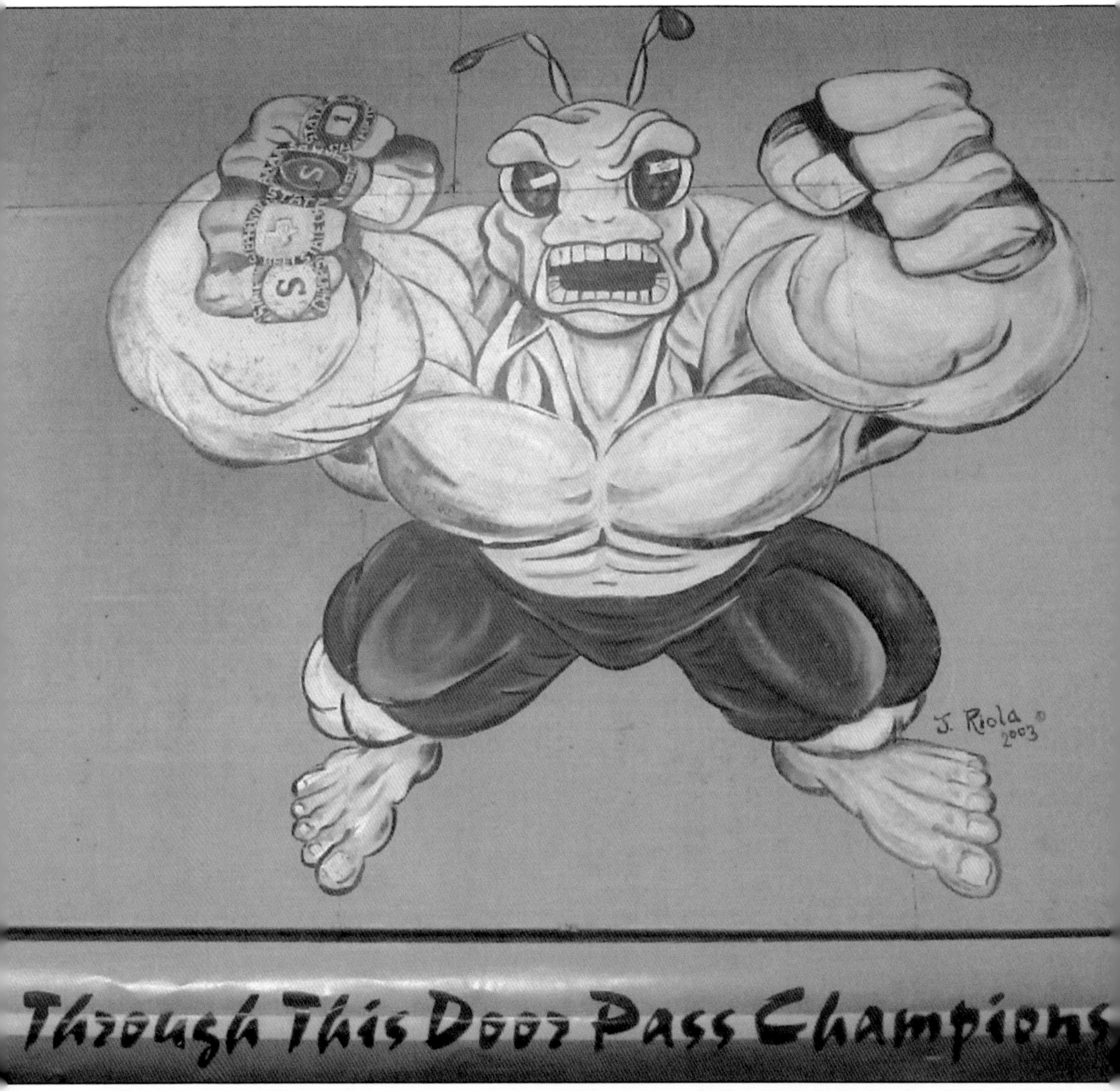

This volume could continue on for many pages. Hundreds of other Yellow Jacket football worthies rightly deserve inclusion. Whether found herein or as part of that larger 90-year-old brotherhood of Jacket football alumni, those who have gone before and those who are yet to come are part of a venerable football tradition that never graduates. Alongside the Green Room sign that reminds players old and new of that same mantra, the muscled Jacket pictured stands watch over players passing into the high school weight room. Four championship rings adorn his fingers. Only time will tell, but history and tradition suggest that before too long, one for the thumb is sure to come. (Author.)

TITLES AND PLAYOFFS

Year	Head Coach	Won-Lost-Tie Record	Conference	Season Achievements
1924	Verne Scott	6-3-0	B	District Champion Bi-District win over Graham Area against Cisco
1929	Joe Brown	3-2-1	B	District Champion Bi-District against Ballinger
1930	Joe Brown	7-1-2	B	District Champion Bi-District against Albany
1933	Joe Brown	7-1-1	B	District Champion Bi-District against Cross Plains
1934	Pleas Stanley	5-2-1	B	District Cochampion District Committee advanced Dublin over Stephenville
1936	Jim Mobley	9-0-0	B Class B played only through Regional round	District Champion Bi-District win over Winters Regional win over Rock Springs
1937	Jim Mobley	9-1-0	A	District 3-A Cochampion District Committee advanced Abilene over Stephenville
1940	Jimmy Marshall	8-0-1	2A	District 9-2A Champions Bi-District tie versus Temple (who advanced on 3-2 penetrations)
1952	Mike Murphy	9-3-1	2A	District 10-2A Champion Bi-District win over Winters Area win over Graham Regional against 1952 State Champion Terrell
1989	Art Briles	9-3-0	4A	Bi-District win over Belton Area against Brewer
1990	Art Briles	13-2-0	4A	District 6-4A Champion Bi-District win over WF Hirschi Area win over Brewer Regional win over Snyder Quarterfinal win over Burkburnett Semifinal against 1990 state champion Wilmer-Hutchins
1991	Art Briles	9-3-0	4A	Bi-District win over Burkburnett Area against Boswell
1992	Art Briles	10-4-0	4A	Bi-District win over Azle Area win over Arlington Heights Regional win over Plainview Quarterfinal against Estacado

Year	Head Coach	Won-Lost-Tie Record	Conference	Season Achievements
1993	Art Briles	16-0-0	4A	District 6-4A Champion Bi-District win over Azle Area win over Arlington Heights Regional win over Sweetwater Quarterfinals win over Andrews Semifinal win over Waxahachie State Champions win over La Marque
1994	Art Briles	16-0-0	4A	District 5-4A Champion Bi-District win over Estacado Area win over Denison Regional win over Borger Quarterfinals win over Sherman Semifinals win over Corsicana State Champions win over La Marque
1995	Art Briles	12-2-0	4A	District 5-4A Champion Bi-District win over Snyder Area win over Sherman Regional win over Borger Quarterfinals against state finalist Denison
1996	Art Briles	8-5-1	4A	Bi-District win over Arlington Heights Area win over Boswell Regional win over Sweetwater Quarterfinals against state finalist Denison
1997	Art Briles	8-4-0	4A	District 8-4A Champion Bi-District win over Eastern Hills Area against state finalist Denison
1998	Art Briles	15-1-0	4A D-2	Bi-District win over Andrews Area win over Denton Regional Semifinal win over Pampa Quarterfinal win over WF Hirschi Semifinal win over Southlake Carroll State Champions win over La Marque
1999	Art Briles	16-0-0	4A D-2	District 5-4A Champion Bi-District win over Andrews Area win over WF Hirschi Regional Semifinal win over Wolfforth Frenship Quarterfinal win over Canyon Semifinal win over Ennis State Champions win over Port Neches-Groves

Year	Head Coach	Won-Lost-Tie Record	Conference	Season Achievements
2000	Mike Copeland	9-3-0	4A D-2	Bi-District win over Western Hills Area against Southlake Carroll
2001	Mike Copeland	7-4-0	4A D-2	Bi-District against FW Dunbar
2002	Mike Copeland	10-2-0	4A D-2	District 8-4A Champion Bi-District win over Western Hills Area against 2002 state champion Denton Ryan
2004	Chad Morris	10-1-0	4A D-2	District 6-4A Champion Bi-District against WF Rider
2005	Chad Morris	13-1-0	4A D-1	District 6-4A Champion Bi-District win over Sherman Area win over Azle Regional win over Plainview Semifinal against 2005 State Champion Highland Park
2006	Chad Morris	10-2-0	4A D-2	District 8-4A Champion Bi-District win over FW Southwest Area against WF Rider
2007	Chad Morris	10-2-0	4A D-2	Bi-District win over O.D. Wyatt Area against WF Rider
2008	Joseph Gillespie	10-4-0	4A D-2	Bi-District win over FW Dunbar Area win over WF Rider Regional win over EP Parkland Quarterfinal against Everman
2009	Joseph Gillespie	9-3-0	4A D-2	District 8-4A Champion Bi-District win over FW Poly Area against 2009 State Champion Aledo
2010	Joseph Gillespie	8-6-0	4A D-2	Bi-District win over Crowley Area win over FW Southwest Regional win over Canyon Randall Quarterfinal against 2010 State Champion Aledo

Top Three All-Time Yellow Jacket Leaders Statistics adapted from Stephenville Yellow Jackets and Honey Bees www.stephenvilleyellowjackets.com		
Passing Yardage	**Single Season**	**Career**
Kelan Luker	4,697 (1998)	8,297 (1996–1998)
Jevan Snead	3,546 (2005)	6,854 (2003–2005)
Kevin Kolb	3,247 (2002)	5,733 (2000–2002)
Rushing Yardage	**Single Season**	**Career**
James Myles	1,853 (2009)	Unranked
Zac "Rabbit" Hunter	1,833 (1999)	4,376 (1997–1999)
Brad Mills	1,830 (2008)	3,452 (2005–2008)
Receiving Yardage	**Receptions—Career**	**Receiving Yards—Career**
Cody Cardwell	213 (1996–1998)	4,241 (1996–1998)
Jeremy Madkins	163 (1999–2001)	2,115 (1999–2001)
Brent McElfresh	141 (2004–2006)	2,953 (2004–2006)
Touchdowns	**Single Season**	**Career**
Brad Mills	25 (2008)	49 (2005–2008)
Cody Cardwell	27 (1998)	43 (1996–1998)
James Myles	31 (2009)	38 (2008–2009)

Yellow Jacket Coaches, 1920–2010 Coach, Season(s), and Career Record (Based on Yearbooks and Newspaper Reports)		
Joe B. Preston (1920) 5-2-0	E.E. Walker (1943) 7-2-0	Sam Taylor (1969–1970) 13-7-0
J.C. Dykes (1921–1923, 1925) 23-13-1	H.H. Hassler (1944–1945) 9-9-2	Leon Manley (1973–1981) 40-46-4
Verne Scott (1924) 6-3-0	Mike Murphy (1946–1954) 48-35-6	Joe Loudermilk (1982–1987) 26-33-1
Joe Brown (1926–1933) 30-25-7	Scott McCall (1955–1958) 15-23-2	Art Briles (1988–1999) 136-29-2
Pleas Stanley (1934–1935) 12-5-1	C. E. Booth (1959–1961) 5-25-0	Mike Copeland (2000–2002) 26-9-0
Jim Mobley (1936–1937) 18-1-0	Kenneth Scott (1962–1966, 1971–1972), 37-33-0	Chad Morris (2003–2008) 49-10-0
Jimmy Marshall (1938–1942) 27-17-2	Johnnie Henderson (1967–1968) 8-12-0	Joseph Gillespie (2008–present) 27-13-0
Cumulative Totals 1920–2010 21 different coaches	Cumulative Record: 567-352-28 (947 games) Win Percentage: 59.8 • 21 coaches over 90 seasons • 16 with winning record (76%) • 5 with nonwinning record (24%) District Titles: 18 (and two co-championships) Playoff Appearances: 28 (31.1% of seasons)	

About Stephenville ISD

The first school in Stephenville was built around 1855, two years after the settlers reached the banks of the Bosque River. At that time, there was only one teacher, a man named McBride. In 1856, school was taught in a little log cabin on the southeast corner of the town square. It was a subscription school charging $2 per month per pupil, and the length of term was three months. A later schoolhouse in Stephenville was the Masonic Lodge, located in a cabin erected by John M. Stephen, founder of the town. Both a church and a school met on the ground floor, and the Masons met on the second floor. Windows and stairs were finally added between 1869 and 1870. Prior to that, entrance to the second floor was by way of a ladder.

Because all county records were destroyed when the courthouse burned in 1866, there is no official count of how many schools operated in Erath County before that time. However, due to a sparse population and Indian raids, it is believed to be very few. By 1875, the school was a stone building located where the Central Ward School was constructed in the early 20th century.

Today, SISD educates over 3,600 students across six campuses—Central Elementary (prekindergarten and kindergarten), Chamberlin Elementary (first and second grades), Hook Elementary (third and fourth), Gilbert Intermediate (fifth and sixth), Henderson Junior High (seventh and eighth), and Stephenville High School (ninth through twelfth). The district is annually funded with a combination of state, local, and federal funds totaling approximately $24 million.

Although Stephenville is proud of being called the Cowboy Capital of the World (because of its many World Champion Rodeo residents), the town is also proud of its school district motto, a Tradition of Excellence. This stems from its numerous successes in both academics and extracurricular events, not the least of which is SHS's four state championships in football. To find out more information, please visit www.sville.us, the website of SISD.

Discover Thousands of Local History Books Featuring Millions of Vintage Images

Arcadia Publishing, the leading local history publisher in the United States, is committed to making history accessible and meaningful through publishing books that celebrate and preserve the heritage of America's people and places.

Find more books like this at
www.arcadiapublishing.com

Search for your hometown history, your old stomping grounds, and even your favorite sports team.

Consistent with our mission to preserve history on a local level, this book was printed in South Carolina on American-made paper and manufactured entirely in the United States. Products carrying the accredited Forest Stewardship Council (FSC) label are printed on 100 percent FSC-certified paper.

MADE IN THE USA